AF477352

BARBARA VISSER IS ER NIET
[edited by Lisette Smits and Barbara Visser]

CONTENTS

PROLOGUE
[Paul Elliman]

The name of this book is *Barbara Visser is er niet*.

For a while this was Barbara's outgoing answer-phone message. I checked an online translator and it gave me *Barbara fishermen are not there*. More realistically it would be something like *Barbara Visser ain't here*, but what is realism to language? Not only does it miss the refrain, a kind of echo on the line that rhymes *is er* with *Visser*, it also loses the special ambiguousness of the *er*, a word that often isn't quite here either.

Not strictly a filler like those *ers, ums* and *ahs* that punctuate the grammar of our conversation — or a *disfluency*, to use the more technical term — in Dutch, *er* is an actual word, even if a shadowy one. In the sentence *Barbara Visser is er niet*, it does mean 'there' (remove it and Barbara, if only in a grammatical sense, ceases to exist). But sentences with *er* could just as often mean the same thing whether the *er* was there or not.

Stef Grondelaers, a researcher at the University of Leuven, is a specialist of the word *er*, an *er*-scholar. And while Grondelaers suggests that its passive form can be connected to the English filler *er*, he's much more interested in the Dutch word's ability to transform itself into a decisive part of the sentence.

A Dutch newspaper article on Grondelaers outlines several *ers* in use in the Dutch and Flemish language: "*Er* is a weakened form of *there (daar)*, it also occurs in combination with prepositions (at it/*eraan*, against it/*ertegen*, therewith/*ermee*), and in combination with numbers: 'How many do you have *there*? I have ten *here*.'" It can also occur — and this is the use that Grondelaers

studies — in combination with indefinite topics. 'A bird sings there' is not the same as 'a bird sings'. The latter sentence could mean that all birds sing. Whereas *there* in 'a bird sings there' addresses, or introduces into the conversation, one specific bird.

By contrast, the common English *er* is a small, chirruping bird of hesitation; never too far from error — think of Alexander Pope's 'To err is human, to forgive, divine.' Not that the spoken filler *er* should only be associated with mistakes or ineptness. It can also be part of the sound of a sentence under construction, a kind of buffering that we now know from streaming audio, as the system stalls to make room for the amount of data being supplied.

Both English and Dutch *ers* tell of a language of parts that are not quite language; ambivalent fragments of signs, gestures and sounds that make up the messages we send, or leave for each other. We like to imagine, in simpler times, that our voices used to only say *here I am* — that they didn't live on in a delayed reflection somewhere else. But for a language that exists for us to make distorted claims about our own presence — me here writing this, you there reading it — the voice is no different. The intimacy of a connection to a body or a place has been undone. As a famous phrase of Gertrude Stein's reminds us, there is no there there. Or no *er* there.

/

The writer Allan Weiss imagined a software programme that, after analyzing sound patterns in a vocal recording, could build it back as an artificial voice able to speak any text entered via a keyboard. Weiss says he thought this was a great sci-fi plot device until he found that the programme had almost been perfected already. Who, he asks, would you choose to leave your outgoing answer-machine message?

'Barbara Visser is er niet' is something Gertrude Stein might also have had a voice for.

A deceptively machine-like repetition is typical of Stein's low-resolution, incantatory language. John Ashberry once described it as being "made up almost entirely of colourless connecting words", like *here, there, where* and *were* — and suggested that Stein was able to transmit a different picture of reality by imitating its rhythms rather than its content. She talked of capturing the sound of the voice in writing, as well as the impact of mass-media on speech, and her work is somehow faithful to the confusion of these things. Heard on recordings, for example, Stein speaks her words with the same unflinchingly fixed-form that printing gives them. In print, her written sentences adopt the grammatical incompleteness of aphasic language.

Dutch and English *ers* also tell us certain things about speech and writing, their differences as well as how they accommodate each other. The Dutch *er* is an example of something that writing has problems with, when the meaning relies on the situation. So-called *deictic* expressions (from the Greek word for pointing) such as Grondelaers' *this bird here,* or *that bird over there,* work more easily in conversational speech where they can be combined with gestural exchanges. The English spoken *er* is thought of as a phonemic gap in meaningful discourse — linguists refer to it as a "neutral vowel sound" as if it were not accountable for anything.

On the other hand, the "colourless connecters" (like the Dutch *er*), as well as, in speech, the filler-pauses (the English *er*), the *disfluencies*, are thought to be a key to fluency in any spoken language. In multi-lingual societies, the formal distinctions that are supposed to separate how we talk from how we write are often abandoned.

Words disappear into the language, somewhere between speech and writing.

A translation of Stein's *there is no there there* (*er zijn geen daar daar*) recognizes in the first *there* a difference that the *er* word is happy to provide, even if Stein may have preferred the ambiguous tone of all *there-s* being equal. Or, given the autobiographical context of her phrase, a language that emerges like a mirage from the remains of a place or person that has changed beyond recognition. *There* for Gertrude Stein, whether it was any longer there or not, was her childhood home, a house on the corner of Thirteenth Avenue and Twenty-fifth street in East Oakland during the 1880s: "It was shabby and overgrown; the houses were certainly some of those that had been (...) yes it might have been Thirteenth Avenue where I had been."

/

Many of the forms that language can take are never easy to translate, or, in some cases, even identify. Often more like a trick of the light, a shift in the wind. Or a change in location (and locution); ways of saying *I'm not there anymore.* Just as languages have different ways of conveying past, present and future tense, technology also carries inflections that can put us in and out of the world around us, in and out of ourselves. Describing an early part of his life in the city of Istanbul — his birth, no less — Orhan Pamuk pauses to add *or so I've been told*. "In Turkish" he explains, "we have a special tense that allows us to distinguish hearsay from what we've seen with our own eyes; when we are relating dreams, fairy tales, or past events we could not have witnessed, we use this tense. I'd have liked to write my entire story this way — as if my life were something that happened to someone else, as if it were a dream in which I felt my voice fading..."

This way of 'remembering' is an important
part of the social structure of language —
an everyday sense of things based on the
perceptions of others *and* the ghost voices
of technology recurring inside us. Not only
is it because he's a writer does Pamuk find,
in this tense of his language, a temptation
to talk about himself as if he were someone
else, somewhere else. As if, effaced by their
own words, their own voice, the person
telling the story is no longer there. *Is er niet.*
Anyone who ever left an outgoing message
on an answer machine can tell you as much
about that.

THE CHOREOGRAPHY OF TIME
[Maria Grever]

One day a picture in a Dutch newspaper caught my eye. There was something odd about it. Against a background of windmills, a man and a woman were looking straight into the camera lens. Their clothes and hair seemed to be from the 1960s. I wondered whether they were Japanese tourists, somewhere in the Netherlands. But somehow, the whole scene looked more like a decor for a theatre production. Who were these people? When and where was this picture taken?

The photograph turned out to be part of a series that played an ingenious trick with time. The man and woman were Belgian actors in Nagasaki. They were posing as Dutch people imitating Japanese tourists. A Dutch artist had placed these imitation tourists against the backdrop of Dutch architectural replicas in a Japanese theme park called *Huis Ten Bosch City*. Ten years ago this park had been constructed so that Japanese people could catch a glimpse of 'historical Holland' without having to travel to the West. The park has several life-size replicas of existing Dutch buildings and cityscapes. They are positioned with no regard for their actual geographical proximity in the Netherlands; in the theme park, windmills and dykes stand next to a cathedral and a castle.

This representation of reality is more perfect than the real one. There is no litter in the streets, and none of the buildings are defaced by graffiti. The garden of the real *Huis Ten Bosch* is unfinished, but the Japanese one has been completed. The perfect construct of the Netherlands illustrates the Japanese view of culture. Japanese tend to see beauty as a synonym for perfection, while Europeans also see an aesthetic value in decay. The photographic representation of the theme park challenges the distinction between 'real' and 'false' versions of reality, between historically accurate representations and entertainment. Interestingly enough, this view of 'Holland' comes from Asia and has, in turn, been manipulated by a Dutch artist. The choreography of time, expressed in the pictures concerned, is a typical example of how we, in post-modernity, relate to the past. They impersonate

A Day in Holland/Holland in a Day
2001
series of colour photographs

A Day in Holland/Holland in a Day
2001
series of colour photographs

temporal experiences linked to the acceleration of modern history, meaning both the historical process and the narrative about this process.

In pre-modern societies history was merely studied for the lesson one hoped to learn from it. Particularly classical antiquity provided historians with many important examples. This instrumental approach to the past presupposed a relatively unchangeable human nature and a static society. From the end of the seventeenth century this attitude gradually started to shift in the Western world, at first only in scholarly circles, but later also among the public at large. Worldviews were historicized and historiography was elevated into a science, resulting in the breaking of the hold of tradition. The past was increasingly perceived as fundamentally different from the present. A new perspective on the future, and especially the idea that the future was malleable, led to a re-interpretation of the past. Particularly between 1750 and 1850 the chasm between past and present became wider than ever before. That was the period in which words like 'progress' and 'future' were first used in their modern sense. According to the historical theorist Reinhardt Koselleck, these terms expressed the temporal difference between *Erfahrungsraum* ('space of experience') and *Erwartungshorizont* ('horizon of expectations').[1]

Dramatic social changes over the last 150 years have pushed the past even further away. The sense of forever being denied access to a time in the past has invoked a nostalgic longing for a past world. This longing has been transformed into

A Day in Holland/Holland in a Day
2001
series of colour photographs

a desire to know, study and objectify the past. The kaleidoscopic choreographies of time and culture at the theme park *Huis Ten Bosch* in Japan by the aforementioned artist illustrate this phenomenon.

The gap between experience and expectations manifested itself in a fascinating way at the world expositions that became *en vogue* since the middle of the nineteenth century. From 1851 onwards, millions of people visited these sites of industry and artisanship in London, Paris, Vienna, Philadelphia, Chicago, Brussels and other cities, to see manufactured goods, tools, machinery, inventions and architecture, primarily from Western countries. The narrative of the expositions popularized the ideas of the Enlightenment, expressed in the encyclopaedic urge to classify every single object, the desire for a visual overview of the world as a whole, and in the extreme emphasis on progress and the future by ingenious choreographies of time.

One of the most impressive choreographies was the Paris *Exposition Universelle* in 1867.[2] Mining engineer Frédéric Le Play had designed an exposition that expressed a utopian desire for a harmonic, rational society. Its 'plot' told the story of the rise, progress and triumph of Western civilization. Le Play had carefully planned every last detail of his exposition's main building. He designed a coherent unity by organizing the classification of displayed objects into an architectural form. Seven concentric oval galleries were built on the *Champs de Mars*. In the roofed-over galleries, all objects were displayed according to specific categories. By touring one gallery, spectators could compare countries in a particular category. The outer ring was reserved for shops, restaurants and cafés from the participating countries. The next ring was full of steel and smoke; there were power looms, spinning machines, typesetting machines, tractors, locomotives and cannons. The innermost ring was devoted to the history of labour since the Stone Age. Sixteen radial cross-sections offered exhibition space to the various countries, so that a pie-shaped cross-section showed all exhibits from a single country. In this microcosm, objective time was expressed as a linear progression. The diachronic layout was intended to represent precise dates and to illustrate industrial changes and improvements. From the innermost ring, which represented the past, visitors walked outwards to larger galleries displaying modern products and production processes. Those who walked from the outside inwards moved backwards in time. Here, the choreography of time was based on the rational and utopian doctrine of progress.

Symbols of modernity and rationality expressed Western European desire to impose standard measures — and especially the French-born metric system — on the rest of the world. The objects on display reflected Western wealth that was partly gained from the exploitation of the non-Western countries represented outdoors. The composition of the building and the surrounding grounds referred to the global balance of power. At the time England and France were developing into fully-fledged imperial empires that saw themselves as the centre of the world.[3] Seen from this angle, the outdoor area functioned as a staging of anachronistic space. With this phrase Anne McClintock refers to colonized human beings who, in a temporal sense, exist in a permanent prehistory, while spatially they live on the fringes of the modern empire. As anachronistic beings, irrational, robbed of any will power, they are the perfect embodiment of the archaic 'primitive' peoples.[4]

The 1851 London world exposition had given a slightly different slant to this imperialist staging of time.

In the *Crystal Palace*, the British colonies formed the central focal point, but they were positioned in such a way that visitors could also survey and judge them from galleries upstairs. Illustrated maps guided spectators through the building, and seemed to bring the 'overseas possessions' within reach.[5] In this way, world expositions domesticized imperialism, while also highlighting ethnic differences.

A stimulating factor were visitors from the colonies themselves. Non-whites attracted a great deal of attention. One of journal Punch's drawings shows the *Crystal Palace* as an exhibit packed with Oriental looking people, with Western spectators gawking at them.[6] Other caricatures depict them as primitive beings. One drawing has black visitors 'from the Cannibal Islands' leering at a child in a restaurant as if the child were a potential appetizer.[7] These drawings and caricatures were the first expressions of a globalizing society. Modern perceptions of time were articulated by staging the difference between civilizations, where so-called 'negroes' lived in the pre-history of Western society. The time difference emphasized racial inequality, an argument that also served to discourage the deplored practice of 'interracial marriage' in the colonies.

At later world expositions, indigenous people from the colonies worked as restaurant personnel, and later still the idea was conceived of putting the people themselves on display. In 1877 one began to experiment with this idea in the Paris *Jardin d'Acclimation*, a plant and animal garden.[8] In the anthropological section of the 1878 world's fair, the public could acquaint itself with the evolution of *homo sapiens*. 'Negro' skeletons were compared to those of apes and other animal species.[9] The 1883 Amsterdam world exposition displayed colonized people in their 'own' habitat; Javanese men and women lived and worked

in a replica of a *kampong* (a Javanese village), while Surinam 'natives' stayed in huts under a big tent.[10] From this period onwards, colonial exhibits with 'real' people were a standard attraction at world's fairs. Entire villages with hundreds of inhabitants were constructed. Sometimes, people were grouped according to race so that visitors could more easily study human evolution.

Sometimes the staged opposition between Western superiority and non-Western inferiority was cancelled out by the interaction between spectators and people on display. This happened for instance with Louise Yda, a black Creole woman who had been brought from Surinam to the *Dutch National Exhibition of Women's Labor* in 1898. Louise Yda did not allow herself to be reduced to a mere object in the West Indies exhibit. As the crowds stared at 'this great attraction', she walked around with self-assurance, communicated with the visitors, and to the amazement of all she appeared to speak perfect Dutch.[11] Burton Benedict points to another phenomenon. War dances and marriage ceremonies were some of the rituals accompanying the original lifecycle of non-Western people. They were grounded in objective time, in the rhythm of the seasons and life-stages. At the expositions these rituals degraded into a weekly spectacle.[12] To the spectators this entertainment signified the ethnic background of the performers. The performers themselves however did not assign meaning to the rituals beyond their entertainment value in the colonial exhibit. The rituals were no longer a consciously perceived marker of objective time. They had lost their temporal orientation.

Eventually, people began to protest against the housing and working conditions for the indigenous black and coloured people at expositions, and there were also complaints about the very fact that they were on display. In 1893, Frederick Douglass condemned the existence of Dahomey village at the *World's Columbian Exposition* in Chicago, claiming that the Africans were made to look like savages.[13] Despite the criticism, nothing much changed, and the villages long remained popular. As late as 1928, the *Dutch Industry Exposition* in Rotterdam featured a 'Negro village' in its Lunapark, housing more than one hundred Senegalese men, women and children in an enclosed pen.

These human expositions were a kind of colonial trip taking spectators in opposite directions: forwards in space and backwards in time. Yet, the backward movement in time did not imply an inversion of time. The exposition's structure — with its deliberate divisions into Western versus non-Western exhibits and modern manufacturing versus artisanship — was intended as a normative portrayal of the world that confirmed the West as the centre of the world and the present as the universal point of reference. The future-oriented concept of time had to be made visible. Pavilions and exhibits displayed the various stages of progressing civilization, from backward and savage to civilized and superior. World expositions not only created a differentiated temporality with different time periods linked to specific locations, but they also constructed new stories about the world.

World expositions had another far-reaching consequence. The escalator, the telephone, electric light, x-ray photography and many other inventions that were first introduced at world's fairs, embodied a future that lay within reach of the industrialized countries. These inventions however also increased the separation from their own past. New technology improved mobility and communication; it made the world appear smaller and accelerated the historical process. Yet, it also pushed the past further away. As a result, the past became an object

on display as well: the world's fairs featured historical villages, which became as popular as the 'Negro villages'. The attraction of these locations proved how ambivalent the bourgeoisie felt towards modernity: they had a nostalgic longing for a historical context that was long gone.[14] The first historical villages — Old Vienna, German Village and Irish Village — made their appearance at the 1893 world exposition in Chicago. They stood along with the 'Negro villages' on the Midway Pleasance, an entertainment park next to the *White City*, the heart of the exposition where serious exhibits about industry, arts and sciences were held. To American immigrants, the historical sites functioned as recognizable landmarks at this immense exposition heralding an unknown future.[15] Later world's fairs included districts like Old Antwerp, Old Brussels, Old Paris and Old Plantation. All these sites were meant to both domesticize and objectify the Western past.[16] Inevitably, the simplification of history in these villages led to reductionist stereotypes, just as in the colonial villages. For example, the *Insulinde Kampong* at the *Dutch National Exhibition of Women's Labor* — a collection of huts where Javanese people lived under the street lanterns of The Hague — was supposed to represent the entire Indonesian archi-pelago.[17] In the same way, historical villages combined historical figures and monuments in one setting, resulting in 'unhistorical' tableaux.

However, there were two crucial differences between historical and colonial villages. For one, the people who worked in the historical villages took their costumes off at the end of the day and went home. They were actors. The indigenous people in the colonial villages were supposed to play themselves and often lived on the exposition grounds. The second difference was that the historical villages staged memorable events from national history, which the spectators could take pride in.

As such, these villages belonged to the so-called invented traditions.

The wave of invented traditions in the late nineteenth century points to experiences of discontinuity. In the industrialized world, traditions were invented or reinvented because the link with the past was no longer self-evident. To prevent social dis-integration, the elite promoted activities that legitimized modern institutions and evoked a sense of continuity. The ritual nature of these inventions engendered the sense of belonging and recognition desired by the masses. The rational focus on the future at world expositions therefore generated its own emotional counterforce: nostalgia.[18] The historical sites at the world's fairs seemed to compensate for the disorder of modern society and the uncertainty of the future. The organizers created a recognizable, heroic image of the past, a visual plot in which history is explained by a configuration of time. Various temporal spaces allowed visitors to experience the simultaneity of the un-simultaneous. As a result, the colonial and the historic were turned into objects of entertainment.

These choreographies of time illustrate the discontinuity experienced by nineteenth century Western people. The kaleidoscopic trick with time that I began this article with, in the photographs by the Dutch artist, articulates the acceleration experienced globally in the twenty-first century. Now we see an Asian country putting a European country's past on display, and this 'Japanese' decor in turn becomes the object of a Dutch photographer's gaze. This visual inversion disrupts the hierarchical choreography of Western superiority versus non-Western inferiority. The gap between the space of experience and the horizon of expectations is only getting wider. However, the human need for a point of reference, for an orientation in time, is as strong as ever. This increasing tension may lead to a desire for rigid and superficial histories. Therefore

the challenge to historians is, in Martin Heidegger's words, to keep 'the future past' dynamic, to remain open to an unconscious, unknown and alienated past.[19] In this way new perspectives from the past might enlighten the present.

This text is an extract of the inaugural lecture **De enscenering van de tijd** *(The choreography of time) by Maria Grever at the Erasmus University Rotterdam in 2001.*

Dr. Maria Grever is professor of Historiography and Theory of History at the Faculty of History and Arts at the Erasmus University Rotterdam, the Netherlands.

Notes:

1) Reinhart Koselleck, 'Erfahrungsraum und Erwartungshorizont — zwei historische Kategorien', in: *Vergangene Zukunft*, 349–375, p. 366. *(Futures Past. On the Semantics of Historical Time)*

2) See also: Maria Grever, 'Tijd en ruimte onder één dak. De wereldtentoonstelling als verbeelde vooruitgang', in: Maria Grever and Harry Jansen ed., *De ongrijpbare tijd. Temporaliteit en de constructie van het verleden* (Hilversum 2001), p. 113–130.

3) Edward Said, *Culture and Imperialism* (London: Vintage, 1993), p. 6–7.

4) Anne McClintock, *Imperial Leather. Race, Gender and Sexuality in the Colonial Contest* (New York/London: Routledge, 1995), p. 30.

5) J.A. Auerbach, *The Great Exhibition of 1851. A Nation on Display* (New Haven/London: Yale University Press, 1999), p. 4–5.

6) Ibid, p. 159–160.

7) Ibid, p. 174–175.

8) They were exposed, first, at the proposal of anthropologists and ethnographers, but soon with commercial purpose, see: Maria Grever and Berteke Waaldijk, *Feministische openbaarheid. De Nationale Tentoonstelling van Vrouwenarbeid in 1898* (Amsterdam, 1998), p. 169–171; also in English translation: *Transforming the public sphere. The Dutch National Exhibition of Women's Labor in 1898* (Durham and London, 2004), p. 142–143.

9) Dutch journal *De Wereldtentoonstelling van 1878 te Parijs*, no. 19, p. 302.

10) Ilja Montijn, *Kermis van koophandel. De Amsterdamse wereldtentoonstelling van 1883* (Bussum, 1983), p. 36–42.

11) Grever and Waaldijk, *Feministische openbaarheid*, p. 192–197.

12) Burton Benedict, 'Rituals of Representation: Ethnic Stereotypes and Colonized Peoples at World's Fairs', in: R.W. Rydell and N.E. Gwinn ed., *Fair Representations. World's Fairs and the Modern World* (Amsterdam: Free University Press, 1994), 28–61, p. 57.

13) Laura Rabinovitz, *For the love of pleasure. Women, movies and culture in turn-of-the-century Chicago* (New Brunswick, 1998), p. 60. Already in 1889, French and Dutch newspaper complained about the treatment of people from the colonies exhibited at the Paris world exhibition, see: Grever and Waaldijk, *Feministische openbaarheid*, p. 171.

14) Lieven de Cauter, *Archeologie van de kick. Verhalen over moderniteit en ervaring* (Leuven: Van Halewijck, 1989), p. 118–119.

15) James Gilbert, *Perfect Cities, Chicago's utopias of 1893* (Chicago, 1991) 77–78, p. 112.

16) See also: David Lowenthal, *The Past is a Foreign Country* (Cambridge 1985), xvii and xxiv.

17) Grever and Waaldijk, *Feministische openbaarheid*, p. 167–181; idem, *Transforming the public sphere*, p. 141–161.

18) Lowenthal, *The Past is a Foreign Country*, p. 4–13.

19) See: Veronica Vasterling, 'De rechte lijn en de lus. Heideggers onderzoek naar de tijd en de geschiedenis van het tijdbegrip', in: Grever and Jansen ed., *De ongrijpbare tijd*, 175–187, p.187.

TRANSFORMATION HOUSE
[Barbara Visser]

I. A house is not a hiding place

The place where we will live is no longer
the self-imposed jail it has been for the past
two thousand years. From this moment on,
the house as we know it will change programme, because people have changed,
or at least the lives of people have changed.

Most of human evolution took place before
the advent of agriculture, when men lived
in small groups, on a face-to-face basis.
As a result, human biology has evolved to
an adaptive mechanism to conditions that
have largely ceased to exist. Despite the fact
that the brain capacity of man has not
notably expanded since the Stone Age, the
social and professional demands of today
call for a radical reconsideration of the way
we view our habitat.

The conditions we live in appear to be
choices, but in fact they depend largely on
availability, coincidence, and most of all,
on pure luck.

The house will cease to be a shelter from
the elements. The notion of a retreat for the
vulnerable un-hairy species is obsolete.
Issues like nourishment, as in: being able to
collect enough food to stay alive, or the
imminent danger to become food for others
yourself, are negligible concerns in this part
of the world. The same applies to
climatologic factors. The primitive reflex to
design dwellings to shut the elements out is
hard to delete from our system, since we
despise the weather in our country so much
that to ignore it seems to be the best
defence.

Another point of interest for the two-legged
mammal is possession: how to obtain it,

London 1977
1977
colour photograph

how to multiply it, and most of all how not to lose it. This led to the false conclusion that a house is a storage place for goods. The need to lock away collected commodities is an endless one. Large groups of people lose their reasoning and move to virtual wastelands, led by the promise of more storage space. Single objects are often interchangeable and can be made of recycled material. Emotional attachment from now on exists only from one living creature to the other — plants included. Please note that the structure at stake here is considered to become one of these living creatures.

It seems that the design of houses has been largely driven by negative factors. Now that all practicalities of living in the 20th century have evaporated into mere theory, former concerns on human housing from the year zero to the year two thousand can soon be looked up in history books.

II. A house is not a home

My parents met in the early sixties, when they were studying architectural engineering in Delft. I was born in 1966, my sister a year earlier. We lived on the highest level of a four-floor apartment block on the outskirts of Haarlem. My father went to work, my mother stayed home with two babies. With little else to do she wondered why so many people like herself were sitting alone in a box stacked on top of another box all day. This depressed the hell out of her. A few years later the four of us moved to Amsterdam, where we had two boxes on top of each other. But my mother remained depressed. She decided to leave the family in 1977, to live elsewhere and study architecture. Her ideal was something called 'Central Living', a form of co-habitation that she promoted in articles and as part of a support group. The idea of Central Living is that a group of people choose to share a

building and its facilities, and sometimes share other, more personal things as well. Meanwhile, she lived alone in a small room she rented. When she finally managed to sublet a more spacious apartment, my sister moved in with her. My father just seemed to work or sleep. One day he came home and announced that he was going to live with a woman he described as 'pearl', who stayed on a house-boat in one of the canals of Amsterdam. He took a bag of clothes and some books and went off.

Now that my parents had left home, I remained in the two-storey apartment, surrounded by the brown and orange furnishings they'd picked according to the fashion a decade earlier. Despite the admiring remarks of my friends about my huge flat, I was relieved to find a student room in the city centre. My father, then over 50, started a new family with 'pearl'. My mother had a Living Apart Together relationship with a law student 15 years her junior.

(continued)

III. Indefinite walls for indefinite futures

The growing variations in professional and personal activities during a persons' life today are poorly reflected in the way houses are designed and built. Change and time are rarely considered useful factors in building plans; it seems to contradict planning-as-we-know-it.

Transformation House revolves around the idea that the location where someone works, sleeps and interacts can be a stable factor in a life marked by transformations, without the structure being the dumb and deaf entity it is today. It leads in the direction of a modular set of connectable forms in different sizes, shapes and materials, from which the owner can assemble a bungalow or villa to fit momentary needs, and add and subtract according to any changes in his/her personal or professional situation. The word modular points to the system as developed by Le Corbusier. This once ideal system will be adjusted to meet the needs of contemporary and future men and women. Apart from the obvious physical changes, like the increase in average size of man, psychological factors become an important part of the equation as well. The fact that the senses are hard to measure does not mean they're not important.

This proposal takes the advantages of the conventional 'box' by allowing private spaces (exit loft-architecture), but eradicates the claustrophobic effects of the fixed scale and rigid proportions, the one we locked ourselves up in, in order to escape the threatening world outside.

The permanently unfinished house can have a radically different appearance, according to the elements used. Included are elements that allow the spaces to be placed at different heights by using poles, or can be placed on wheels for easy re-location on the premises itself. For radical and almost instant transformations in the interior, walls sliding and rotating in every direction are appropriate.

IV. A house is not a museum

Imagine living in a world where the *Rietveld-Schröder House* had not turned into a museum. Imagine that the ideals as articulated in that house had rooted themselves into the considerations of mainstream architects and builders, and a large amount of people had embraced the idea of living in a space that allowed for a series of transformations.

Transformation House
2006
computer-animation

Amsterdam, May 29th, 2006

Dear Gerrit,

A few weeks ago, my father quit his job at the **Rietveld-Schröder House.** *Having worked as an engineer for the National Building Society all his life, he considered the house you've designed for and with Truus Schröder-Schräder an appropriate environment for a post-career volunteer job, where he could make use of his love for architecture and design, guiding groups of tourists around the house.*
He explained his resignation by giving just one reason. He said that the ride to Utrecht from his home in Almere is too long if it is merely made to tell the same story every time.
My father however did enjoy the questions of the visitors, he told me. He's kept a record of the ones he could not answer, to look for the information later, at a moment when the visitors themselves were already on their way back to Tokyo, or busy seeing another important European sight.

In most of the literature about the **Rietveld-Schröder House,** *as romanticized as that may sometimes be, your relationship to Mrs. Schröder is described in technical terms. It's probably unprofessional to consider personal circumstances when reviewing a designer's work. But isn't the* **Rietveld-Schröder House** *the ultimate metaphor of the radical changes in your personal life at the time? The idea of transformation is expressed most clearly in the changeable structure inside; rooms can change size and shape, appear and disappear according to their function and the needs of the inhabitant at any moment of the day or night. It's tempting to think of the 'hidden' storage places in terms of psychological as well as practical signs.*

The big changes you've made in your personal life may have been quite a scandal at the time. Here, in the 21st century, it's common practice that people change habits, houses, jobs, spouses, age, offspring, language, looks, foods and time-zones within days, hours, sometimes minutes. What remains a mystery to me is why a lot of the ideas as formulated in the **Rietveld-Schröder House** *— so clearly ahead of their time, have become relics: things to be visited and*

Transformation House
2006
computer-animation

*looked at in retrospective admiration, instead of
having naturally developed into general parameters
for building in the 20th century.*

*The paradox of the time I am writing to you from, is
that one is expected to have conflicting personalities;
on the one hand be a stable and decisive person, and
at the same time being able to adapt to an infinite
range of social and professional situations. The form
of living for a person under these demands, is to be
further developed, starting from your heritage that,
unjustly so, has remained unique.*

*Yours truly,
Barbara Visser*

V.

One of the qualities of *Transformation House*
is that it would never work as a museum.
It only has meaning when its form is not
fixed in time. If neighbours were to be part
of the system as well, a number of variations
could be on display at the same time.
Transformation House is a proposal for a way
of building that is more related to the reality
of people's lives today. It is not bound to be
an artefact to be guided through in 2086,
but one example of a structure, which by
then has become an intrinsic part of the way
homes are designed and built.

*Transformation House
2006
computer-animation*

LECTURE ON LECTURE WITH ACTRESS [BIS]
[Barbara Visser]

"If the aim of the artist is to approach reality as closely as possible, what am I doing here, sweating in the dark?"
Lecture on Lecture with Actress, Berlin, 2004

Actress:
Good evening. My name is Barbara Visser. *Lecture on Lecture with Actress* takes place in Berlin, September 2004. The location is a new hangout for art people, called *The Münz Club*. You can't see me, but I'm standing on the other side of the wall, behind the actress. I will be there for 45 minutes. It's noisy as hell. I'm blocking the passageway to the toilets. I am standing facing a small door, whispering a text into a microphone.

This is the start of a performance, where I prompt an actress playing me. From my dark spot, I am trying to live up to my own ideas. Speaking as clearly as I can, I'm wondering if my words are reaching the actress, performing on the other side of the wall. A young art critic from Germany has invited me for a show with the ambiguous title: *Funky Lessons: the trouble with didactics, and how it's tackled.* Art people from around Europe have gathered here tonight. While waiting, they chat about their expectations. They came to get a funky lesson. To meet their needs I'm presenting them an artificial version of myself.

To force the actress to speak in a specific way, my intonation is over-acting during this lecture about my work. The actress follows without hesitation. She has no choice, since her failure would be public. She's somewhat out of place here, the Dutch actress in this German setting receiving English words to reproduce.

Lecture on Lecture with Actress
2004
performance, registration on DVD

No one seems to notice the fact that the brunette is an empty shell, mechanically repeating the words she receives through a small device in her right ear. To produce these words is easier this time than in 1997; this time I have written text in front of me that I read aloud. The actress registers and repeats simultaneously, and I continue talking while she listens and speaks at once. The audience sits quietly. Her pace and tone are so convincing, that the audience shows no second thoughts. Her behavior is smooth, like a stewardess in full action.
I tell the actress a video clip is coming up, of my appearance in a Lithuanian soap-series. Our looks can be compared here. The resemblance between the dark-haired woman on stage and me is striking.
The audience is reassured. They say to each other: my, she hasn't changed at all in seven years! At this moment it occurs to me that one can also be too convincing. Even her mistakes appear to be natural; the robot has come to life.

To create confusion about the identity of the speaker isn't easy at this point. I am somewhat discouraged by seeing how easily the audience complies with the situation presented, and wonder if this is becoming a problem. The audience is half-drunk and patient, a rare combination. Even without a moderator, a form of direction is called for. From my dark passage I tell myself I'm in charge.

A play is not a play when the audience doesn't know what they're looking at. There are no other actors around for guidance, there's only the screen showing *Lecture with Actress* from 1997, which the actress is instructed not to look at.

Her attention is starting to show flaws because my directions are lost. The activity in the passageway is too noisy; this is a club, after all. The actress seems to manage anyway. Her lines come out well enough,

Lecture on Lecture with Actress
2004
performance, registration on DVD

since she knows by profession how to
believe her lines and transmit this belief to
anyone in front of her.

The centre is a great place to be. But what
one tends to forget is that being in the
centre has one great disadvantage: you cease
to be a spectator who observes from behind
a black curtain. Let's remain here, living in
the illusion that Barbara Visser is a friendly
brown-haired flight attendant pretending to
be an artist. Not all exposure is good
exposure. It really doesn't matter if something is true, what matters is whether there
is meaning in it.

Last Lecture
2005
photomontage for performance

UNCOVERED: THE MYTH ABOUT...
[Jörg Heiser]

Prior to writing this piece, I was asked to conform to two 'obstructions': "1. Do not mention 'the artist Barbara Visser' — neither name nor profession. 2. Do not refer to actual works in the past tense — to a past context, space, situation or time." Do I already violate the obstructions by quoting them? Furthermore, I was asked to write about 'myths' in relation to these works. I like a game, so I will try to play to its rules. In my case, these rules form a strong, interesting tension to the very subject matter, 'myths'. You can read the two obstructions as a means to take apart the myth of a linear, causal relation between someone's biography, intention, and publicised work. In that sense, the obstructions would be anti-mythological. But ironically, you can also see them as the ultimate mythologization: the person turns into a phantom — the 'person who cannot be named' is usually God — while his or her works become living beings, or rather: mythical beings.

Before we can continue exploring this schism between the mythical and the anti-mythical, we need to gain some clarity on the notoriously unclear notion that it is based on. To start with, a myth is a cultural expression, or as Roland Barthes has described it, a type of speech. It can have almost any content, but the form or scheme of which establishes a particular set of connections between the appearance or identity of humans (including cultural artefacts and technology) and that which seemingly transcends them (the cosmos, nature, deities, 'higher' spheres and causes etc.). A myth is formed historically, as Claude Lévi-Strauss has stressed, by the interplay of all the ways in which it is narrated and passed on. It is a means to gratify the urge to gain access to some kind of truth or knowledge beyond ordinary, everyday life knowledge.

The critical impetus of exposing myths can be compared to Hans Christian Andersen's story of the Emperor's new clothes, in which a naïve child exposes what all others were to cowardly to say or even think, the fact that the Emperor is actually naked. But what complicates the matter is that if one was to continue this 19th century story into the late 20th and early 21st, the point would be that the nudity fashion would catch on; that it would become popular to actively expose oneself as purified of myths and that the story would have to be reversed: the naïve — or would it already be cynical? — child would have to exclaim that the Emperor, counter to what is claimed, still wears something. This 'striptease' of the mythological, as Odo Marquard has aptly called it, inevitably turns into strip-poker: who exposes whom first of still 'wearing' myths? Who keeps aces up their mythology-sleeves?

Not to get lost here: this doesn't mean to denounce enlightenment, as it often has been done, as the greatest myth. Rather, it means not only to expose how the gesture of demystifying can become mechanical, or manipulative, and thus fall back onto being mythical itself, but how even this exposure of the exposure cannot escape the illusory: namely, the illusion that it was possible to cleanse the world of myths. The point is that enlightenment possibly works most effectively when it is less about denouncing than 'organising' myths, making it possible to experience them in competition and interference with one another; to read them differently or 'subversively' rather than allowing any of them to become ideologically dominating. In effect this means to favour, as Odo Marquard has argued, the poly-mythical over the mono-mythical. Sounds like a hell of a mishmash relativism, but the point is to really understand this concept of enlightenment as an active social and discursive 'navigation' amongst competing myths, ensuring that they remain in competition, instead of a passive, indifferent tolerance towards all of them.

In art, hence, the schism between the mythical and the anti-mythical turns out to really be the schism between the mono-mythical and the poly-mythical. It is this schism in which interesting art is situated; it sits on the fence between striving for and dismantling mythical hegemony. It is egotistic and self-negating, it clothes and strips, it interferes and retreats, praises and mocks, entertains and disturbs, fucks up and beautifies, often all in one go, while resisting the urge to identify itself merely with the role of either prosecutor or defender. Thus the history of art, to some extent parallel to the history of the Enlightenment, can be told as a struggle between the mono-mythical and the poly-mythical.

What in the 20th century follows the old myth of the genius artist in touch with higher powers (whether through talent or madness) is that of the artist as hard worker, even manager. Lévi-Strauss compares the mythological way of thinking with the improvisational methods of the bricoleur, juxtaposing it with the supposedly systematic methodology of the engineer. Jacques Derrida in turn 'exposes' the engineer as a myth created by the bricoleur. The relation between bricoleur and engineer seems analogous to that between the classical modern Cubist or Surrealist on the one hand, and Constructivists on the other; or between Modernism in general and the first generation Conceptualists — with the ironic turn that the Conceptualists were 'engineers' of exposing myths, turning the 'strip-poker' of exposing the myths of Modernism into a systematic method,

often neglecting their own debt to it. However, 'Romantic' Conceptualists, such as Bas Jan Ader or 'Tropical' Conceptualists such as Lygia Clark, were countering the all too easy denunciation of the image as kitsch, the act as faux-authentic, and the object as fetish, with the very means of conceptualism. In other words, they favoured the poly-mythical over the supposedly anti-mythical strip-poker which is ultimately mono-mythical. Warhol would be another example of an artist whose attitude towards the bricoleur vs. engineer schism took the form of a kind of Russian nesting doll of mythical personas and images; Warhol as both hardworking and bored'n'lazy, genius and dilettante, sociable and semi-autistic, etc.

Which finally brings us to... (oops I almost mentioned her name) and her work. It can be read as an intricate set of experiments exploring three distinct ways of 'navigating' myths, and a possible notion of truth that we inevitably need in order to do so. These three different ways, I would argue, correspond to the three different types of empirical knowledge as defined by Donald Davidson: knowledge about what's in my mind, in the world, and in other people's minds. The point for Davidson is that you can't have one without the other, that these three types of knowledge rely on each other to gain some kind of stability like the three legs of a tripod: that for example you only can know what you think by comparison, via communication, with what other people think, against the background of what's in the world. And that truth, as inaccessible as it may be, is the only 'intersubjective standard' that ultimately allows that comparison. A statement you have to take with a pinch of salt as Davidson makes quite clear that it's easier to say what truth is *not*, than what it is.

The 'knowledge about what's in my mind' corresponds to the kind of work that predominantly explores what could be called 'performing the myth'. *Philippa* consists of shots of a 17th century aristocratic Amsterdam house called the van Loon house, after the family who owned it from the 19th century onwards. A woman wearing three kinds of lady-style attires (elaborate hairdos, high heels,

Philippa
1998
video, set photographs

expensive looking dresses) moves 'hysterically' through heavily decorated period rooms, using secret doors and sliding down the richly ornamented copper banister, signalled by slapstick, silent-movie type accelerated speed. She is basically three women at once — decadent, odd, idiosyncratic — who look for each other, or hide from each other, yet miss each other all the time, while a female voice keeps calling out for *Phiiilliiipa!?* Philippa in that sense is a phantom, a ghost. According to descriptions of the piece, the protagonist is supposedly the 'real' Philippa van Loon, last descendent of the van Loon family who spent her childhood in the house. But we can't be sure that this is actually the case, as according to the website of Museum van Loon, Thora Egidius, wife of Willem van Loon, was the last resident of the house until her death in 1945. And we don't need to be sure. Because ultimately it feels like we are watching glimpses into the mind of a single woman who is stuck with different options of making sense for herself in terms of playing her social role. The labyrinthic house becomes both an allegory for the psyche, in its trap doors, hidden rooms, staircases, its phantoms and ghosts, and for the mythical identification of women with the domestic sphere, that was accelerated, if not 'invented', by the new kind of capitalism so characteristic of the Dutch Golden Age. A monitor displaying the work is located in the rustic kitchen — the kitchen obviously being the most blatant site of that mythical identification — while ironically the protagonist roams anywhere around the house but the kitchen. The mono-myth of the woman-as-domestic, in the mind of *Philippa*, turns into a poly-mythical farce.

'Knowledge about what's in the world' seems to correspond to the kind of works that at first glance seem to simply 'represent' some ordinary aspect of the

Philippa
1998
video, set photographs

Philippa
1998
video, set photographs

Philippa
1998
video, set photographs

world. Starting with the title, the ten-minute video loop *Decorealism* creates the impression of a focus on what could at first seem arbitrary aspects of everyday life: the decorum that supposedly is just a derivative side-aspect of the 'real thing'. We see a static total shot of a modernist cinema building, and entering the frame from the front, an old couple in grey Sunday best are slowly walking backwards towards it, as if the film was running backwards. Yet in the background we see other passers-by (two teenagers entering the cinema, a person with a dog leaving it) going forwards. We realize the couple must have been instructed to move that way. What could be the establishing shot for a movie scene — extras instructed to provide a realist background for what the actors are doing in the foreground — is twisted and made the 'actual thing' by a single inversion. Later on in the piece, we return to the cinema, shot from the same angle, and this time two women with prams first stand still before a silly bell sound rings and they move slowly away, leaving the site, which ends the scene — the impression of instructed extras is being emphasised.

Another short scene of an equestrian on a large horse in front of a temple-like building is hilariously deadpan: the horse, like a donkey, obstinately resists desperate attempts to make it move (in a later return to the scene, another person tries to help, but to no avail). Often the short scenes, which are divided by unhurried fades to black, have the same generic birds-in-the-park-soundtrack; otherwise there are almost no voices except for cryptic utterances that seem to stand for film set instructions. 'Knowledge about the world' comes in the disguise of the way it is manifested as media reality (film, TV etc.), as the 'deco-realist' milieu for what goes on in our minds, or other people's minds. The extras — turned main protagonists by the way their movements are stopped, inverted, instructed etc. — are enacting the struggle to make sense of the world and our place in it, along the way.

'Knowledge about what's in other people's minds' finally corresponds to the works that predominantly deal with the impersonation of a character based on a real person. In regard to *Philippa*, we are sure that what we see is an impersonation of three characters by the same person, while we have doubts about the claim that the person, Philippa van Loon, actually exists. It is the other way round with pieces like *Interview with Duiker, Gimines, Lecture with Actress*, and *Lecture on Lecture with Actress*:

Decoralism
1999
video, still

Decoralism
1999
video, still

here we may have doubts about who is actually providing the impersonation, yet we can be pretty sure that this impersonation does refer to an existing person (an architect, an actress, an artist). Otherwise, these pieces would be kind of pointless: because they would render irrelevant the question of what's in the other person's mind (the architect's, the actress's, the artist's). In other words, this relative stability of reference to an authentic person highlights that despite of that stability, we still have no direct access to what's in that person's mind.

Images, with typical technical transmission errors, show a Methuselah giving grumpy answers to a journalist's questions. Yet a little bit of research would easily reveal that Duiker already died in 1935. The point of the piece however is not just the funny fake, but the way it projects the question of how 'original' generations of producers in early Modernity, if they were still alive, might think about the way their work is perceived in the post-1960s world of late or Post-Modernity. It provokes you to imagine what would be 'in other people's minds' if they hadn't died.

Interview with Duiker consists of what seems like a short satellite-TV interview with the famous Dutch architect Johannes Duiker, who designed the classical Modernist cinema in which the piece is shown.

Gimines is based on a participation in a Lithuanian sitcom of the same name (meaning 'relatives'), in which the char–acter of a Dutch artist named Barbora [sic] Visser appears (introduced as the wife of a Lithuanian surgeon living in the US). The point is of course that we can assume that for the predominant part of the TV audience, the question of whether this character is based on a real character or not, has no relevance whatsoever. However, presented in the art context, this 'irrelevance' bounces back ironically onto the image of the authentic artist, emphasising and highlighting the way her 'performance' as a person does not provide privileged access to what's in her mind, lest her work.

Interview with Duiker
1994
set photograph

Gimines
1995
video still of set

Gimines
1995
video, stills

Gimines
1995
newspaper clipping

In *Lecture with Actress*, this mix-up comedy aspect is transferred into the plot itself: at a symposium on 'reality as fiction', the artist is played by an actress that looks and behaves quite differently from her. Because of the fact that she receives her lines through an earpiece and repeats them hesitantly and mechanically, the situation becomes slightly surreal, even more so as a video presentation of *Gimines* reveals the fact that the person who plays the character Barbora Visser and is supposedly the same person now present in the room looks completely different. We don't know what's in the actress's mind, but we do get an idea of what is *not* in her mind: most of the things she mechanically says. Yet a large part of the audience seems to continue to accept that the person they are listening to is the one they think it is. *Lecture on Lecture with Actress* turns the screw once more: it starts with a woman standing in front of a screen, introducing herself as "Barbara Visser", telling the story of *Lecture with Actress*. It becomes increasingly impossible to untangle the conundrum, because you would have had to have been familiar with these earlier works to distinguish who was playing whom. In other words, our knowledge of 'what's in other people's minds' relies heavily on our knowledge of what's in the world and of knowing what's in our own mind.

Actor and Liar is even more of a 'meta-work' in terms of providing, in its 'explicit' content, a discussion of the interrelation between Davidson's triad of knowledge. Like *Philippa*, it delves into how we relate to what's in our mind, but like *Decorealism* it does so predominantly by looking at manifestations in the world, while — like *Lecture with Actress* — pointing to the ques-tion of how a person's behaviour relates to what's supposedly in that person's mind.

Actor and Liar is a double back-to-back video projection on a suspended screen.

It begins with a certain Mr. van Watermeulen on one side, reading from a letter he wrote to a certain Mr. Neuman, who has been sent to prison for fraud: for selling pieces of the moon. In his letter Watermeulen argues that Neuman had obviously sold an idea, not an object — apparent due to the fact that someone buying a plot of land on the moon would evidently have no access to it — and thus did something that is a tradition of Conceptual Art: to hand over a certificate to confirm that an idea has been sold. Neuman — seen on the other side of the screen sitting in a prison cell, and played by the very same actor — listens attentively, before responding by saying, with slight sarcasm, that Mr. van Watermeulen should have been his lawyer, as he could have saved him from his prison sentence with that very argument. Watermeulen in turn says: "In the book *The Psychology of the Liar*, I read that the intention of lying is to convince another person of something the liar believes is false." The interesting point here is that there is a distinction made between lying and believing something to be true or false; which includes the possibility that someone could state something as supposedly true that he believes to be false, yet which actually turns out to be true.

This points to the classic philosophical paradox of Epimenides of Knossos, who stated that "all Cretans are liars". If Epimenides, being a Cretan himself, believed what he said to be true (that all Cretans — including him when making that statement — lie), then he would not have been lying when making this statement. However if he believed what he said to be false, then he would be lying, but the Cretans, including him, would not be liars. Both possibilities remain paradoxical, and the only 'solution' is to simply state that a sentence like this can be 'neither true nor false'. In the case of the 'liar' selling pieces of the moon, we have a similar ambiguity. One could argue that he simply convinces others of what he believes is true; that it is possible to 'own', in some imaginative way, a piece of the moon through the transaction he offers. However, it is not possible to make that argument without knowing how precisely the transaction took place and was argued. For example, if the context makes clear that a buyer was buying under assumptions and suggestions of an 'actual' ownership of juridical viability — which is clearly not the case — then the 'liar' is knowingly allowing that assumption to be an implication of that transaction, and then he is in fact a liar (Davidson: "Our speech acts reveal our underlying attitudes towards our sentences; *but often indirectly.*")[1]

It is this question of how much we know about the concrete context of a 'transaction' — or more generally of some form of communication — that is the defining line in terms of dealing with notions of the mythical, and the true. Admitting that we can never know *everything* about a concrete context (the precise relation between what in a given case was/is in my mind, in the world, and other people's minds) is to admit that the potential of 'unravelling myths' in terms of something being true or false exists, but we inevitably have to live with and 'negotiate' myths as we can never fully master that potential (unless we assume to be God, which would be the ultimate myth). As Donaldson puts it: "Realism, with its insistence on radically non-epistemic correspondence [i.e. the philosophical belief that truth is 'objective', completely independent of what is in people's minds], asks more of truth than we can understand; antirealism, with its limitation of truth to what can be ascertained [i.e. the philosophical belief that truth is 'subjective', completely dependent on what's in people's minds], unnecessarily deprives truth of its role as

an intersubjective standard. If we want to speak the truth about truth, we should say no more than need be."

Truth as an 'intersubjective standard' — rather than being either what radically cannot be ascertained or only that which can be ascertained — is a kind of navigational tool in-between, between the known and the unknown, between what I know and what I don't know about what's in my mind, in the world, and in other people's minds. That implies it's a 'tool' that is subject to revision and recalibration. Davidson's proposal to see truth as neither completely detached from communication and experienced reality, nor only residing within the limits of what we can access via communication and experienced reality, can also be read in relation to the mythical versus the anti-mythical: while we 'navigate' competing myths, we may assume that we test their truth-value, but must be aware that we can never have full access to all necessary data to ultimately determine it. 'We should say no more than need be' expresses that remaining uncertainty.

It's a beautiful irony that on the cover of Donald Davidson's book *Subjective, Intersubjective, Objective,* the designer used a cropped portrait of the bald-headed philosopher wearing a turtleneck and put a kind of glowing aura around it, making him look like the leader of a Sci-Fi sect. This tension between the pragmatic tone of Davidson and the way he's presented as a freaky guru corresponds nicely to the works discussed in this essay: because they sit on the fence between embracing the humbleness of a statement like 'if we want to speak the truth about truth, we should say no more than need be' and at the same time pointing out that it is actually not that humble: that stressing the importance of not saying too much can easily make you sound like an oracle, or phantom.

Actor and Liar (Liar)
2003
back-to-back video-projection

Actor and Liar (Actor)
2003
back-to-back video-projection

This should also make clear that these works are not an expression of a kind of trickster scepticism that simply asserts that we have no access to truth because everything could be a lie. Rather, by way of suggesting tensions between intentions and utterances, these works navigate the line between what can be 'revealed' and what cannot, between the known and the unknown. The 'two obstructions' encourage the contributors of this volume to do this as well, making them a part of that endeavour.

Notes:

1) Donald Davidson, *Subjective, Intersubjective, Objective*, Oxford University Press, 2001, p. 190

2) Donald Davidson, op. cit., p.191

ACTOR AND LIAR
[Barbara Visser]

Actor:
Dear Mr. Neuman, I recently read an article about your activities in selling property on the moon, as well as the consequences of those activities. Although what you did appears to be punishable, I actually think it's a wonderful idea: it's obvious that for the foreseeable future, anyone who purchases a plot on the moon will not be able to visit that plot. As such, it is clear that this is a concept. The rest of his or her life, owners of a piece of the moon will probably have to leave it to their imagination in order to enjoy their possession. The beauty of the entire undertaking lies precisely in this detail. The way I see it, what you sold was an idea.

Liar:
Selling property on the moon was a huge success. In newspapers and magazines they called me a failed entrepreneur. Do you call selling 8000 pieces of land a failure? The fact that I'm sitting here now has little to do with my business — what I did was completely legal. It was even approved by the highest authorities in America.

Actor:
I'm an actor. My work centres around the questions, 'What do we see?' 'What do we hear?' 'What is believable and why?' In the visual arts, when a conceptual piece — which consists solely of an idea — is sold to a collector or a museum it is usually represented by a certificate. This has been common practice for decades, and to my knowledge no artist has ever been jailed for 'selling air', as you were. Although they are intangible, ideas are the fuel that has fed art for centuries.

Liar:
I should have hired that guy as my lawyer.

Actor and Liar
2003
document

Actor:
I'm very curious about your motives, about people's reactions, and about the regret you expressed, which was mentioned in the article. I would like to hear what it is you're sorry for. Perhaps I could come visit you sometime?

Liar:
It was immediately clear to me that he wanted to do more than just talk. The warden of my unit approved his visit. The prison fence is there in order to keep prisoners in, not to keep the world out. In his second letter, Mr. van Watermeulen asked if I would speak about myself in the third person, using he instead of I. No idea why.

Actor:
(reads from letter) Neuman wrote: "Dear Mr. van Watermeulen, Many thanks for your visit and your letter. I understand the questions, and will do my best to answer them. At first, your request that I replace the word 'I' with 'he' seemed not to be a problem, but a bit of self-evaluation proved that it is more difficult than I thought. I hope you don't mind if I make a mistake once in a while and accidentally use 'I' instead of 'he'." The first question is, 'Does Thomas Neuman know who he is?' I asked him what he wanted to be when he was a child. It seemed like a good question to start with.

Liar:
I'm actually a good actor. I've been a salesman for years. There's no better training. You cultivate an attitude: self-confident with a hint of arrogance. And always wear a suit. Mr. van Watermeulen asked me whether it was possible to sell an idea, just an idea. I told him, 'Yes. If you're wearing a suit. If you're wearing a suit, you can sell anything. Even the moon.'

Actor:
I asked him, 'Does the moon belong to anyone?' If you're going to sell people a piece of land on the moon, of course they're going to want to know who will be writing out the parking tickets *(laughs)*. He replied: 'Nobody governs the moon. That's not yet necessary. But the United States keeps an eye on that, to make sure that nothing unwanted happens.'

Liar:
People always have a ready answer to the question about what they wanted to be when they grew up. If I did know then, I certainly can't remember now. I don't think I knew back then, either. I'm a sort of chameleon. Maybe that's my problem. Here, they call it a 'compulsive disorder'. They think it's something you can learn: to stop making things up. I hope so.

Actor:
In the book *The Psychology of the Liar*, I read that the intention of lying is to convince another person of something that the liar believes is false. That is exactly the difference between Thomas Neuman and myself. But we have the same motive: to do everything in our power to make life less banal.

Liar:
Mr. van Watermeulen asked me rather puzzling questions. One of them was if I would be portrayed by an actor in this film, what the actor would have to do in order to play the role convincingly.

Actor:
The average person lies 1.5 times per day. How many is that for Neuman? In reference to him, lying suddenly becomes a compulsive disorder. Is this due to the frequency of his lying or to its sophistication? In our society the power of imagination on this subject is limited, of course.

Liar:
At the moment, Marlon Brando is making an educational DVD entitled *Lying for a Living*. In it, he teaches average people how to use the lie of acting in everyday life. I'm in the process of developing a similar idea to exploit when I'm free again. Mr. van Watermeulen will be able to help me with this. It is a social project for fighting injustice in the world. I can't say too much about it yet. The project is called *Diana*, after my ex. It's a simple name. Easy to remember.

Actor:
I approached Neuman because I think that I can learn a lot from him. When he says that you have to put on a suit in order to be convincing, at first I don't feel like I'm hearing anything new. But you have to know how to interpret his words. What he's talking about is the meaning the wearer gives to the suit. Neuman has not just put on the suit in order to come across as respectable. No, he was born in that suit.

Liar:
If I had become an actor, everything would have been different. I'm 100% sure of that. The temptation to make things up is so strong. But I'm not the only one who's responsible. When you see how easily people will believe something, you're compelled to make things up. The world is asking for it. And once you've started, there's no going back. Through talking with Mr. van Watermeulen, perhaps I'm getting more of a grip on reality.

Actor:
According to Cicero, faith is a kind of impression that is made upon our inner selves, and the gentler and more malleable we are, the easier we are to influence. Just as a scale will immediately tip down when you place a weight on it, our souls yield to obviousness.

Liar:
The world must change. I must change.

Actor:
Wouldn't we be constantly repeating ourselves, if we would always use the term 'unnatural' or 'strange' as soon as we came into contact with something we couldn't comprehend? If we consider the fog through which we are forced to gropingly come to know most things that pass through our hands, we would surely discover that it is not so much our knowledge of things but rather our getting used to them that removes their strangeness.

SCRIPTED SPACES
[Alexis Vaillant]

*"If we try to adopt a more realistic approach to the
absolute nothingness of space, we become like those
people floating in sensory deprivation chambers,
who are disturbed when the only perceptible external
reality enters our own minds"*
J.G. Ballard, 1974

"Take a photo, it will last longer!"
John Waters, 1999

<u>A trip to nowhere</u>

In 1999, I looked for her everywhere.
Having obtained her telephone number,
I left several messages on her answer phone.
At that time, I was preparing a workshop
with young artists, devoted to television.
Five years earlier, she had spent some time
in Lithuania where she appeared in a *soap*
as the artist Barbora Visser, but this was
a vague rumour. We wanted her to come
to San Sebastian to talk about her time on
the small screen. She never replied to us.
Without a doubt she did not exist at that
time. We met two years later on the Côte
d'Azur in a white convertible. We quickly
turned the conversation to other matters.
In the space of two years, she had become
a myth, for which I never would have an
explanation. Like an unidentified work,
access to this story was not forthcoming.
It took a further five years to obtain an
'explanation' from its author. Here it is:

"Barbora is a character that originates in
a moment of despair. The demand to make
a work in a country (Lithuania) in circumstances and in a culture that is virtually
impossible to understand by a foreign artist,
made me look for a solution that was close
to my own world (fiction) and close to
my own character (Barbara). The idea to
propose to play myself and have the

dramatic story synchronized with the actual
situation — a Dutch artist in Vilnius to make
a work — was in fact a solution to a
problem. Barbara had a lot of trouble to be
herself though; the cast of Lithuanian stars
were not her natural environment, and the
question 'how does one play oneself' seems
an easy one to answer, but in fact led to
an existential crisis. One of the intentions
was to blend in with the exotic environment
yet to confirm the position of the outsider.
Another interest was to be an uninvited
guest in 80% of the homes in Lithuania who
were watching the popular show. The
writers of the episode felt it necessary to
give Barbora an interpersonal reason to be
there (a romance with a doctor), whereas
I felt she could have a more marginal
existence, someone who was just passing
by... One of the most interesting outcomes
is that it turned out to be the work seen by
the most people (a TV audience) outside
of art, and by the fewest inside of art.

Gimines
1995
calendar of 1996

This made it a piece of conceptual art, since
it was not the work itself but rather the idea
of the work that people talked about.
The tangible result is a photograph on the
December page of the 1996 calendar."[1]

And I understood why I had the feeling of
going nowhere, precisely because I wanted
to know. This ghost of a thread, which
became an intrigue and then a quest, is,
as Piero Manzoni once said, the proof that
"there is no art without myth". Thus
initiating an ambiguous discourse situated
nowhere between truth and lies, this quest
represents an open source to our projections
and (mis)understandings. An open source
with no solution. A jumble, a hybridisation,
just like in any important experiment.

XM
1994
video, still

XM
1994
video, still

In 1994, a black Citroën crosses the woods at full speed to the sound of the title music of *Black Beauty* — a TV series that made every child cry in the 1970s. The layouts, framing and duration are respected, but an XM replaces the 'black prince'. The sound-track for this series awakens the unconscious fan that slumbers in all of us. The 'déjà vu' effect becomes more refined, it becomes a 'psychological déjà vu', which turns out to be a "first"[2], because the image is totally new. This revival therefore has the distinctive feature of also derailing the memory that we had of the subject, at the very moment when it resurfaces in our lives by means of music. And the fact that the horse has become a car literally shows that this horse is going nowhere, and we with it. We experience the exercise of re-remembering, imposed on us by *XM*, as a performance. A psychological performance asking whether, now that we know that channel hopping is to remain in our memories and that to remember is to forget, going nowhere is reassuring to us — or not.

From 'déjà vu' to never seen

Yoko is visibly bored in her room at the Amsterdam Hilton. The room is ghostly. On the windows are slogans/memories: 'Hair Peace' and 'Bed Peace'. John is not there — he's dead of course. It's 1994 and Yoko still looks very young behind her enormous sunglasses. Is it Yoko, her picture, a look-alike, a doll? No further explanation. Between dream and hidden drama, the parameters of this situation — which could equally have been captured by a photographer or a camera with a self-timer — grate more than purr, since the re-enactment is lethargic. The 'déjà vu' is completely twisted.

Hilton Piece
1994
video stills

Hilton Piece (Bed II)
1994
three colour photographs

Hilton Piece (Bed II)
1994
three colour photographs

Entering *Ars Futura* in Zurich (still in 1994),
a photograph leads you to understand that
in the very place where the photo is pinned,
Pollock 'tags' had been made and then
erased. A video of a frenetic love-dance
with the walls had been recorded without
an audience and without the gallery director
even being concerned about it. You ask
yourself what period you are in: are you too
early or too late, has the exhibition gone
wrong, been moved or cancelled? In other
words, are we capable, today, of forgetting
the chronology of events when we visit an
exhibition, look at a work of art, or come
across a story that already exists?

A Day in Holland/Holland in a Day is a series
that sets tourist clichés and imagery back to
back. A couple made up as Japanese tourists
take a tour of Holland in a day (a full
program in itself) and have themselves
photographed in their best clothes (total
Burberry-look) in front of the country's best
known 'sights'. The 'country' in question is
Huis Ten Bosch Stad, a theme-park in Japan in
which certain urban Dutch landscapes have
been meticulously recreated. The tourists
blend in with the decor, or is it the decor
that absorbs them? Holland and *Huis Ten
Bosch Stad* = same contest. This combination
demonstrates that it is not only the
backgrounds that are interchangeable in
the world of the image, but also that they
themselves interchange, i.e. that the tourist
(non)experience offered by Holland and
Huis Ten Bosch Stad are identical. The change
of scene that's sold by the "procurers of
different experiences"[3] now has a tourist
clone.

Ars Futura
1994
colour photograph

Ars Futura
1994
set photograph

A Day in Holland/Holland in a Day
2001
series of colour photographs

A Day in Holland/Holland in a Day
(Charlotte II)
2001
series of colour photographs

A Day in Holland/Holland in a Day
2001
series of colour photographs

A Day in Holland/Holland in a Day
2001
series of colour photographs

A Day in Holland/Holland in a Day
2001
series of colour photographs

A Day in Holland/Holland in a Day
2001
series of colour photographs

Have you ever assessed, when faced with the photo of the famous 'savaged' chair, to what point the image has become an 'untouchable'? *Detitled*, literally a series of those with no name, as well as those that are destitute and discredited, has become its benchmark. Famous pieces of furniture are photographed in show-house type environments with stag horn ferns, cosy 1950s veneer and calfskin rugs; weightless on a white floor in front of a white curtain; in a gallery type atmosphere or that of a workshop with a red brick floor or bare grey floor, all recreating design type shots. These 'unbreakables', fossilized by their images, are not unbreakable any more. This proves that they live, age and suffer terrible injuries. It doesn't really matter whether these are caused by a Kalashnikov or Photoshop, whether they are laid bare, have lost their feet or bottoms, whether they are 'leaning' against a wall (like a ballet dancer at the bar); these objects have been photographed in a previously unseen condition. An operation that removes them from the perfect image that had neutralised them, giving them a future anti-life — and all it took was for one Eames to appear

broken in two with a slashed footrest, for all Eameses to have this in them: their dark side.

The fact that this is a series, leads us to believe that these 'uncanny and fetish style' monsters have willingly participated in the casting of their symbolic desecration, a type of occult rite of passage. And, as if to accelerate the establishment of their 'new image' and to increase its strangeness, their circulation is guaranteed on postcards. This deviant imagery touches the heart of the perfect darkness in which these cult design objects have been hidden. These objects themselves have a soul.

Besides BV says that she "is searching to promote a place of confusion... (knowing that it is) more difficult to produce an image that resists interpretation than a shocking or beautiful image"[4]. This place of confusion is an area of instability, which destabilises the fossilized state in which all

Detitled/EAARS20001205/FT/S/bw
2000
series of photographs

Detitled/AAS19992010/FT/S/bw
2000
series of photographs

objects that have achieved the status of an
image find themselves. We need to
understand the extent of this in this time
of generalised formats, in precisely the same
era in which Madonna continually changes
her image in order to continue to exist.
Examining BV's body of work from this
angle, is to measure or to begin to measure,
its political impact. If certain objects or
situations may have a soul, it can only be
materialist, corroded and collapsed. Insofar
as it inverts the aura, we could say that
the feeling is more science fiction than
cosmetic. Logical, as "we are after. After
modernism, post-modernism, after post
post-modernism. After all neo-movements.
In what you described as the realm of the
B-series".5)

Detitled/AAC19990303/FW/L/bw
2000
series of photographs

Detitled/AAC19990303/RW/L/bw
2000
series of photographs

Detitled/JC19991211/RT/S/bw
2000
series of photographs

Animism & Science Fiction

Every age attempts to construct the past in its own image, either as an ideal, of which the present, in its decline, retains only a few traces (the idea of a golden age), or as a childhood state of blissful innocence on which, little by little, is built the impressive edifice of modernity (the idea of evolution). It appears that the positivist age, which has characterised the recent past — until 1989 for historians and until the year 2000 for advertisers — favoured the notion of evolution.

No doubt because evolution always aims to free itself a little more of the illusions and beliefs of the Middle Ages — a dark period, unsettled by magic, uncertainty, animism, the occult and a lack of clarity.

Detitled/BABC19990910/TQT/S/c
Detitled/AAS19992010/ST/S/bw
2000
series of photographs

Detitled/PT-C19992510/FT/L/c
2000
series of photographs

Detitled/EGG19992811/FT/L/c
2000
series of photographs

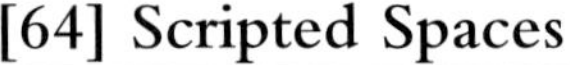

Detitled/MVB20001505/FT/S/c
2000
series of photographs

From a rationalist point of view, animism represents a derailment. This doctrine, which philosophers adopted from Aristotle, states that the soul is the principle of organic life and thought. It is also a creed or religion that believes that nature is governed by souls or spirits similar to human will.
In short, objects have a soul, can live their lives and therefore figure in ours. Works of art are not exempt from this rule, appearing like 'special effects' in a world seen and experienced as an infinite fixed image.
This appearance is animist in nature, and everyone is free to accord its importance or not. Since rationalism has historically taken the lead, any animist interpretation operates on a second level. We play at having a life with objects or ideas. However, today, the formats are so fixed that this type of logic upsets their stability. As a result there are moments when things are turned upside down, which is what the best works of art do. In this, they are completely con-temporary. A work of art (far from being just an image) is, by definition, available.
It is exposed to the most diverse reactions, comments, readings, desires, fantasies, (mis)understandings, until it vanishes, re-emerges, etc.

As soon as he has created a work, Maurizio Cattelan says that it no longer belongs to him because he cannot control it.
He believes that "a work needs to fight its own battles and define itself" in order to exist. Nevertheless, placing a visual image, not just an advert or an ego trip, into circulation, in a world that is built on symbols and appearance — a world that is just as artificial and fake as that in *Total Recall;* a world in which "experience passes for a totally created experience, adopting artifice as a constituent dimension of truth"[6] — always produces a special effect.
In 2000, the black Eames-chair acquired a special soul. The famous chair was photographed broken in two. By bringing this new image into circulation, the piece of furniture was lifted out of the design iconography in which it had been neutralised. The new identity left its mark on the old one, which persists, thereby giving it a materialist soul. This kind of reversal mechanism allows us to believe that any alternative that is individually intelligible to the prevailing representation-

Detitled/EAFS19991012/ST/L/c
2000
series of photographs

Detitled/RDH19990410/ST/S/c
2000
series of photographs

Detitled/EACH19991012/ST/L/c
2000
series of photographs

Maison Grégoire 118%
2000
colour photograph

Maison Grégoire 118%
2000
b/w photograph

Maison Grégoire 118%
2000
b/w photograph

Maison Grégoire 118%
2000
b/w photograph

regimes, supported by the alliance of the media, the economy and social concerns, will now be effective once it has been slotted into a history that turns it upside down, like a 'special effect'.[7]

Maison Grégoire is a private residence in Brussels. In *Maison Grégoire 118%* we move on to the world of image fabrication. The photographic scene is as follows: a woman is posing in a doorway that opens on to a terrace. The following photo shows a man advancing down a corridor inside the house (near the office) and coming across the woman posing in another doorway. He looks enormous and she looks tiny. The scenario turns into a slightly bizarre demonstration: once sitting in a *Barcelona chair* designed by Mies Van der Rohe, he appears really small. Here, the true-false dialectic that is typical of image-trickery (from retouching to virtualisation) poses another question: will we adapt our visual codes to future technology or will we continue to move from one scale to another in order to configure the extent of our personal and collective histories?

2050, final date of the future. All media flip out. Yet, none of them recognise that when you "take a photo, you are never taking a picture of the present but of the future".[8] The photographic tableaux and videos by BV disturb the certainties generated by the world of the image. Their irony is devastating. In *Philippa*, three women, as if speeded-up, move from one room to another in the former residence of Philippa Van Loon, while calling her name. The echo of their call recalls the place where she once lived, which summons up her spirit. As we float through the cloud of her spirit, it is not her past we are dealing with but her future, a future which "is a better key to the present than the past", as Ballard wrote in 1971; an animist future in which, "what you see depends on what you are looking for"(BV).

Notes:

1) E-mail correspondence with the artist, June 2006.

2) Paolo Virno, *Miracle, Virtuosité et 'déjà vu'*, éditions de l'éclat, 1996, p. 14. *(Miracle, Virtuosity and 'déjà vu')*

3) Victor Segalen, *Essai sur l'exotisme, pour une esthétique du divers*, Paris, le livre de poche, 1999. *(Essay on exoticism, in favour of a diverse aesthetic)*

4) Maxime Matray, 'La position du touriste couché', in: *Le monde appartient à ceux qui se lèvent tôt*, Nice, Villa Arson, 2002. *('The position of the sleeping tourist', in: The world belongs to early risers)*

5) 'Che fare?', a discussion between John Armleder, Cristina Farwood and Parker Williams, in: *Never Say Never*, Zurich, Offizin, 1996.

6) Mehdi Belhaj Kacem, *Pop philosophie*, interviews with Philippe Nacif, Paris, Denoël, 2005, p. 396.

7) In *The Vatican to Vegas, A History of Special Effects* (New York & London, The New Press, 2004), Norman Klein analyses the seduction of special effects and establishes a parallel between our history and the development of special effects, from Baroque architecture to the casinos of Las Vegas. In 'scripted spaces' that we must physically cross, our spirit lives through an 'exercise of fantasy', being both the 'site and process of imagination'. "By decoding scripted space, we learn how power was brokered between the classes in the form of a special effect", p. 11.

8) William Burroughs, 'Old photographer', in: *The Burroughs File*, San Francisco, City Lights Books, 1984, p. 122.

Philippa
1998
video, set photograph

Twee Projecties/Two Projections
2005
video and slide projection with sound

TWO PROJECTIONS
[Barbara Visser]

Grandmother:
My name stays out of it, right?
I mean, my name is not mentioned,
I prefer to do this anonymous.

Barbara:
But people do know I have made this.

Grandmother:
That's your problem.

OK. Let's go.
My mother left when I was two.
It was 1918, and my father was serving in
the war. I don't think she could bear the
loneliness. She was salesgirl at *Gerzon*.
They didn't take just anyone there. They
were always special girls. She met a man at
a party in The Hague. He was the Cuban
ambassador to Holland. She married him
and went to Cuba. My father was given the
custody. I met her in the late 1950s. She
visited me twice for a month.

But it wasn't like in *Spoorloos★*, where people
embrace warmly when they meet their
parents again. No, it wasn't like that at all.
But at the airport, even from a distance,
I could see it was her. I recognized her
clearly. But it was quite a cool greeting, not
at all like on TV.

Barbara:
Where did she live then?

Grandmother:
In the Vanderbilt Hotel, in New York.
She fled to Miami when Castro took over in
Cuba. The ambassador had a nervous
breakdown and was being nursed in a
private villa.

When she arrived in New York, she told
Castro: "I want my pension!"

And he said: "Come and get it". Of course
she didn't do that. In New York she
followed a course and became an interior
decorator. That's how she earned her
money.

Barbara:
You grew up with your father and a woman
you thought was your mother. They ran an
art store in Bergen, and later one in
Amsterdam. One day you came home and
announced that you wanted to be an
architect.

Grandmother:
I heard my parents saying to each other:
"That's not going to happen, or she'll end
up like 'that woman'".
Only later I understood that 'that woman'
was my real mother, who had studied
interior design in the US.

Barbara:
At the age of sixteen, you discovered that
your mother was not your mother. Then
the story suddenly changed into a classic
dark fairytale.

Grandmother:
I couldn't care less. During an argument she
shouted: *"I don't have to look after you, I'm not
even your real mother!"* I said: "Oh, that doesn't
surprise me at all". Then I also understood
why I was not allowed to be an architect.

Barbara:
You said that you were, in all respects,
a simple child.

Grandmother:
Well, to give you an example: when I was
sixteen, I knew next to nothing about sex.
I honestly wasn't concerned with it. I didn't
even know where children came from; I
had never thought about it. I mostly played
with boys. In that respect I was backward.

Barbara:
But you knew that you wanted to be an architect.

Grandmother:
I apparently was interested in that. If something interests you, you concentrate on it and other things stay unnoticed. Or maybe I liked the artists who visited us, and I listened to their conversations.

Barbara:
How did you live?

Grandmother:
In Bergen we lived in a house called *The Barque,* designed by a well-known architect.**) It was shaped like a ship. The bedrooms upstairs had porthole windows. A row of them. Because of the boat form there was a gap behind the bookcase. My father had it custom made because we had a lot of large books and they wouldn't fit in a normal bookcase.

In Amsterdam, where we had the art shop, our interior was a little in the style of Berlage. We always had mats on the floor. Sand-coloured coconut mats on dark marmoleum. That was very rare at that time. People had rugs. Factory-produced rugs with a border or with flowers. But never something real, hand-made. Anyway, they wouldn't be able to tell the difference.

We had a divan. It had a green baize cover. That was also unusual. You didn't see that bright green at that time; everything had to be soft and pretty. And we had specially designed chairs with detachable, woven cane seats. A frame with three bars and a rosette on top. It sounds a bit smug, but they were very special chairs. I am very sorry that I got rid of them. I had put them up for auction when I suddenly had to clear the whole house. My father was taken away by the Jerries, my stepmother got sick and the house stood empty. I didn't know what to do with the things.

Twee Projecties / Two Projections
2005
video and slide projection with sound

Barbara:
After that, how did you decorate your own living space?

Grandmother:
Particularly in left-wing circles, the fashion was a table and chairs in plain oak, and the fruit bowl in the middle. That was *the* thing. To get rid of all the dead weight and have everything in plain oak. And the table was no longer allowed in the middle. Before it had *always* been in the middle. And no covers. That was sacrilege. And a Van Gogh on the wall.

Barbara:
What was that all about?

Grandmother:
Probably because they had jettisoned the ballast of their parental homes, and a different interior was part of it. It's the remaining ten per cent of that survey, I think.

Barbara:
Which survey?

Grandmother:
About how people decorate their homes: ninety per cent of people decorate their home like their childhood home. I think this group was the other ten per cent who wanted something different. And we also found such a suite of furniture beautiful. We had ordered something like that from a man on the Ceintuurbaan, but we heard nothing. When we passed by later they were still not ready, and the man who was supposed to make them was drunk. So we said: "To hell with your furniture!" That was a relief because then... then we saw the Gispen chairs. We were walking through town and I saw them in a shop window on the Leidsestraat, and said straight away: "That's it, that's what I want". My fiancé said: "Yes, but only if they're comfortable". They were

comfortable, but for the time they were unbelievably expensive. One chair cost a *tenner*, twelve guilders, and these chairs cost twenty-five guilders. And everyone said we were mad: who buys office-furniture? Most people were too polite to say they found them ugly. Other people were astonished that they worked so well at home. At first they were upholstered with tomato-red corduroy. But I have had them re-covered many times.

Barbara:
Not that expensive when you've enjoyed them for sixty-six years.

Grandmother:
Do you know what people say when they first enter here? "It is so modern!" I never know what to make of that, because when people say something is modern, it is just ugly. I don't know; it doesn't really exist. What is modern? Something different than usual, or what?

Barbara:
Do you think it is a hollow term?

Grandmother:
'Modern' has nothing to do with design or function. It is often something expensive, which people call modern.

Barbara:
And what does that sort of 'modern' look like?

Grandmother:
It is rarely beautiful. It is usually ugly. But it depends a bit on who it is, that thinks it is modern. Some people come here and think it is terribly modern, even though there are things from 1939 here. So I don't really understand the term 'modern'.

Barbara:
Did you once think, as some Modernists did, that in the future everyone would live

in good, beautiful and functional surroundings?

Grandmother:
No, I never thought that. I have always thought that most people have no taste, or are not interested in design. And I don't think that will change. The most 'modern' interior out of these 300 homes is by that man, the one who lives in a house like a castle.

Barbara:
Jan des Bouvrie.

Grandmother:
(You won't get in trouble for this?)

Barbara:
(I don't care)

Grandmother:
They call that modern. One resident has that, but for the rest it's fat upholstered armchairs, flowers and little ornaments. As long as there's a lot, as long as it looks rich.

Barbara:
Is that the most important thing, that it suggests wealth?

Grandmother:
Wealth, prosperity, yes. I think that I am, as far as interiors and taste goes, quite stubborn. Uncompromising. I cannot be talked into something. Like with that clock. That was also in the late 1930s. We spent the whole day *schlepping* around Amsterdam looking for a clock, but found nothing. And then we saw it in a clockmaker's window. And we both said: "That's the one". It was a second-hand clock but still it cost twenty-five guilders.

Barbara:
Have you ever thought: time to buy another clock?

Grandmother:
No, I am still happy with it. At the time I thought: if I don't find anything better I'll just get a kitchen clock. After all it's for telling the time, not for its looks. But when we saw this one, we were both delighted. Look around and you'll see that there are no beautiful clocks.

Barbara:
A while back I went to buy a watch for you at *HEMA*, and you said: "it must be as simple as possible". When I returned with a simple watch you said: "I would prefer it a tiny bit simpler, a simpler one must exist".

Grandmother:
I can believe that about myself. I am mainly concerned with function.

Barbara:
But if it's really about the function you could wear any old watch.

Grandmother:
What kind of watch could I wear then?

Barbara:
You could wear any watch if it is really only telling the time that matters.

Grandmother:
You are right. Yes, but I wouldn't want that. For example, I would find a decorated watch unbearable.

Barbara:
Why?

Grandmother:
Each time I looked at it I would think: 'ugh, what a monster.' I have the same problem with that thing with the hanging blobs my neighbour gave me. It really irritates me, but I don't want to upset her. But it remains ugly. One never gets used to it.

Twee Projecties/Two Projections
2005
single slide

Twee Projecties / Two Projections
2005
single slide

Barbara:
What do you find so irritating about it?

Grandmother:
It is not kind to the eye. It is not aesthetic.
It has no purpose because in the middle
there is a small wick, so is it actually a
candle, but the function is apparently not
important for the form. That is stupid, isn't
it? That annoys the hell out of me.

Barbara:
Your furniture has never gone out of
fashion. Why is that?

Grandmother:
No, but I believe — that is another cocksure
statement — something that is beautiful has
nothing to do with fashion.

Barbara:
Does your spouse have to have the same
taste to ensure a good marriage?

Grandmother:
I can speak only from experience.
My husband actually knew nothing about
such things. He came from a very different
background. I think he had never thought
about it. I taught him to appreciate things
and slowly he began to think as I did.
Maybe it is important that you eventually
develop the same taste.
I say eventually.

Barbara:
Were you also concerned with the form and
function of things during the war?

Grandmother:
Not at all. So many things were broken or
lost, that I couldn't be bothered. You think:
as long as we stay alive. Imagine, with two
young children, to make sure you have
something to eat. And above all the threat,
a husband in hiding. We had a large
trapdoor in the floor to disappear through in
case of danger.

And when I would return from getting food
my husband would say: "I was underground
again because German soldiers came
looking for blankets".

At the time I had a very simple oak buffet.
When I briefly came back to that house, to
give birth, I saw that my sister-in-law's
boyfriend had stubbed his cigarettes out on
it. My first reaction was: 'oh, how terrible',
and then immediately: 'well, it's not really
important, we survived, that's what counts'.

Barbara:
What do you find really ugly?

Grandmother:
Cane chairs in a normal interior. That's an
idée-fixe I have. When you put a cane chair
between steel or wooden furniture, it upsets
the balance. And if I put a different chair in
the same spot it doesn't worry me, but with
a cane chair something isn't right. It's very
strange. I can't explain it. It's probably some
kind of phobia.

Barbara:
Something else.
You have always worn trousers. I don't
think I have ever seen you in a skirt. Was
that a statement? Was there something
behind it?

Grandmother:
I just found them comfortable.
In Haarlem, where we lived at the time,
you never saw another woman in trousers!
When I did shopping people turned and
pointed at me.

Barbara:
What year was that?

Grandmother:
I think 1952. But I can still see people's
faces, the disapproving glances and nudging
each other. I didn't care what people
thought. About six months later everyone

was wearing jeans. And I had blouses made
of curtain fabrics. Always *raglan* blouses with
stripes. Because I had a seamstress once a
week and I had to keep her busy. And then
I had the idea to make nice jackets from the
curtains. That was another thing that got
me funny looks.I wore them with great
pleasure. Sturdy material.

Barbara:
And the furniture you wanted hardly
existed, so you designed it.

Grandmother:
As for the black chairs: my mother-in-law
needed new chairs.We looked at each other
and said: "Oh God, what will that be",
because she had an old-fashioned interior.
You can't just put steel chairs in, that
doesn't work. So, we gave her advice.

Barbara:
What kind of advice?

Grandmother:
"Keep it simple, mother. And no
decorations. And they must be comfortable.
And you must remember that it's an easy
chair and not a dining chair." She wasn't
stupid. She listened. We said: "That Van
der Elsken, on the Middenweg, has nice
furniture and if you say what you want you
might get something that suits you".
We went there and my husband had
sketched an armchair — but not a tub chair
— and Van der Elsken understood
immediately. The upholstery had to be what
she called warm, so it got a sort of taupe-
coloured plush. And those chairs were
perfectly acceptable. When she died we
decided to keep them. But we had to get rid
of these covers.

Barbara:
And now you have adapted them with an
extra cushion.

Twee Projecties / Two Projections
2005
video and slide projection with sound

Grandmother:
That's because when you get older you can no longer sit so low. Actually I already need a higher cushion. Of course I think it's more beautiful without it, but then I sit too low.

Barbara:
Is sitting a verb?

Grandmother:
Then where do you relax?

Barbara:
In bed?

Grandmother:
But is bed the only place where you can relax? I can really relax in that chair. No, I don't see it that way.

Barbara:
It was Rietvelds' defence to his critics.

Grandmother:
The chairs are no good then.

Barbara:
Some Modernist designers at the beginning of the Twentieth century thought that mass production would make their furniture available to more people. However, they were still expensive things.

Grandmother:
We didn't have much money. But if you find something beautiful and you really want it, you can sacrifice other things. However, it is not the designers who earn the most, it is the retailers. That is capitalism. The designers were on the breadline.

Barbara:
Can you describe the interior of a random home in this complex?

Grandmother:
Yes, that's very simple. They all have the same interior. A buffet with a glazed middle section and two doors underneath. An average wooden table and four hard square wooden chairs. Their form is not so bad, but you can't sit on them. And then the sofa: always overstuffed, with homemade patchwork cushions. Yes, with most of them the sofa is the showpiece. That is probably the most expensive piece of furniture. That always steals your attention. When you enter, the first thing you see is an enormous TV. That is also expensive. Always the same. It has to look rich. They even compare with each other. When my neighbour first visited me and looked around he said: "you must certainly save a lot". I looked at him in surprise. I think he thought it looked really poor. He knew that my husband had been in education so he had expected something more luxurious. I didn't answer him because I found it rude, but also strange.

Barbara:
Other people do not make the careful choices you make.

Grandmother:
They have other motives. They don't imagine how things will look in a room. They don't choose things based on function; whether a sofa is comfortable. I would never have bought my own sofa nowadays, although I like it, because I can't sit on it anymore. They don't think of that. They don't look at colours at all. Combinations? They don't have a clue. What are they thinking? Everything on one side, full up. No idea behind it.

Barbara:
Does your interior and your taste have something to do with a life vision?

Grandmother:
Of course you can turn your style into a sort
of style-worship, and then it becomes a
religion. In any case, politically, I am very
sober. And I don't see that changing, even
if I am a member of a left-wing party. I live
here with old people and see how little they
care... But I'm no revolutionary. I once
was. I still believed that I could contribute
to change.

Barbara:
What was your contribution?

Grandmother:
I immediately went to talk with the director
of social housing about accommodation,
because they were receiving streams of
Turkish homeless people. A group of us
started squatting houses. They were driven
by a kind of idealism but they were not
talented otherwise. We had an ex-burglar
who checked whether a house was empty
and ensured when we could get in. And if
there was any furniture there, it all went
into a locked room. We would then ring an
official to inform them we had squatted.
It was not like here in Amsterdam with all
those battles. It was an exciting period,
but the pain was that another woman and
myself were the only ones who could write
a proper letter or speak nicely. Before you
knew it you were the leader of the group.
That was not my intention at all.

Barbara:
And now you are 89.

Grandmother:
Yes. No obligations anymore.
Apart from that: I have visitors now and
then. But that is nothing. The people you
could speak to here, stay at home like me.
They don't go downstairs to the
'conversations' either.

Barbara:
Why not?

Twee Projecties/Two Projections
2005
video and slide projection with sound

Grandmother:
What can you do with these people?
I can't talk to them. They don't read. They
watch TV and talk about that. 'My, terrible
things happen', they say. Nothing interests
them.

Barbara:
What do they talk about besides TV?

Grandmother:
About each other. They gossip.

Barbara:
Are you glad that your daughter has become
an architect?

Grandmother:
I never pushed her. She knew that I would
have liked to become one, but if she had
become something else I also would have
been happy. It was her own, free choice.
And you are working with design as well.
It must be something genetic.

Barbara:
What do you think: is taste hereditary,
or learned?

Grandmother:
I think it's inheritance, because it is based
on feelings and it is not entirely cerebral,
but also slightly emotional.

Barbara:
And you can't learn that, you think.

Grandmother:
No, no. That's exactly what my wilfulness
derives from as well because if something is
based on feeling, it's maintained much
longer than something intellectual; people
can talk you out of it.

People can't change your mind about things
you sense, and honestly feel. That's just
how you feel it.

Note:
*) *Spoorloos* is a Dutch TV program where
   children seek to trace a lost parent, in order
   to be united.

**) J.F. Staal

MEDIUM GIRL, LIVING BARBIE
[Jennifer Allen]

I haven't played Barbie in ages. And never with a living woman. My Barbie was a small doll that fit into my lunchbox if I folded up her plastic body. This girl discovered a special trick to bring her doll to life; like my Barbie, hers is blonde, blue-eyed and buxom with perfect skin and perfect hair and perfect everything — plus, her doll walks, breathes and blinks her eyes. Her doll is so real that it towers over the little girl, like her mother does. The girl is dark-haired and plain; she looks at her doll with admiration: I want to be like you when I'm big, but in the meantime, I'll pretend by dressing you up. The girl has lots of old retro clothes for her doll: white laced kerchiefs, some aprons, a big black skirt, a golden dickey. She even has bobby pins to do up the doll's hair — to fix her thick braids, this way, that way — although she has to stand on a bed to reach the doll's head.

Barbie has a date, as she always does. Barbie has a date with Ken, but first she is going to meet her secret friend Barbara whose name can't be mentioned to anyone in the world. Barbara always wants to play civilisation; it's her favourite game because lots of other people can play, too. Barbie and Barbara are going to meet in the museum because that's where you are sure to find civilisation. Anything that ends up in the museum has to be civilised, even the visitors wandering around inside. But the girl has a plan, she dresses up her doll, not for a trip to the museum, but like a painting hanging on the wall in the museum, maybe like Vermeer's *Milkmaid* in the Rijksmuseum. The girl dresses up the doll to look like a maid and sits her down in a chair right beside the window. The light from outside hits her face, which glows in its frame of white lace; she even glances out of the window, as if she were waiting for a love letter from Ken instead of Barbara. A mirror hanging on the wall reflects everything inside the room, including the girl, who admires her work. Barbie looks beautiful, even in a maid's uniform. She's an artwork; she's an Old Master, she's a new master, it doesn't matter. Barbie can be anything.

Barbara has no trouble finding Barbie; she aims her camera at the doll and reduces the scene from a majestic painting to a postcard image, without leaving her own reflection in the mirror. Barbara's invisible, after all. The girl decides that this game was too easy; it's time to play hide and seek, not in the museum, but somewhere in the Netherlands. She dresses up her doll in a traditional costume to go to the market, maybe at Noord-Beveland in Zeeland. Getting dressed for the market is a complicated ritual, with strict rules for each place that have been handed down from one generation of women to the next. The doll is Protestant, so she must wear a rounded kerchief on her head in Noord-Beveland (the square ones are for Catholic women living there, or maybe it's the other way around); she wears a golden dickey because she is rich; an extra white kerchief because she is not married (at least not yet); an apron because it is market day; and a voluminous black wrap because it is the autumn season. But Barbara finds her in a split second because there are hardly any women wearing traditional costumes anymore and certainly no young women walking around in 'mooi-tooi'. The costumes are part of a dying civilisation that may as well be in the museum along with the Old Masters.

Anyway, the doll is bored in Noord-Beveland and wants a more modern and glamorous life. Her blue eyes have an empty gaze waiting to be filled with more exciting visions, if not blinded by the storm of flashbulbs that illuminate famous people. She wants to be part of Western civilisation,

A Day in Holland/Holland in a Day
(Jan IV)
2001
series of colour photographs

A Day in Holland/Holland in a Day
2001
series of colour photographs

A Day in Holland/Holland in a Day
2001
series of colour photographs

where everyone gets to be famous and everything can be bought, even civilisation itself. She is going to become world-famous as the fashion model whose face graces every single Dutch product that leaves the country: *Edam cheese* with the red wax seal that you can squeeze in your fingers, *dubbelzoute drop* and, her favourite, *stroopwafels*. She could even do the advertising campaign for *Flower Bomb* perfume by Viktor & Rolf. The girl can make her doll into any image to sell any commodity, from a bag of licorice to a perfume bottle. If the doll wears her kerchiefs like a tall crown, her head could appear on coins, just like Queen Beatrix's head, and travel around the Euro zone, moving through hands and pockets and purses and cash registers. No: The doll will travel in person and represent Dutch civilisation around the world. She is going to make an appearance at the living museum *Huis Ten Bosch City* in Nagasaki, which is more Dutch than anything in the Netherlands. Or she'll live on Holland Street in Disneyland, the best place on earth. She could be the Dutch ambassador's wife, although she's not sure if Disneyland has a Dutch embassy. But it doesn't matter; she'll be so famous that she'll end up in wax at Madame Tussaud's, where everyone will take her picture.

Wherever the doll's face appears, Barbara recognizes her right away: winking on the cheese wheel, looking regal on the coins, smiling at the tourists. The girl has yet another trick: she puts Barbie in a burqa. She covers up the doll's face with several white kerchiefs, which easily double as headscarves; the doll's head and body disappear under black skirts and wraps. Only her big blue eyes are visible, along with her hands, which rest with the fingers spread on her lap. The doll looks like a traditional Muslim woman; she also looks like a citizen hidden behind the voting booth. It's important to be anonymous; in certain situations, no one should be able to see your face. But there is a problem. An inevitable clash of civilisations. The doll is sitting on a chair by a window in a police station in Antwerp because women are not allowed to wear a burqa in public in that city. "Except for certain holidays like the carnival," explains the policeman, "masked people in Western culture are up to no good." But the doll does not want to pay a fine because she has civil rights, which protect everyone's freedom of religious expression. The policeman says that he is not discriminating against her religion; she is simply breaking the civil code of conduct by covering up too much of her face. The police will fine her, whether she's in a burqa or a Mickey Mouse mask.

Medium Girl
1996
video, still

Medium Girl
1996
video, still

Medium Girl
1996
video, still

The game of hide and seek is over. The girl has to come up with a punishment: Barbie and Barbara must civilise the barbarians. That will teach everybody a lesson. The task is endless; there are all sorts of barbarians. There are the children, the lower classes and the riff-raff who need to be taught hygiene and manners: how to keep your ears clean, how to chew properly at the dinner table, how to walk in high heels while signing autographs on the red carpet. There are the backward people, who live in primitive conditions and need more technology to be modern, like toilets, space ships and milkshake mixers. Then there are the primitives themselves, who idolise magical wooden carvings instead of one God and a bunch of movie stars; the primitives don't know how to read and to write. Sometimes, they eat people; sometimes, they don't wear clothes. Just jewellery, headdresses, feathers or scars, which probably mean something, like the kerchiefs, aprons and golden dickeys. If only the primitives could learn how to wear more clothes on their bodies, which is important to get a job. The girl fashions an

apron into a halter top by tying the apron around her doll's neck; it's too hot to wear anything more than an apron where the primitives live. But the doll just sits there watching with a void expression on her

Medium Girl
1996
video, still

face, as she if were an anthropologist, a living blank tape that records a way of life while witnessing it disappear. Whoever the barbarians are — children or primitives — they will be civilised into history. Into extinction.

Civilising all of the savages is far too much work; it's impossible to finish the job before dinnertime. Plus, nobody seems to like being civilised; everyone is discontent; they just want to enjoy their own cultures: low, high, somewhere in-between, native, foreign, exotic, pop. The girl decides to travel far back into the past, all the way back to a period before such confusing distinctions. The name of their destination appears on the dressing table right in front of the mirror: *Loutraki Ivi*, a Greek brand of bottled water that comes from the springs at Loutraki. Indeed, there's no civilisation without water and Greece. Life begins with clean drinking water; then you have to add some Ancient Greek philosophy and democracy (while ignoring the taste of polytheism and mythology). But the girl wants to relive the myth of Pygmalion; she wants to be the sculptor who fell in love with his creation and brought the inanimate figure to life. The doll is her living statue Galatea. And Barbara is her assistant who has to trek deep into the mountains and steal some marble to make a pedestal for

Medium Girl
1996
video, still

the statue, without being seen by the gods. The girl lovingly strokes the doll's face while trying to decide which clothes would look best. The doll behaves exactly the way that the girl wants her behave; her body bends to the girl's every gesture, more like warm wax or wet clay under the fingers than stubborn marble. The metamorphosis is already complete. The doll walks, breathes and blinks her eyes, but she never says a single word. If she could speak, wonders the girl, what would she say about civilisation? The girl stands in front of the mirror, watching her creation. Barbara arrives and watches the girl watching her creation. We watch everything.

<u>The world belongs to early risers, the world belongs to tourists</u>

Now the image itself has come to life. We are no longer passive spectators, watching the scenes of civilisation that appear before our eyes. We can walk around inside of the image and choose our own perspective. We do not want to civilise people; we do not want to be civilised ourselves; we just want to take pictures, wherever we go. Our trip starts at a bus stop on the long avenue that runs parallel to the beach. As we wait for the bus, we see a glossy ad in the light box inside the bus shelter; instead of showing a product, the ad displays an

Medium Girl
1996
video, still

image of the beach lying right in front of us. In the image, people are tanning on towels; in the distance, closer to the shore, a few people are playing with some plastic toy for the water. The image must be a marker, which means that the beach is authentic and worth seeing. We take a picture of the ad because then we can remember what beach we saw. Unlike a traditional historical site, the image does not have an explanatory plaque; we know we are in front of something significant, but we are not sure why. The only text is the front page of *Corriere della Sera*, which the biggest sunbather in the image is reading. The headline reads: "Impronte digitali per gli immigranti." We forgot our dictionary at the hotel. It must be a warning about immigrants who steal digital cameras on the beach.

The bus arrives; we get on, only to get off at the very next stop. After all, we're doing the bus tour to get the authentic insider local view of the city. At the next bus shelter, a similar beach image welcomes us again, like a guide leading on us along the right track. The image looks about the same, except that we are getting closer. Moving inside the image for a closer look, we get to see just how fat and tanned the next sunbather is, after the newspaper reader. We see that the group is not inflating a plastic toy but taking a picture of someone lying on the beach. Maybe someone drowned; maybe the headline was a warning about illegal immigrants drowning at sea. The toy turns out to be one of those reflectors used by fashion photographers, not police photographers. Maybe the headline read: "We are looking for digital images of immigrants". Could we pass as immigrants? We could get pictures of ourselves working as models; we photograph the image, just to remember this moment. The bus arrives; we get on and travel to the next stop, which takes us even deeper inside the image, closer to the body lying on the beach.

Le monde appartient à ceux qui se lèvent tôt/
The world belongs to early risers
2002
5 full colour offset posters

Le monde appartient à ceux qui se lèvent tôt/
The world belongs to early risers
2002
5 full colour offset posters

Le monde appartient à ceux qui se lèvent tôt/
The world belongs to early risers
2002
5 full colour offset posters

Le monde appartient à ceux qui se lèvent tôt/
The world belongs to early risers
2002
5 full colour offset posters

Le monde appartient à ceux qui se lèvent tôt/
The world belongs to early risers
2002
colour photograph

Le monde appartient à ceux qui se lèvent tôt/
The world belongs to early risers
2002
colour photograph

He looks way too beautiful to be drowned, although the photographer's assistants are holding other tools, besides the light reflector: a white sheet to cover up dead people and a striped band for crime scenes. One man is holding his hand to his chest, maybe in regret. Next bus stop, next close-up: the man's hand looks well groomed but he doesn't have a police or a press badge. We continue, from bus stop to bus stop, from shelter to shelter, until we finally arrive at a close-up of the beached man's face. We seem to be seeing what the photographer sees through his lens: a tanned young man, freshly shaved, with one eye slightly open. He can't be dead; he's a model; everything is a prop. And we are definitely not tanned enough to get our picture taken as immigrants on the beach.

That seems to be the end of the tour. How much closer can you get? We decide to go to the beach; we can work on our tans and look at our photographs. As we walk from the shelter towards the sea, everything is there: the man reading the *Corriere della Serra,* the fat tanned man closer to the shore, the group of photographer's assistants holding their props, the photographer and the model. We ask them about the headline. Was it a plaque, a warning or an audition call? "No," they tell us, "this is part of an artwork." They are doing a photo-shoot of a photo-shoot; the images appear in the bus shelters near the beach. We tell them that we just saw all of the images on the bus stop tour! "Then, you're all part of the artwork," they tell us. Wow, we are art. We take a picture because otherwise no one is going to believe us. Who else goes to the beach and gets to be part of an art project? Maybe this experience is inauthentic, due to its patent artifice; but that claim would take us back to the divisive terms of civilisation. The process of looking for authentic markers — and trying to interpret them — joins all tourists with each other, whatever their origin, whatever their destination.

We wonder what the plaque says; we make our translations; we keep moving until we end up at a scene that satisfies us; we say "It's like *Alice Through the Looking Glass* meets Antonioni's *Blow-Up*" and argue; we say things were good; we heard they were bad; and we always take pictures to continue the conversation with other people in other places.

ABC
[Works by Barbara Visser]

A

<u>Actor and Liar (2003)</u>
Back-to-back video-projection in which
the exchange of letters between an actor
and an imprisoned pathological liar are
intertwined. Based on conversations and
letters of the artist with the convicted R.V.,
who sold 2000 plots of land on the moon
through self-made certificates.
(Advaney Collection)

<u>Ars Futura (1994)</u>
Installation at Ars Futura Gallery. Colour
photograph, video on monitor and
electricity plug in gallery space. A painting
action took place in Ars Futura gallery in
Zurich, without any spectators.
A photograph was taken before the walls
were painted white again, with the
exception of one electricity plug. This
picture was shown in the otherwise empty
space, together with a video on a
surveillance monitor. The video showed
the artist doing a pantomime of an 'action
painting' in an entirely white gallery.

B

<u>Barbie Conventie/</u>
<u>Barbie Convention (1993)</u>
Series of small colour photographs mounted
with pushpins on board. *(Collection Rob van de
Ven and Corinne Groot, Amsterdam)*

<u>Bellen in de baas z'n tijd/Private calls
during working hours (1996)</u>
Textbooks. Series of scripts featuring
transcribed private telephone calls of the
staff of Stedelijk Museum Bureau
Amsterdam, which they made during their
work as receptionist. Originally made for
the exhibition *Gedraag Je! Behave! Tiens Toi!
Benimm Dich!* at SMBA.

<u>Berlin Chair Loveseat (2001)</u>
Wooden object, acrylic paint. 'Coseuse' or
Loveseat based on one of Gerrit Rietvelds'
best known chairs.

<u>Boom-Box (1998)</u>
Video on DVD, surround sound. In a bird's
eye perspective on a 'Märklin' landscape,
a red VW Golf is seen cruising through the
valley carrying along the increasing sounds
of a Boom-box.

<u>Boris (1991)</u>
B/W photograph, offset printed postcard.

*Boris
1991
b/w photograph, postcard*

C

Ca. 1991/ C. 1991 (1991)

Series of b/w photographs. As a homage to Breitner, photographs were taken from windows on the first floor of the members-only artists' club *Arti et Amicitiae* in Amsterdam, which look out onto the Rokin, a busy street. Small classical-framed photographs romanticize modern life with impressionistic images of a motorcycle racing by, tourists, lunatics and a tram-accident. *(Collection Vendel & de Wolf, Amsterdam, Collection van der Sleen – Peerdeman, Amsterdam, Collection J.M. Visser, Almere)*

Collage I (2003)

Panorama made out of printed architecture.
(Collection/Verzameling De Bruin — Heijn)

Collage II (2005)

Panorama made out of printed architecture.

Computertekening/ Computerdrawing (1991)

Ballpoint pen drawing on rice paper. In the beginning of the 1990's many full-page advertisements of information technology companies appeared in the newspapers. Using symbols from nature and natural sciences, they sought a way to bridge the gap between computer and man.
An eleven meter long drawing shows the tracing of almost all the advertisements that appeared in 1990–91.

Crossing (1995)

16mm film transferred to video, DVD 37'. In a combination of drama and documentary, Carl Gustav Jungs 'drastic actions of the unconscious' are being examined through various subjects, such as Gary, the car mechanic who has been abducted by aliens; Steve, who suspects his house is hosting poltergeist; Ms. Ross, who films Ufos regularly from her bedroom window; Steve, who dedicates his life to 'Nessie', and more. Filmed in Scotland, originally made for the exhibition *The Unbelievable Truth* at Tramway, Glasgow. *(Collection De Vleeshal, Middelburg)*

Collage 1
2001
panorama

D

**A Day in Holland/
Holland in a Day (2001)**
Series of colour photographs, DVD 12' 10"
(see also: Watersnoodramp Zeeland 1953/
Japan 2001). *Huis Ten Bosch City*, an artificial
Dutch Town and theme park in Japan,
is the backdrop for a series of photographsin
which two artificial Japanese tourists
take a walk through the town. *(Advaney
Collection , Collection Frans Hals Museum,
De Hallen Haarlem, Collection Marianne Visser,
Amsterdam, Collection Vermeulen-Kokken,
London)*

Decorealism (1999)
Video loop. Series of short choreographies
of everyday movements, performed
by inhabitants of Dunaujvaros (Hungary),
a 1950s communist model-town built to
house the workforce of the local steel-plant.

Detitled (2000)
Series of colour photographs, poster.
Photographs of violated classic design
chairs. Originally made as an insert for art
magazine *A-Prior*. *(Private collection, courtesy
Annet Gelink Gallery, Amsterdam, Collection
David Fleiss, Frac Nord – Pas de Calais,
Dunkerque, Georg Kargl, Wien, Collection Mireille
Mosler, New York, Collection Florence and Philippe
Ségalot, New York, Collection Juan Regas
Collection Marja Visser)*

E

Exchange-Datsja-Ninotchka (1994)
Installation with audio CD, photo-
textbook, armchair. Audio CD with the
soundtrack of the Ernst Lubitsch movie
Ninotchka, featuring Greta Garbo as a
Russian agent, accompanied by a book
depicting the same movie in thousands of
stills. The page numbers in the book refer
to track numbers on the CD. Installation
for the exhibition *Exchange-Datsja*.

F

Flat (2003)
Fifteen colour photographs of abandoned
apartments in the Bijlmer (a neighbourhood
in Amsterdam South-East) with an identical
architecture, but with different decorations.

Future Greetings (2004)
Set of 12 postcards, featuring images of
possible future provincial museums in the
province of Zuid-Holland, The
Netherlands.

G

**Die 10 Gebote des K.L./
The 10 commands of K.L. (2005)**
Inkjet and permanent marker on paper,
depicting a plastic bag from the Karl
Lagerfeld collection for H&M. *(Chadha
Art Collection, Wassenaar)*

Gimines (1995)
One episode of the Lithuanian drama series
Gimines, calendar. Guest appearance in
the popular television series *Gimines*
('Relatives'), where the artist doubles reality
by appearing as Dutch artist Barbora [sic]
Visser, to make a site specific artwork in
Vilnius. For this cameo, some scenes were
filmed in the Contemporary Art Centre of
Vilnius, where the opening of *New Balance,
Twelve Dutch Artists* served as a backdrop to
the storyline of the series.

**Groeten uit Vijfhuizen/
Greetings from Vijfhuizen (2005)**
Set of 5 full colour postcards. The fortress
in Vijfhuizen, The Netherlands, now
hosting an art centre, is depicted showing
five different futures for the building.
Made on the occasion of the exhibition
In this Colony, curated by Sven Lütticken
and Maxine Kopsa.

Gullivers' Pocket (1989)
Three transparent plastic zip-lock bags in which the remains of Gullivers pocket are shown. Made for the travelling exhibition *A Voyage to Lilliput*. Lost.

H

Het Huwelijk/The Marriage (1993)
One day event in Moscow. Symbolic marriage to a Russian artist, as an attempt to interact with Russian artists for the occasion of *Exchange*, a show in public space in Moscow with 15 Dutch and 15 Russian artists. The wedding dress was acquired in a public underpass, from a woman that had previously worn it herself. Soon after the event and the departure of the Dutch group of artists, the groom exchanged the wedding ring for a bottle of Vermouth.

Hilton Piece (1994)
Video, original 52', currently 8'. Video made during *ArtHotel*, an art fair located on one floor in the Hilton International Hotel in Amsterdam. Filmed in the 'restored' John & Yoko Honeymoon Suite, the work features an androgynous guest, a mixture between an Asian businessman and a Yoko Ono look-alike. In deliberately rough and home-video style video-images, the creature appears mainly to be bored. Continuously played through the internal TV channel of the Hilton hotel.

Hilton Piece (Bed II) (1994)
Three colour photographs. *(Museum voor Moderne Kunst Arnhem)*

I

Interieurs/Interiors (1995)
Posters. Interior C.R., Interior R.K., Interior P.V. & S. de W., Interior B.V.

Interieurs/Interiors
1995
colour photographs

Interview met Duiker/Interview with
Duiker (1994)
Video, 15'. A factional dialogue between
a journalist and the architect of the former
news-cinema *Cineac*. In the monumental
building, a 'live via satellite' connection is
made to the unknown location where the
architect resides. The reception is troubled
by the technical difficulties of live
transmission, such as a-synchronicity and
frequent black outs of image and sound.
The conversation itself is marked by the
young interviewer's nostalgic perspective
on modernist architecture, which 104-year
old Duiker does not appreciate: once a
modernist, always a modernist.

Invisible Uniform (2001)
The full staff of the Casino d'Art
Contemporain received two sets of
underwear, with a stainless steel stylized
casino-logo sewn onto it, to be worn
underneath their daily clothes when at
work. Made for the exhibition *Audit*,
curated by Boris Kremer at Casino d' Art
Contemporain, Luxembourg.

J

Jan die alles zag/ Jan who saw it all (2004)
Insert in the book 10 YEARS Stedelijk
Museum Bureau Amsterdam. Like the
book, also the insert features all the
exhibitions, but told from memory by a man
who has seen all of them; the man has been
employed in the institute from its start.
Made for *Wunderland Unframed*, SMBA.

John & Yoko, Paris 1993 (1993)
Colour photograph.

K

De Kunstberg (2000)
Video and sound, 12'. An exploration of
the immense hollow space underneath De
Kunstberg in Brussels. Collaboration with
Sven Augustijnen. *Made for Brussels Cultural
Capital* 2000.

L

Lezing met Actrice/
Lecture with Actress (1997)
Performance, registration on DVD. An
actress with no previous knowledge of
Barbara Visser's work was hired to do a
lecture on Vissers' work, on the occasion
of an evening of philosophical discussion
about reality and fiction. The actress was
equipped with an invisible earpiece, and
repeating — almost in slow motion —
what the artist was prompting her.

Lecture on Lecture with Actress (2004)
Performance, video 15'. This work is a
sequel to *Lecture with Actress*. It shows a
different actress, again as Barbara Visser
giving a lecture, commenting on the first
performance and illustrating her talk with
video footage. Self-(re)presentation
becomes entangled in conceptual strategies

John & Yoko, Paris 1993
1993
colour photograph

that result in carefully choreographed confusion. Made for the exhibition *Funky Lessons*, curated by Jörg Heiser at Büro Friedrich, Berlin.

Lot, Frankrijk/ Lot, France (1994)
B/W photo series. Series made for Dutch literary magazine *Tirade*.

Luna Park (2006)
Series of colour and b/w photographs. Photographs taken in an abandoned attraction park in the mountains near Bilbao, Spain. Erected in the 1980s and abandoned in the middle of the 1990s, the very particular architectural shapes of that period are overgrown by plants, creating an array of 'contemporary ruins'.

Lot, Frankrijk/Lot, France
1994
series of b/w photographs

M

Maison Grégoire 118% (2000)
B/W and colour photographs. Photographed in Henry van de Velde's *Maison Grégoire*, a villa in the suburbs of Brussels. The human figures in these photographs are digitally downsized, making the space proportionally 18% larger. This is the enhancement needed to translate the piece of modernist architecture to contemporary standards — a 'correction' to the modernist conviction that scale should be linked to the average physical size of man. Three photographs are permanently installed in the villa. *(Collection Thomas Simon, Brussels, Collection Gemeentemuseum Den Haag)*

Luna Park
2006
series of colour and b/w photographs

<u>Medium Girl (1996)</u>
6 Videos of approx. 30 seconds.
Choreography of a Danish and a Greek girl
struggling with a Dutch folkloristic
costume. Initially made for broadcasting
on the television channel of the province
of Zeeland, in the south of Holland.
Commissioned by De Vleeshal, Middelburg.

<u>Mikro Video (2003)</u>
Video work made for a television-wall in an
electronics store in Tilburg. In collaboration
with Lucas Maassen and Dries Verbruggen.
Made for Shopping, Fundament
Foundation.

<u>Mondriaan (1991)</u>
Colour photograph. *(Collection J.M. Visser,
Collection Rob Schröder)*

*Neuflize Vie / ABN AMRO, Collection Armand
Mevis, Amsterdam, Collection MuHKA
Collection Vermeulen - van Winkel, Antwerp)*

<u>Museumstuk/Museumpiece (1992)</u>
Installation of a cylindrical wooden wall
(220 x 700 cm), video monitor, camera,
sound system. A monitor on a pedestal in
front of the wall shows the action — which
cannot be seen by the spectator — that
takes place in the wooden arena: a man is
practising with a set of knifes and axes,
as the loud blows coming from the space
suggest. Semi-live installation made for the
exhibition *Peiling '92* at museum Boijmans
Van Beuningen, Rotterdam.

<u>Myra (1991)</u>
B/W photograph, postcard. Made in
collaboration with Jan Visser. *(Collection
Mireille Mosler, New York)*

<u>Le monde appartient à ceux qui se lèvent
tôt/The world belongs to early risers (2002)</u>
Series of 5 photographs, offset printed on
120 x 176 cm posters, distributed through
the city of Nice on 200 publicity panels;
two newspapers; series of colour photographs of the same posters in stu.
By mixing photographic genres, this work
subsequently questions to what extent
documentary photography is staged and
aestheticized; and how images for publicity
purposes are presented and perceived.
(Collection Stedelijk Museum Amsterdam, Collection

Mondriaan
1991
colour photograph

Myra
1991
b/w photograph

N

O

P

Philippa I & II (1998)
Video/DVD, set photographs. A video
filmed at museum Huis van Loon in
Amsterdam, which permanently displays
period pieces from the van Loon heritage.
Childhood residence of Philippa van Loon
— who herself plays all three characters in
the video — the house is being used as a
décor for a farce about a Dutch, a French
and an English aristocrat.
(Rabo Kunstcollectie, Collection B.J. van Egteren.
Private Collection, courtesy Annet Gelink Gallery,
Amsterdam. Collection Bakker/Gelink. Collection
Fundación NMAC)

Photographs by Barbara Visser selected by Henry Bond, photographs by Henry Bond selected by Barbara Visser (1994)
The two artists exchanged their complete
photo-archives, to make a choice of
pictures, and show them together on
opposite walls.

Ping-pong for the People (2001)
Concrete chairs. Three 'Zigzag' chairs of
Rietveld, made out of concrete, are placed
on a square in a residential area of Tilburg.
The square already hosts a vast collection of
vandal-proof public furniture such as: park
benches, garbage cans, pick-nick bench-
tables, a ping-pong table, a fenced dog-shit
area and a small collection of 'wip-kippen'
(playground chickens).

Playtime (1991)
Chairs, children figures. Site specific
installation in the community centre
of Munster, France

Podium (1993)
Installation at Bloom Gallery, Amsterdam,
photograph. The two female gallerists are
relocated within the gallery, to work on
a 30 cm high podium in the centre of the
gallery space. From this spot, gallerists
Annet Gelink and Diana Stigter were
proposed to work for the duration of the
whole exhibition.

A Poorshow (1993)
Mixed materials, video. Collaboration with
artist Erik Weeda, bearing no signature of
either artist. Experiment.

Portret van de Kunstenaar/ Portrait of the Artist (1992)
18 Drawings, photographs, text. Portraits
of the artist made by eighteen street artists
in various countries in Europe and the US.
Originally each drawing was shown by a
document indicating duration, costs and
location of the drawing, including a small
b/w photo of the street artist. *(Collection*
Museum Boijmans Van Beuningen, Rotterdam)

Podium
1993
installation at Bloom Gallery, photograph

Portret van de Kunstenaar/
Portrait of the Artist
1992
18 drawings, photographs, text

Proposal for a Statue of Mathias Rust (1993)
Billboard-size realist painting shown on
a panel in Central Moscow, made by the
classically-trained Russian artist Iwan
Razumov. The painting depicted the future
statue of the young Mathias Rust, which
was to be erected at this location, next to
one of the many empty sculpture pedestals
in the city. The piece was stolen within
twenty-four hours, never to be found again.

Q

R

Rutger (1989)
Two b/w photographs.

S

T

Transformation House I & II (2006)
Text (I), computer-animation (II) in
collaboration with Olivier Campagne.
TH-I is a text, submitted for an architectural
competition to design an alternative
dwelling for the new city of Leidsche Rijn,
The Netherlands. *TH-II* is an animation film
made to visualize this plan, which is based
on the idea that the current way of building
does not consider the multiple social
transformations of many lives today.

Terug naar Fictie/ Back to Fiction (2004)
Letter and response letters, which were
being sent to and received from visual artists
and architects, who have been working on
the buildings of the Star Network (Sternet).
Star Network is a series of buildings in
The Netherlands, designed to facilitate the
postal system, but which turned out to be
an expensive mistake. Made for the
exhibition Cultureel Erfgoed op het Spoor,
NAi, Rotterdam.

True Lies (1995)
Video. A popular Hollywood movie is
hand-filmed in the cinema and distorted to
abstraction, to be projected again at cinema
size. The storyline is directed by the sound-
track only. Originally made for Casco,
Utrecht.

Tunes for Pre-metro/ Melodies pour
Pre-metro (2000)
Audio CD. Sound piece for the tunnels
and stations in the pre-metro of Brussels.
The usual muzak is replaced by the tones
of an anonymous male voice, the sound
emanating from the tunnel. Craftsman
Salvatore Blasco sings excerpts of operas,
chansons and the popular hit *Mexico(oooo)*.
Made for the exhibition Metro>polis.

Twee Projecties/Two Projections (2005)
Video and slide projection with sound, 30'.
Constructed interview with the 90-year
old grandmother of the artist, depicting
her life through objects and furniture in
her personal environment, showing choices
based on Modernist ideals of the 1930s.

Rutger
1989
two b/w photographs

Two Fighting Prostitutes (1991)
Colour photograph.

U

V

W

**Watersnoodramp Zeeland 1953/
Japan 2001/The Flooding Zeeland 1953/
Japan 2001 (2001)**
DVD 12' 10". Video work based on a
theatrical Japanese depiction of the Dutch
flooding of 1953. The audio track is used
as the basis for a work where the subtitling
tells a whole new story; an invisible group
of actors is rehearsing the Dutch flooding
spectacle, using garbage and a wind-
machine with little effect.

X

XM (1994)
Video, 2'.
A day in the life of a Citroën XM.

Y

Z

Z.T. (Zusjes)/ N.T. (Sisters) (1990–91)
87 B/W photographs on green felt.
Photographs of women who have been
called the artist's sister. *(Collection Bakker /
Gelink, Amsterdam)*

Two Fighting Prostitutes
1991
colour photograph

Z.T. (Zusjes)/ N.T. (Sisters)
1990–91
87 b/w photographs

CURRICULUM VITAE
[Barbara Visser]

1966
Born in Haarlem (NL)

1985/1991
Gerrit Rietveld Academy, Amsterdam
1989
Cooper Union, New York
1998/1999
Jan van Eyck Academy, Maastricht

1996
Charlotte Köhler Prize
1999
Prijs Jonge Belgische Schilderkunst/
Prix Jeune Peinture Belge
2000
Friedrich Vordemberge-Gildewart Prize

Selected Solo Exhibitions

2006
*Vertaalde Werken/Translated Works,
Barbara Visser 1990 – 2006,* De Paviljoens,
Almere

2003
Beauty is the Victory of the mind over matter,
Annet Gelink Gallery, Amsterdam

2002
The world belongs to early risers, Underground
Gallery, Athens; *Le monde appartient à ceux qui
se lèvent tôt,* Villa Arson, Nice

2001
A Day in Holland/Holland in a Day, Stroom
HCBK, The Hague

2000
Detitled, Exedra, Hilversum (with Sam
Durant)

1997
Gillian Wearing & Barbara Visser, Bloom
Gallery, Amsterdam (with Gillian Wearing)

1995
Gimines, Bloom Gallery, Amsterdam;
True Lies, Casco, Utrecht

1994
Ars Futura, Ars Futura Gallery, Zurich
(with Kiki Lamers and Paul de Reus);
*Photographs by Barbara Visser selected by Henry
Bond, Photographs by Henry Bond selected by
Barbara Visser,* Bloom Gallery, Amsterdam

1993
A Poor Show, W139, Amsterdam (with
Erik Weeda); Bloom Gallery, Amsterdam

Selected Group Exhibitions

2006
How to Live Together/Como Viver Juntos,
27th São Paulo Biennial, São Paulo
House for Sale, Beyond, Leidsche Rijn,
Utrecht; *I (Ich) Performative Ontology,* Wiener
Secession, Vienna.

2005
Now and Again, Utrecht Manifest, Utrecht;
Pursuit of Happiness, Beyond, Leidsche Rijn
Utrecht; *In this Colony,* Kunstfort Vijfhuizen;
Life, Once More, Witte de With, Rotterdam;
H x B x D = De Rabo Kunstcollectie, GEM,
The Hague; *Constructed Moment,* KW–14,
Den Bosch

2004
Schöner Wohnen, BE-PART Cabk, Waregem;
Funky Lessons, Büro Friedrich, Berlin; *Making
Public,* CBK Dordrecht; *This is not a home, this
is a house,* Observatoire Galerie, Brussels;
Traffic d'Influences, Lille Capitale Culture
2004, Lille; *Surfacing,* Ludwig Museum,
Budapest; *Wunderland Unframed,* Stedelijk
Museum Bureau Amsterdam; *Cultureel
Erfgoed op het Spoor,* NAi, Rotterdam; *Royal*

Wedding/L'épuisement du Réel, **MAMCO**, **Geneva**; *Mediascapes*, **Fundacío La Caixa** **(travelling exhibition)**, **Lleida (2004)**, **Tarragona (2004)**, **Girona (2005)**; *Migrating Identities*, **Arti et Amicitiae**, **Amsterdam**

2003
Shopping, **Fundament**, **Tilburg**; *Urban Dramas*, **De Singel**, **Antwerp**; *Regarde, il neige*, **Centre d'Art Contemporain**, **Vassivière**; *Histoires Contemporaines*, **IAC**, **Lyon**; *Stop & Go*, **Frac Nord – Pas de Calais**, **Dunkerque**; *Retrospective View*, **De Hallen van het Frans Hals Museum**, **Haarlem**; *Schoonheid...*, **Festival a/d Werf**, **Utrecht**; *M_ARS, Art and War*, **Neue Galerie am Landesmuseum Joanneum**, **Graz**

2002
Haunted by Detail, **De Appel**, **Amsterdam**; *It's unfair!*, **De Paviljoens**, **Almere**; *Faces, People and Society*, **Frans Hals Museum**, **Haarlem**; *Married by Powers*, **TENT**, **Rotterdam**; *Waiting for the Ice Age*, **Georg Kargl Gallery**, **Vienna**

2001
Set, **Castello di Rivoli**, **Turin**; *Audit*, **Casino**, **Luxembourg**; *Silhouettes 'n Shadows*, **Fundament**, **Tilburg**; *Mangistan*, **Oud Amelisweerd**, **Utrecht**; *Helle Nächte*, **Kunstverein van Binningen**, **Bottingen**, **Reinach**; *Neue Welt*, **Frankfurter Kunstverein**, **Frankfurt**; *Remedy for Melancholy*, **Edsvik Kunsthalle**, **Stockholm**

2000
For Real, **Stedelijk Museum**, **Amsterdam**; *Internationales*, **Maison Grégoire**, **Brussels**; *Import/Export* **(travelling exhibition)**, **Salzburger Kunstverein**, **Salzburg**; **Museum voor Moderne Kunst**, **Arnhem**; **Villa Arson**, **Nice (2001)**; *Metro>polis*, **subway Brussels**; *Ville Vacant/Stad op de Helling*, **Brussel 2000**, **Brussels**

1999
Spiral TV, **Wacoal Art Centre**, **Tokyo**; *The Dialectics of Progress*, **ICA**, **Dunaujvaros**, **Hungary**; *Prix de la jeune peinture Belge*, **Paleis voor Schone Kunsten**, **Brussels**
1998
In de sloot..., **Stedelijk Museum**, **Amsterdam**; *Sutemos/Twilight*, **CAC**, **Vilnius**; *Enough*, **The Tannery**, **London**; *Altered States*, **Festival a/d Werf**, **Utrecht**; *Roommates*, **Museum van Loon**, **Amsterdam**; *Shot without Reason*, **Bloom Gallery**, **Amsterdam**

1997
International Film Festival, **Rotterdam**; *Verbindingen/Jonctions*, **Palais des Beaux Arts**, **Brussels**; *Ecce... en Nietzsche*, **Trusttheater**, **Amsterdam**

1996
Gedraag je!/Behave!/Benimm Dich!, **Stedelijk Museum Bureau Amsterdam**; *Album*, **Eight Floor**, **New York**; *Push-ups*, **The Factory**, **Athens Fine Art School**, **Athens**; *The Unbelievable Truth*, **Tramway**, **Glasgow**

1995
Bits and Pieces, **Arti et Amicitiae**, **Amsterdam**; *New Balance*, **CAC**, **Vilnius**; *Selfmade*, **Grazer Kunstverein**, **Graz**

1994
Cinema Actuel, **Stedelijk Museum Bureau Amsterdam & Cineac cinema**, **Amsterdam**

1993
Exchange-Datsja, **Almere/Moscow**; *Ieder kind is van marmer*, **Bloom Gallery**, **Amsterdam**; *Art Hotel*, **Hilton Hotel**, **Amsterdam**

1992
One Hour Art, **Museum Fodor**, **Amsterdam**; *Het Ideale Portret/The Ideal Portret*, **Beurs van Berlage**, **Amsterdam**; *Peiling '92*, **Museum Boymans van Beuningen**, **Rotterdam**

BIBLIOGRAPHY

Catalogues and books

cat. *How to Live Together/Como Viver Juntos*, 27th São Paulo Biennial, São Paulo, Brazil, 2006

cat. *Happy Magazine (Pursuit of Happiness)*, text by Arjan Reinders, Bureau Beyond, Utrecht, 2005

Sven Lütticken (ed.), cat. *Life, Once More. Forms of Re-enactment in Contemporary Art*, Witte de With, Center for Contemporary Art, Rotterdam, 2005

cat. *Unlocked #2, Rabobank Art Collection*, GEM/Rabobank Nederland, The Hague, 2005

Sven Lütticken & Maxine Kopsa (ed.), cat. *In this Colony/In deze Kolonie*, Kunstfort bij Vijfhuizen, municipality of Haarlemmermeer, 2005

Jörg Heiser (ed.), cat. *Funky Lessons*, interview by Jörg Heiser, Revolver, Frankfurt, 2005

Montse Badia, Andreas M. Kaufmann (ed.), cat. *Paisatges Mediàtics*, Fundació La Caixa, Gerona, Tarragona, Lleida, Spain, 2005

cat. *Schöner Wohnen*, Be-Part, Waregem, Belgium, 2004

cat. *Who if not we...? Surfacing*, text by Lívia Páldi, Ludwig Museum Budapest/ Revolver, Frankfurt, Germany/Hungary, 2004

cat. *Migrating Identity — Transmission/ Reconstruction*, Arti et Amicitiae/Artimo, 2004

cat. *Link, Voorstel tot Gemeentelijke Kunstaankopen Fotografie 2002–2003/Proposal for Municipal Acquisitions Photography 2002– 2003*, Stedelijk Museum Amsterdam/Nai publishers, Rotterdam, 2003

cat. *M_ARS — Kunst und Krieg*, Neue Galerie am Landesmuseum, Graz/Hatje Cantz Verlag, Germany, 2003

Barbara Visser, *Le monde appartient à ceux qui se lèvent tôt*, Villa Arson, Nice, France, 2002

Barbara Visser, *The world belongs to the early risers*, supplement by cat. *Haunted by Detail*, texts by Els Hanappe, Basak Senova, Alexandra Koroxenidis, Natasa Petresin, De Appel, Amsterdam, 2002

cat. *Commitment*, Fonds BKVB, Amsterdam, 2002

cat. *Contemporary Art from The Netherlands*, European Central Bank in co-operation with De Nederlandsche Bank, Frankfurt, Germany, 2002

Boris Kremer (ed.), cat. *Audit*, Casino Luxembourg — Forum d'art contemporain, Luxembourg, 2001

cat. *Bra mot melankoli/Remedy for Melancholy*, Edsvik konst och kultur, Edsvik Kunsthalle, Baltic Art Center, Sweden, 2001

Barbara Visser, *A day in Holland/Holland in a Day*, text fragments by Joris Karl Huysmans, Stroom HCBK, The Hague, 2001

cat. *Neue Welt*, text by Vanessa Joan Müller, Frankfurter Kunstverein, Frankfurt/Lukas & Sternberg, New York, Germany/USA, 2001 cat. *Internationales*, Maison Grégoire, Brussels/Artimo, 2001

cat. *Import Export*, text by Jeroen Boomgaard, Salzburger Kunstverein, Salzburg; Museum voor moderne Kunst, Arnhem; Villa Arson, Nice; Austria, the Netherlands, France, 2000

cat. *Metro>Polis, Bruxelles Souterraine/ Metro>Polis, Ondergronds Brussel*, ASBL/VZW Bruxelles/Brussel, Belgium, 2000

cat. *This is for Real*, Stedelijk Museum, Amsterdam/Nai publishers, Rotterdam, 2000

cat. *Spiral TV, The 3rd Art Life 21*, Waocoal Art Centre, Tokyo, Japan, 1999

Barbara Visser. Prix de la jeune peinture Belge/ Prijs jonge Belgische schilderkunst, text by Tony Godfrey, Bruxelles/Brussels, Belgium, 1999

cat. *Roommates*, Museum van Loon, Amsterdam, 1998

cat. *Voorstellen Gemeentelijke Kunstaankopen 1997/Proposals for Municipal Acquisitions 1997, (cover)*, Stedelijk Museum Amsterdam, 1997

cat. *Ecce... en Nietzsche, Waan van werkelijkheid*, Trusttheater Amsterdam, 1997

cat. *Push-ups*, The Factory, Athens Fine Arts School, Athens, Greece, 1996

cat. *Casco 1995*, Casco, Utrecht, 1995

cat. *Self made*, Grazer Kunstverein/ Steirischer Herbst, Graz, Austria, 1995

cat. *The Wall*, Sotheby's Art Foundation Amsterdam, 1994

cat. *Europa '94 — Junge Europäische Kunst in München*, Hypo-Kulturstiftung, Munich, Germany, 1994

cat. *Peiling '92*, Museum Boijmans-van Beuningen, Rotterdam, 1992

Articles

Moritz Küng, *Interview with Barbara Visser*, in: Metropolis M, no.5, 2006

Edo Dijksterhuis, *Vadermoord op een Eames-leunstoel*, in: Financieel Dagblad, 22.10.2005

Domeniek Ruyters, *De openbare ruimte, dat ben jij*, in: De Volkskrant, 08.09.2005

Maaike Bleeker, *Nostalgia for an age that never existed. Over Life, Once More*, in: De Witte Raaf #114, March 2005, Belgium, 2005

Domeniek Ruyters, *Re-enactment haalt het verleden dichterbij*, in: De Volkskrant, 14.02.2005

Sandra Smallenburg, *Met re-enactment herhalen kunstenaars de geschiedenis: Een lichaam opgraven*, in: NRC Handelsblad, 04.02.2005

Harm Tilman, *Barbara Visser — Terug naar fictie*, in: De Architect, 2004

Sven Lütticken, *Reality Studio — over Barbara Visser*, in: Jong Holland: Authenticeit in de beeldende kunst, no.4, 2003

Andreas Schlaegel, *Aperto Amsterdam*, in: Flash Art, January/February 2003

Rutger Pontzen, *Afgrijzen en schoonheid*, in: Vrij Nederland, 10.08.2002

Georgette Koning, *Wounded*, in: Dutch #34, 2001

Hans den Hartog Jager, *Alles kantelt — Barbara Visser in Japan*, in: NRC Handelsblad, 22.07.2001

Nina Folkersma, *Kleine utopieën met de eigen buur — Barbara Visser, Reneé Kool en A.P. Komen & Murphy,* in: **MetropolisM no.4, 1996**

Marietta Franke, *Du sprichst über etwas, was du weisst, aber nicht fühlst,* in: **Work in Progress no.3, Cologne, December 1994/January 1995**

Sandra Smallenburg, *Barbara Visser en Henry Bond,* in: **Ruimte, 1994**

Roel Verhallen, *Een bruid, een arrestant en een spijbelende dichter -* **Exchange**, *kunst in de stedelijke ruimte van Moskou,* in: **Kunst & Museum journaal, Jaargang 5, no.4, 1994**

Tineke Reijnders, *Terugblik,* in: **Kunst & Museum Journaal, Jaargang 4, no.4, 1993**

Dominic van den Boogerd, *Barbara Visser in Bloom Gallery,* in: **MetropolisM no.4, 1993**

Saskia Gaster, *Rijke armen — De kinderen van Beuys op bezoek bij de kinderen van Kabakov,* in: **De Groene Amsterdammer, 11.08.1993**

Publications by Barbara Visser

Contribution, in: Re-Magazine No.12, Hester: Depressed, winter 2004–2005

Contribution, in: Open No.7, SKOR/Nai publishers, Amsterdam/Rotterdam, 2004

Barbara Visser, *Blurring Boundaries,* in: Lier en Boog No.15, Amsterdam, 2000

Barbara Visser, *Detitled,* image contribution in: A-Prior No.2, Brussels, Belgium, 2000

KPN calendar, KPN (Royal Mail, the Netherlands), 1996

Image contribution, in: Tirade, G.A. van Oorschot, Amsterdam, 1994

Barbara Visser, *Morgen gemaakt,* in: Arti, Art et Amicitiae, Amsterdam, 1993

Barbara Visser, Renée Kool, Erwin Slegers, *Avis, 13 jaar audiovisuele afdeling van de Gerrit Rietveld Academie,* Gerrit Rietveld Academy, Amsterdam, 1992

Cover photo, in: Lelijk gebouwd Nederland, SDU uitgeverij, The Hague, 1991

COLOPHON
[Barbara Visser is er niet]

Editors:
Lisette Smits & Barbara Visser

Texts:
Jennifer Allen, Paul Elliman, Maria Grever,
Jörg Heiser, Alexis Vaillant, Barbara Visser

Graphic design:
Mevis & Van Deursen, Amsterdam,
in collaboration with Felix Weigand

Translations and proof reading:
A1 Translations (text Alexis Vaillant),
Emily Pethick

Print:
NPN Drukkers, Breda, The Netherlands

Photography:
Barbara Visser, Olivier Campagne,
Nadine Hottenrott, Ilya Rabinovich

Acknowledgements:
Annet Gelink Gallery, Amsterdam (The
Netherlands); Museum de Paviljoens, Almere
(The Netherlands); Villa Arson, Nice (France);
Bureau Beyond, Utrecht (The Netherlands);
Museum Huis van Loon, Amsterdam (The
Netherlands); CAC, Vilnius (Lithuania); Hilton
International Hotel, Amsterdam (The
Netherlands); ICA Dunaujvaros (Hungary); Büro
Friedrich, Berlin (Germany); Artefactory, Paris
(France); Huis ten Bosch Stad, Kyushu (Japan);
cultureel centrum De Badcuyp, Amsterdam
(The Netherlands); Maison Grégoire, Brussels
(Belgium); A Prior Magazine (Belgium);
Fundament Foundation, Tilburg (The
Netherlands); Brussels 2000, Brussels (Belgium);
Kunst en Fietswerk, The Hague, (The
Netherlands); NAi, Rotterdam (TheNetherlands);
Stroom Den Haag, The Hague (The Netherlands).

Sven Augustijnen, Veronica Ditting, Annelieke
van Halen, Jaap Hoogstraten, Wendela Hubrecht,
Il Kyu Hwang, Elsa de Jong, Renée Kool,
Maxine Kopsa, Mirjam Linschooten, Philippa
van Loon, Sven Lütticken, Lucas Maassen,
Line Nissen, Liutauras Psibilskis, Pieter Roodhorst,
Christine Rothuizen, Gabrielle van der Sleen en
Herman Peerdeman, Evaldas Stankevicius, Diana
Stigter, Saskia Temmink, Dries Verbruggen, Tim
Vermeulen, Sabine Visser, Jan Visser, Marianne
Visser, Miep van der Sleen-de Vries, Simone de
Vries, Jan Vermeulen en Charlotte Kokken,
Astrid Vorstermans, Jolien Wanninkhof, Steven
van Watermeulen, Erik Weeda, Andrea Wiarda.

Made possible with the generous support of:
Annet Gelink Gallery, Amsterdam; Advaney
Collection; Collection/Verzameling De Bruin —
Heijn; Fonds voor beeldende kunsten,
vormgeving en bouwkunst, Amsterdam; J.M.
Visser, Almere; Werner Vermeulen, Antwerpen.

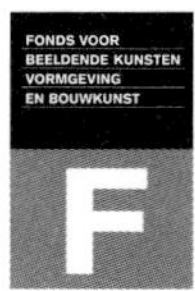

Distributed by:
JRP|Ringier
Letzigraben 134
CH-8047 Zurich
T +41 (0) 43 311 27 50
F +41 (0) 43 311 27 51
www.jrp-ringier.com
info@jrp-ringier.com

ISBN 10: 3-905770-25-3
ISBN 13: 978-3-905770-25-4

JRP|Ringier books are available internationally
at selected bookstores and from the following
distribution partners:

Switzerland: Buch 2000, AVA Verlagsauslieferung
AG, Centralweg 16, CH-8910 Affoltern a.A.,
buch2000@ava.ch, www.ava.ch

Germany and Austria: Vice Versa Vertrieb,
Immanuelkirchstrasse 12, D-10405 Berlin,
info@vice-versa-vertrieb.de, www.vice-versa-
vertrieb.de

France: Les Presses du réel, 16 rue Quentin,
F-21000 Dijon, info@lespressesdureel.com,
www.lespressesdureel.com

UK: Art Data, 12 Bell Industrial Estate, 50
Cunnington Street, UK-London W4 5HB,
info@artdata.co.uk, www.artdata.co.uk

USA: D.A.P./Distributed Art Publishers, 155
Sixth Avenue, 2nd Floor, USA-New York,
NY 10013, dap@dapinc.com, www.artbook.com

Other countries: IDEA Books, Nieuwe
Herengracht 11, NL-1011 RK Amsterdam,
idea@ideabooks.nl, www.ideabooks.nl

For a list of our partner bookshops or for any
general questions, please contact JRP|Ringier
directly at info@jrp-ringier.com, or visit our
homepage www.jrp-ringier.com for further
information about our program.

jrp|ringier

printed in the EU

BARBARA VISSER IS ER NIET
[edited by Lisette Smits and Barbara Visser]

CONTENTS

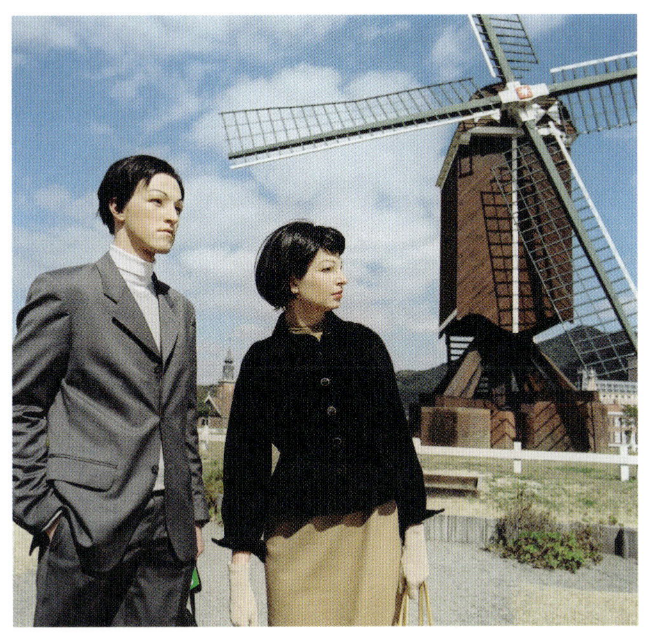

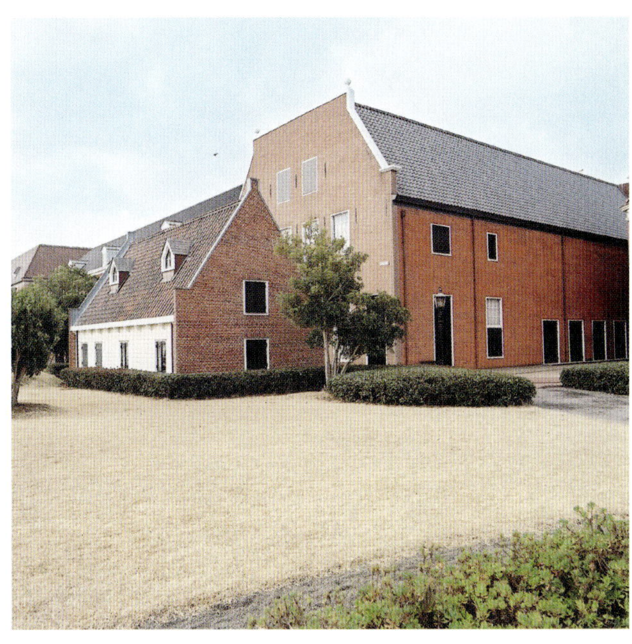

A Day in Holland/Holland in a Day
2001
series of colour photographs

A Day in Holland/Holland in a Day
2001
series of colour photographs

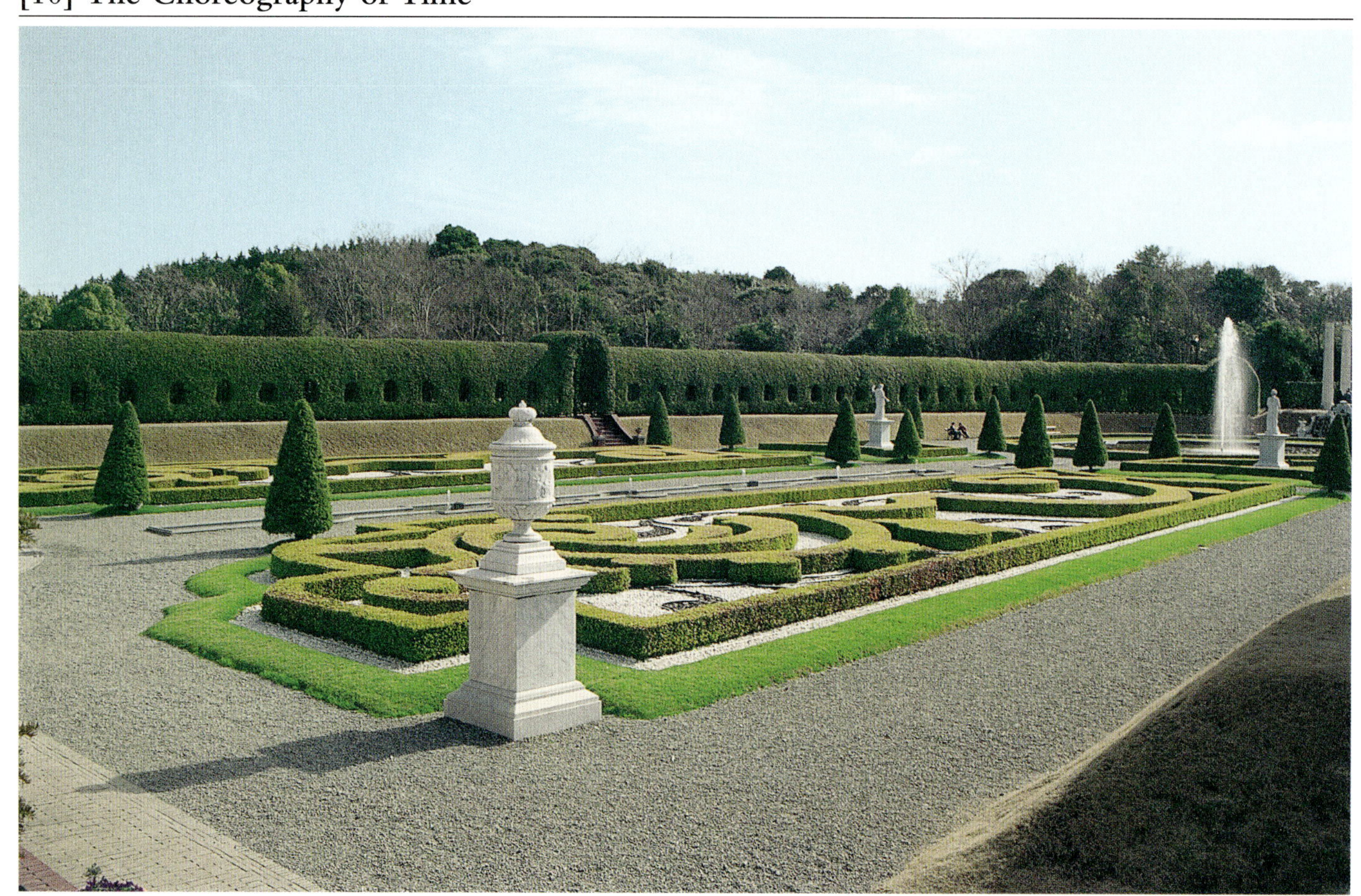

A Day in Holland/Holland in a Day
2001
series of colour photographs

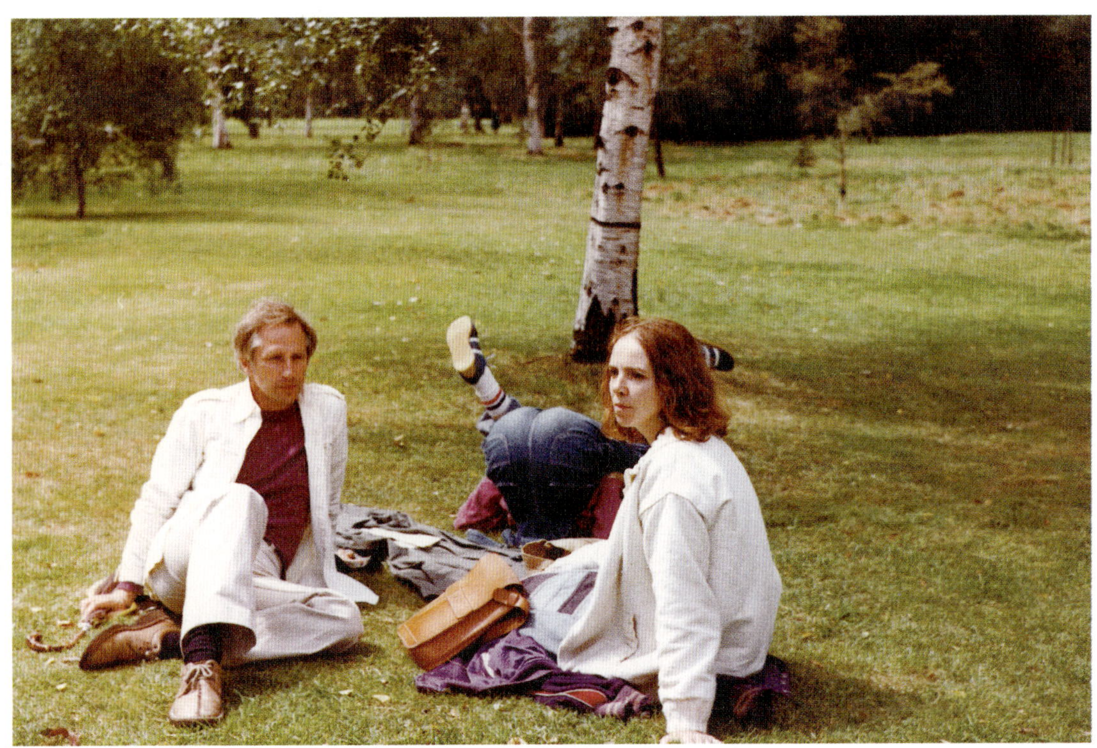

London 1977
1977
colour photograph

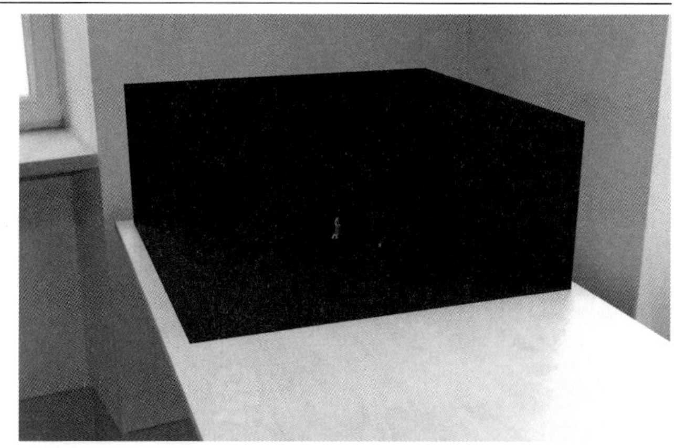

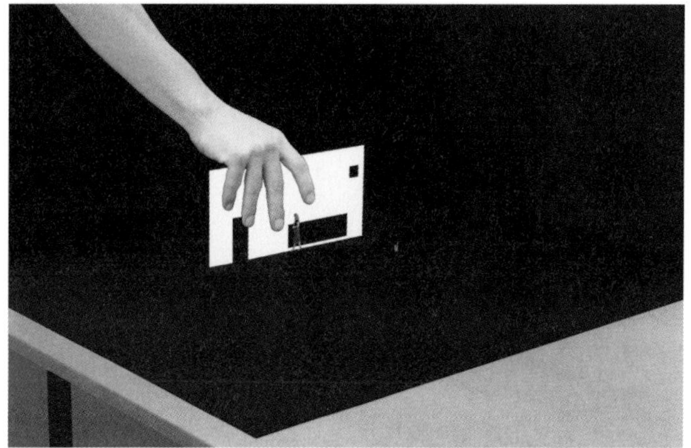

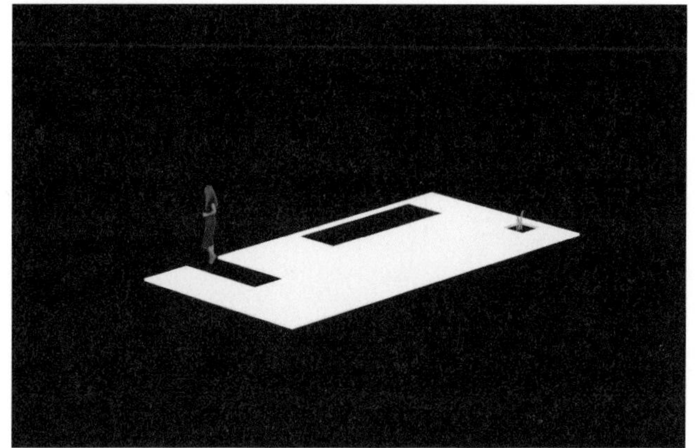

Transformation House
2006
computer-animation

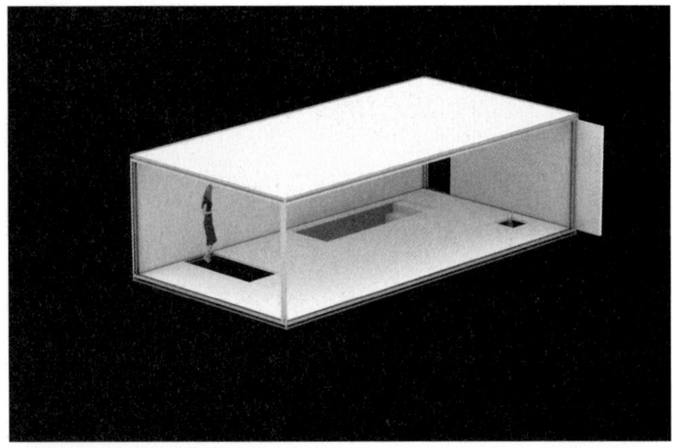

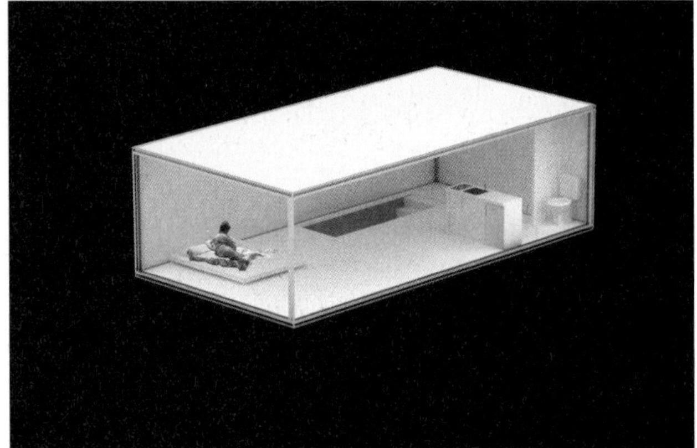

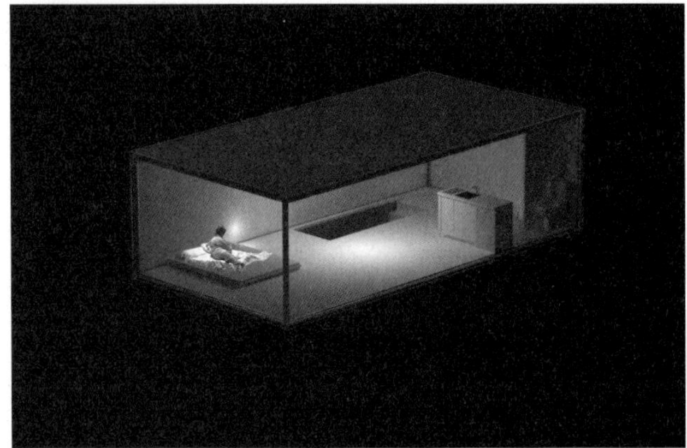

Transformation House
2006
computer-animation

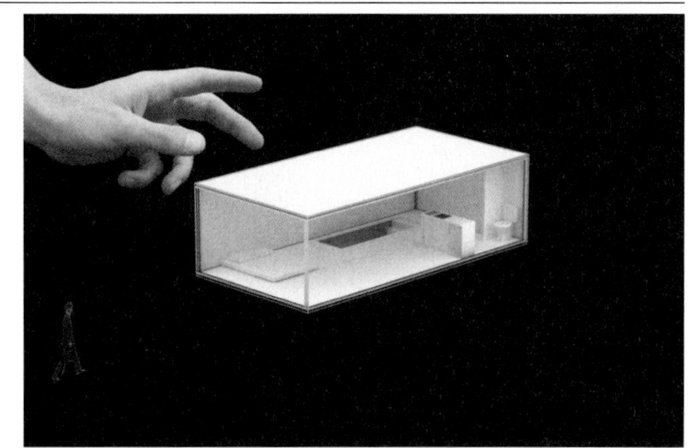

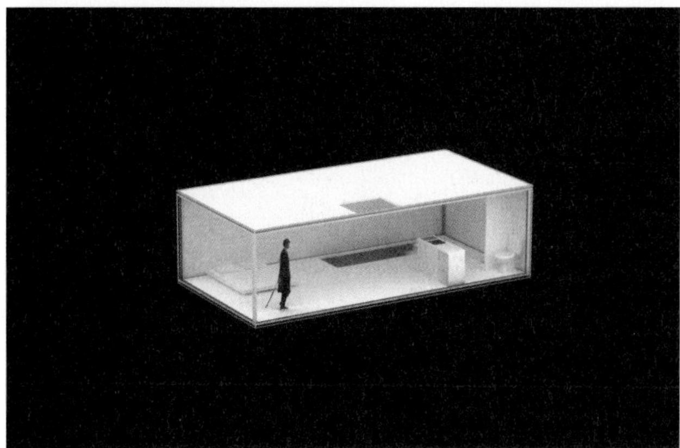

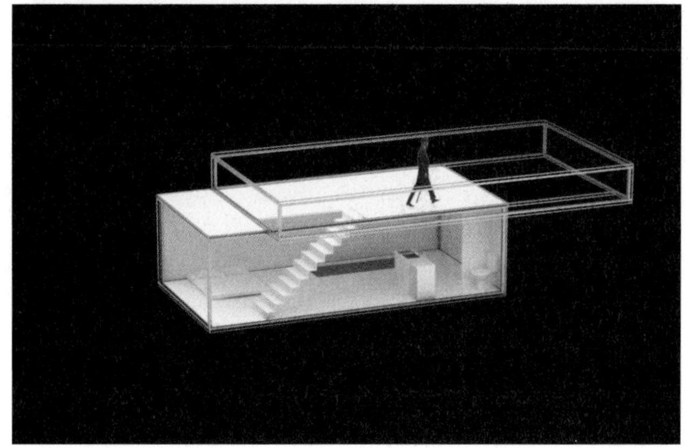

Transformation House
2006
computer-animation

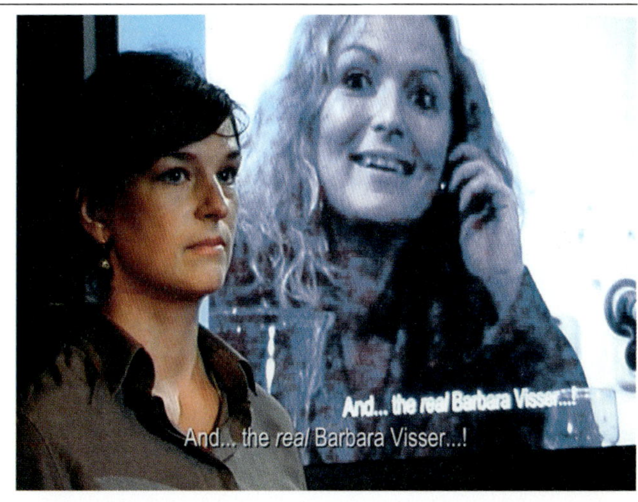

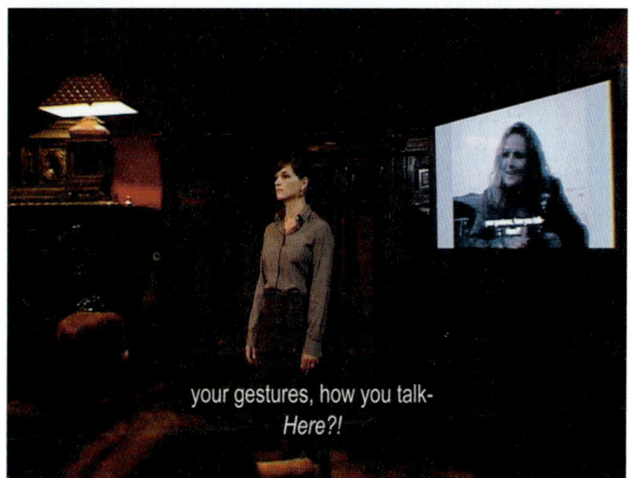

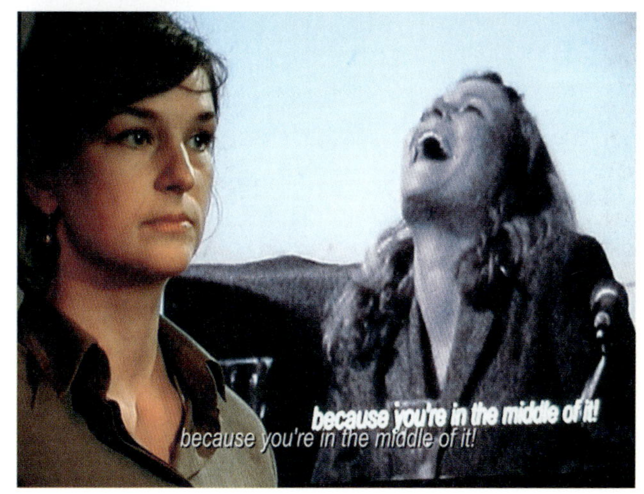

Lecture on Lecture with Actress
2004
performance, registration on DVD

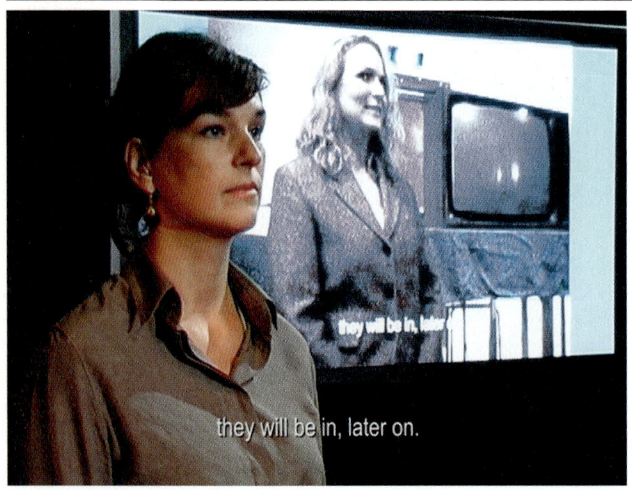

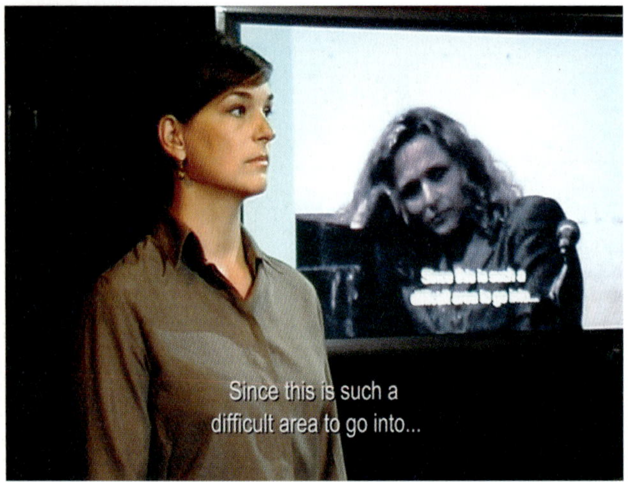

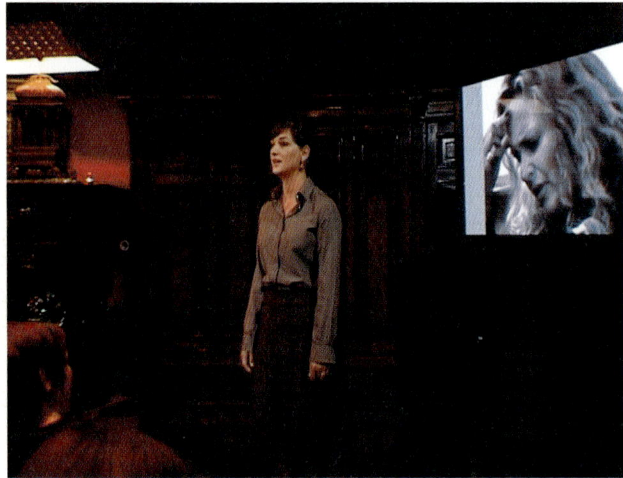

Lecture on Lecture with Actress
2004
performance, registration on DVD

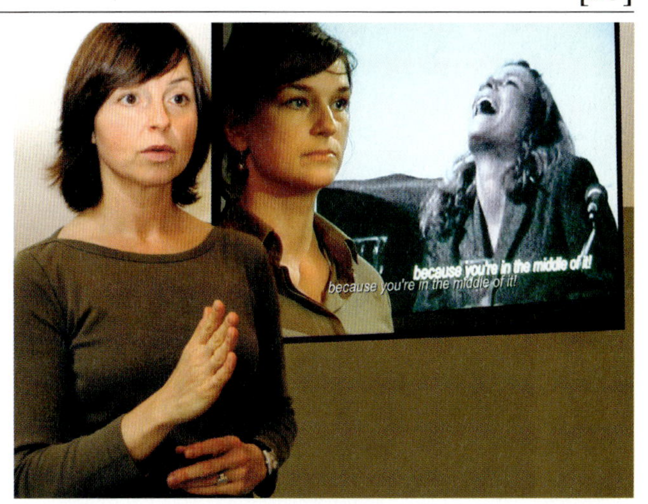

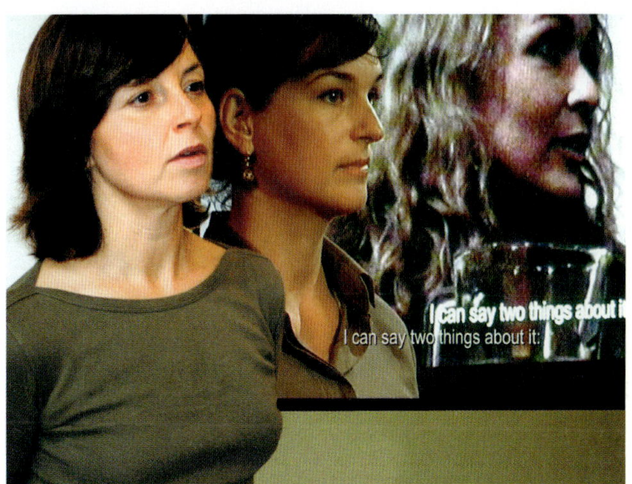

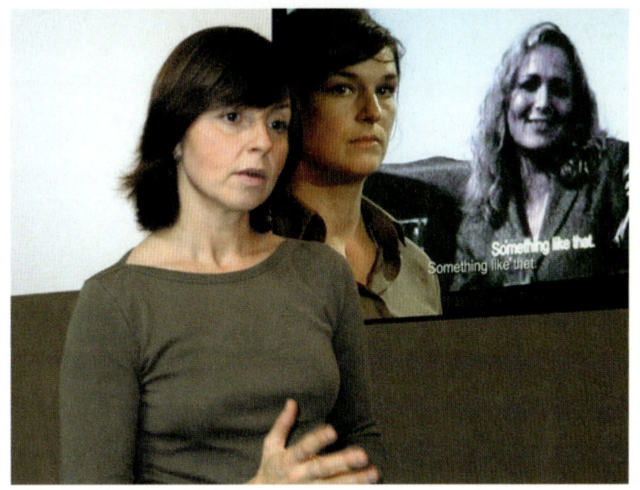

Last Lecture
2005
photomontage for performance

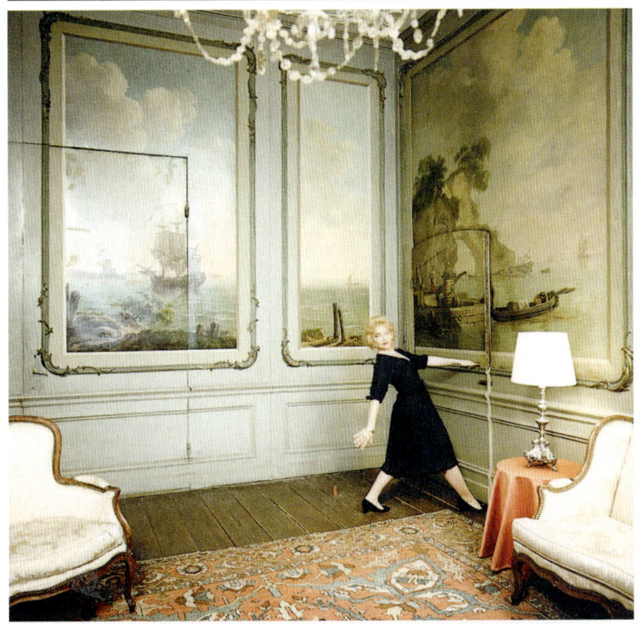

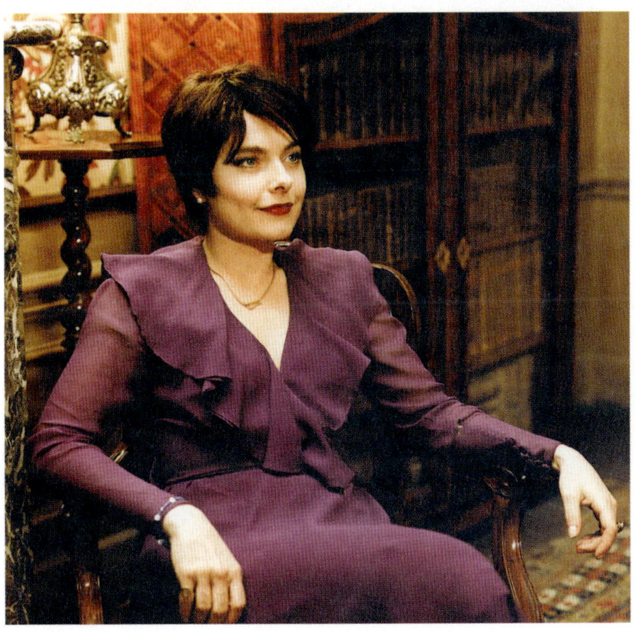

Philippa
1998
video, set photographs

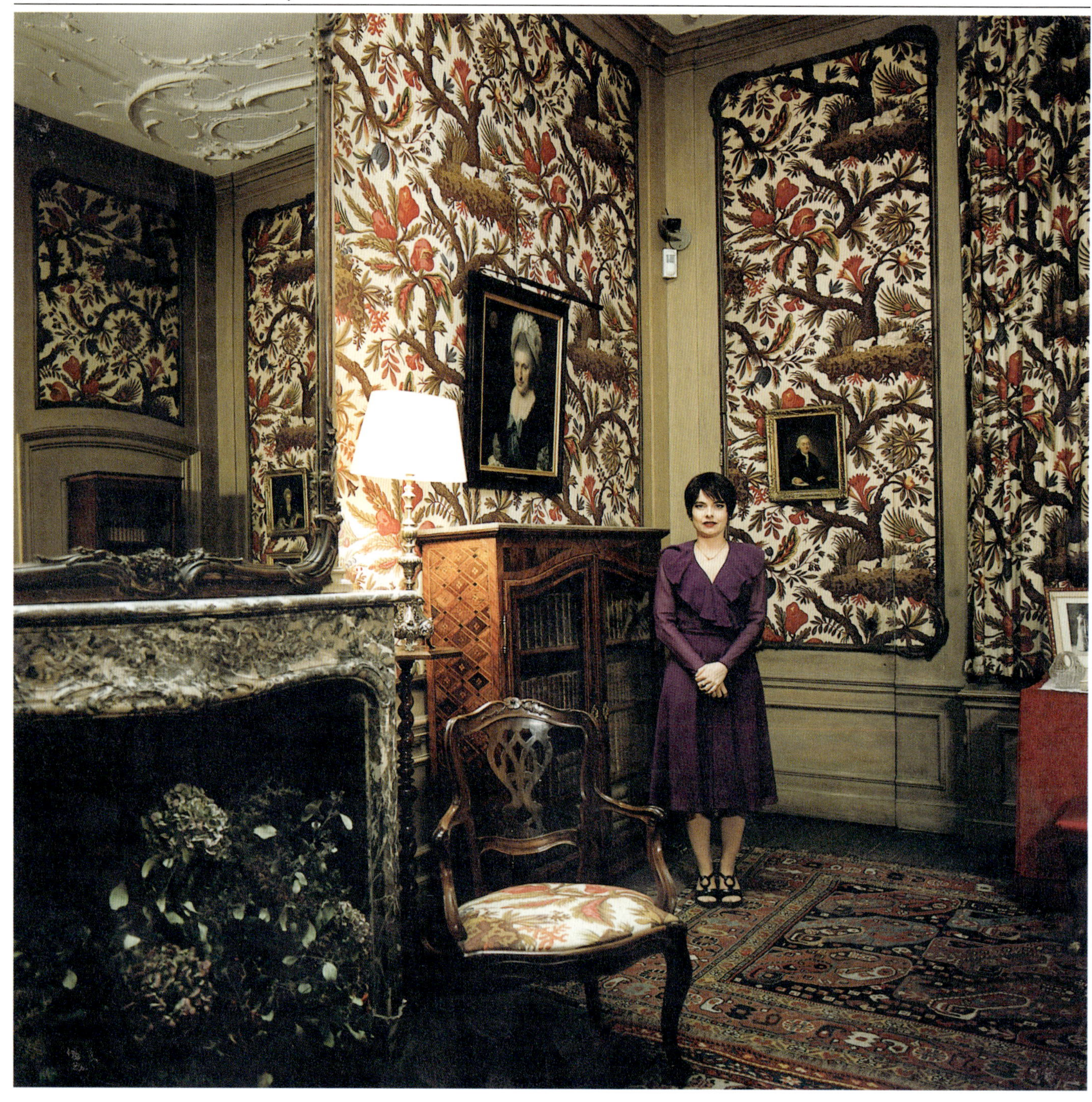

Philippa
1998
video, set photographs

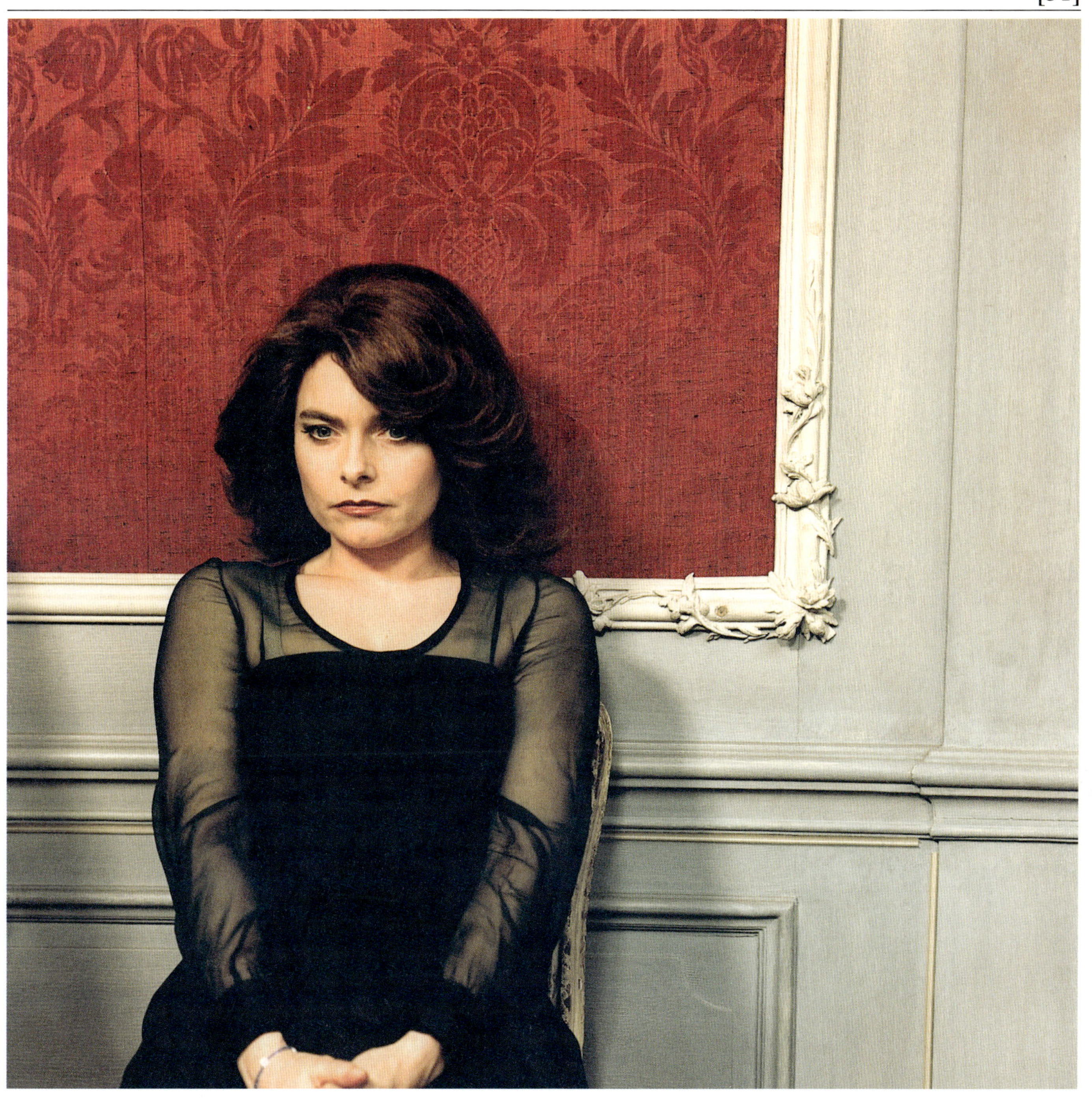

Philippa
1998
video, set photographs

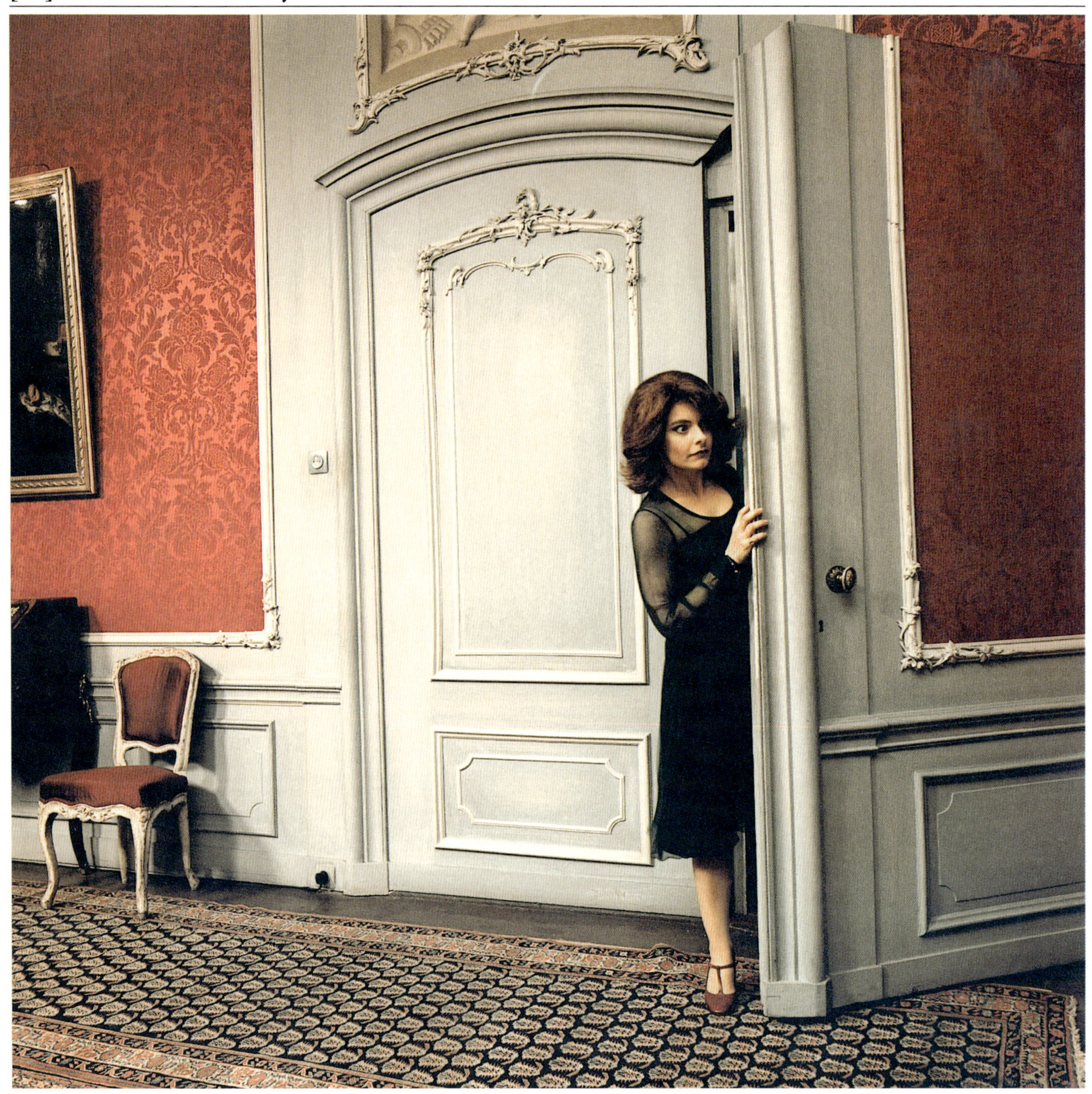

Philippa
1998
video, set photographs

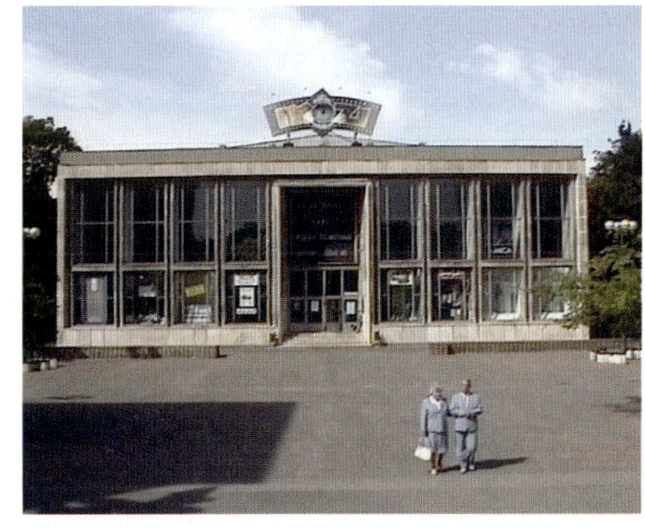

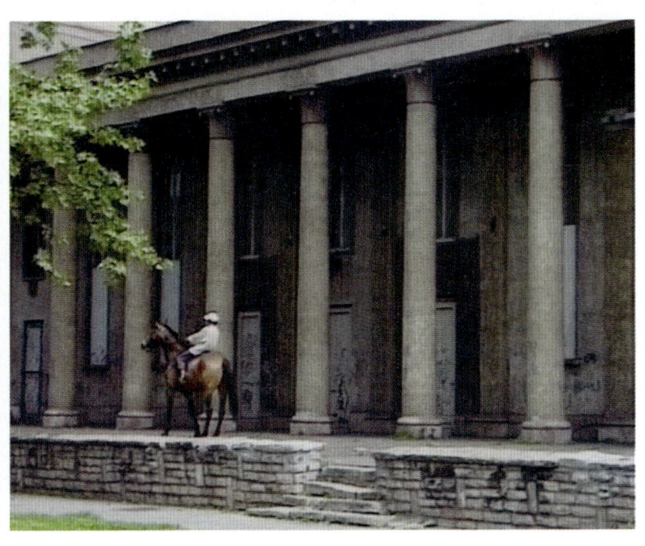

Decoralism
1999
video, still

Decoralism
1999
video, still

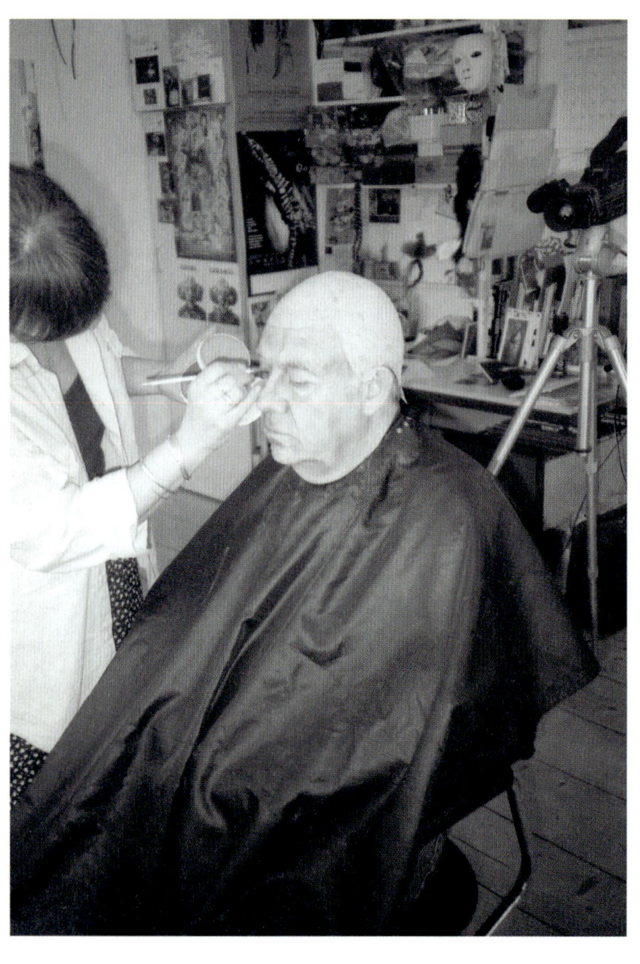

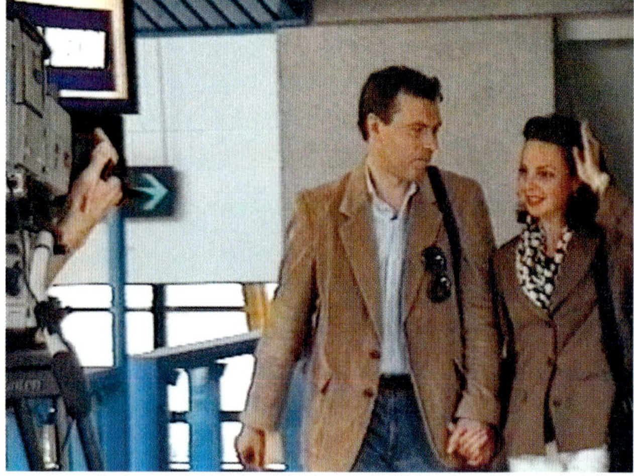

Interview with Duiker
1994
set photograph

Gimines
1995
video still of set

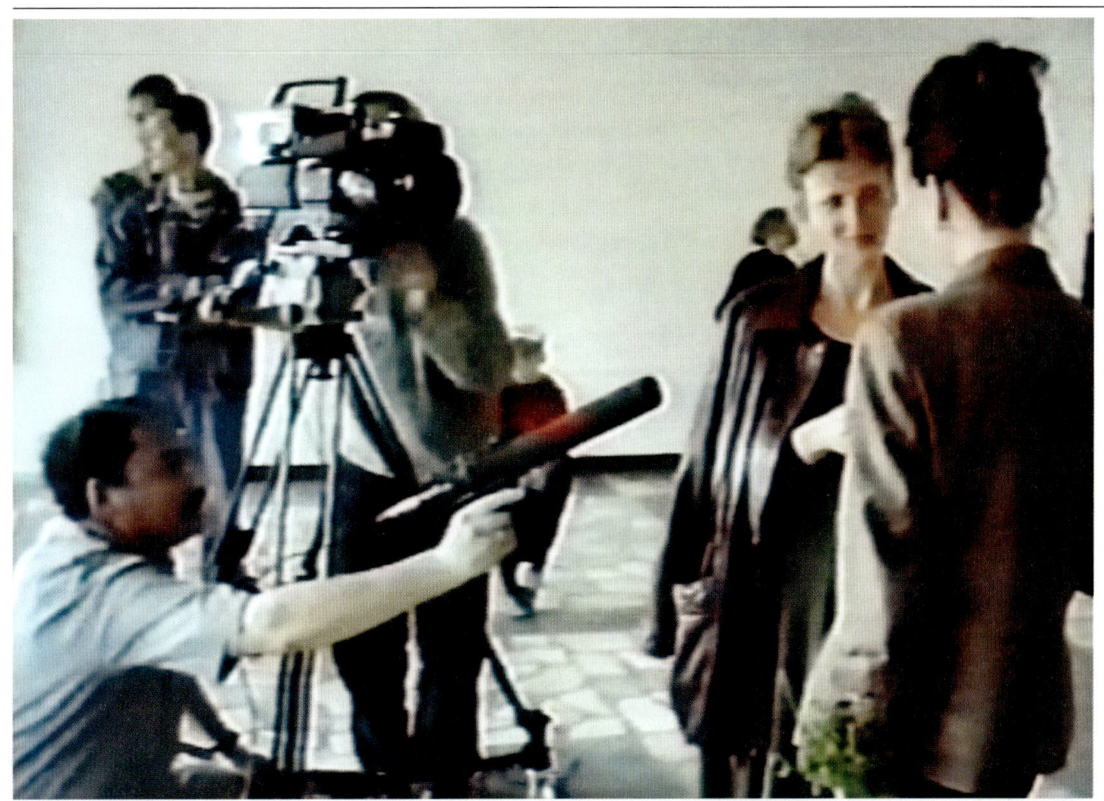

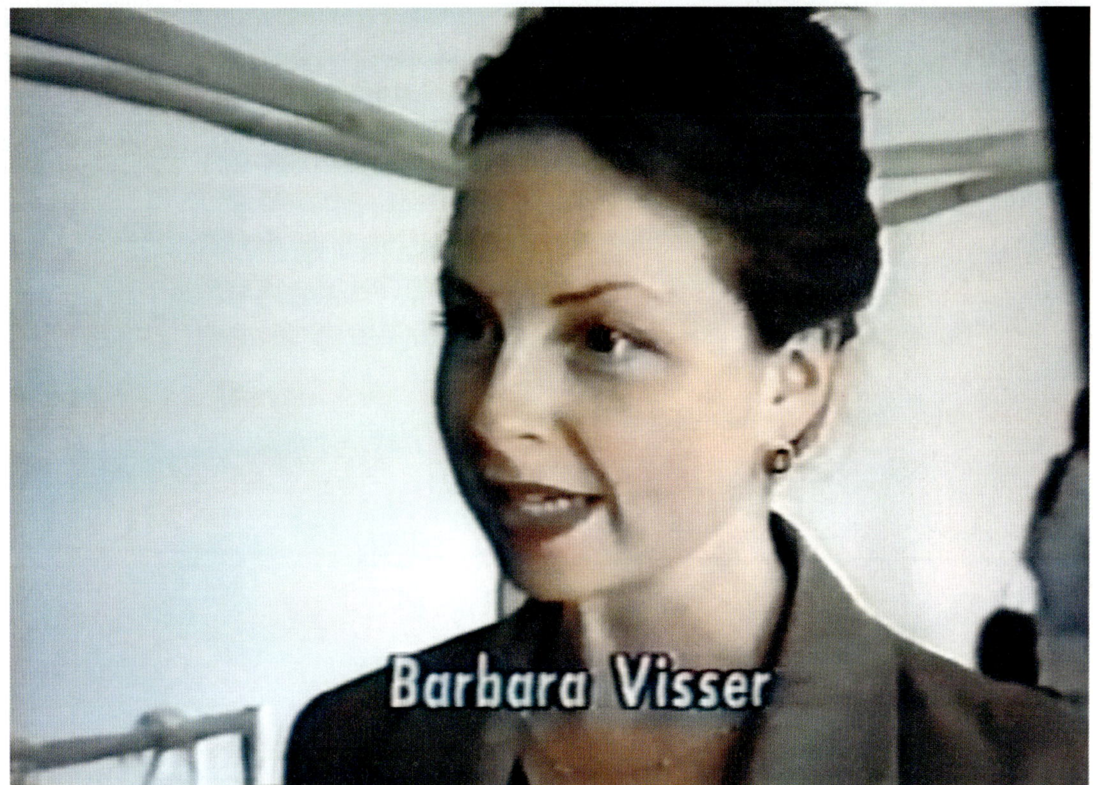

Gimines
1995
video, stills

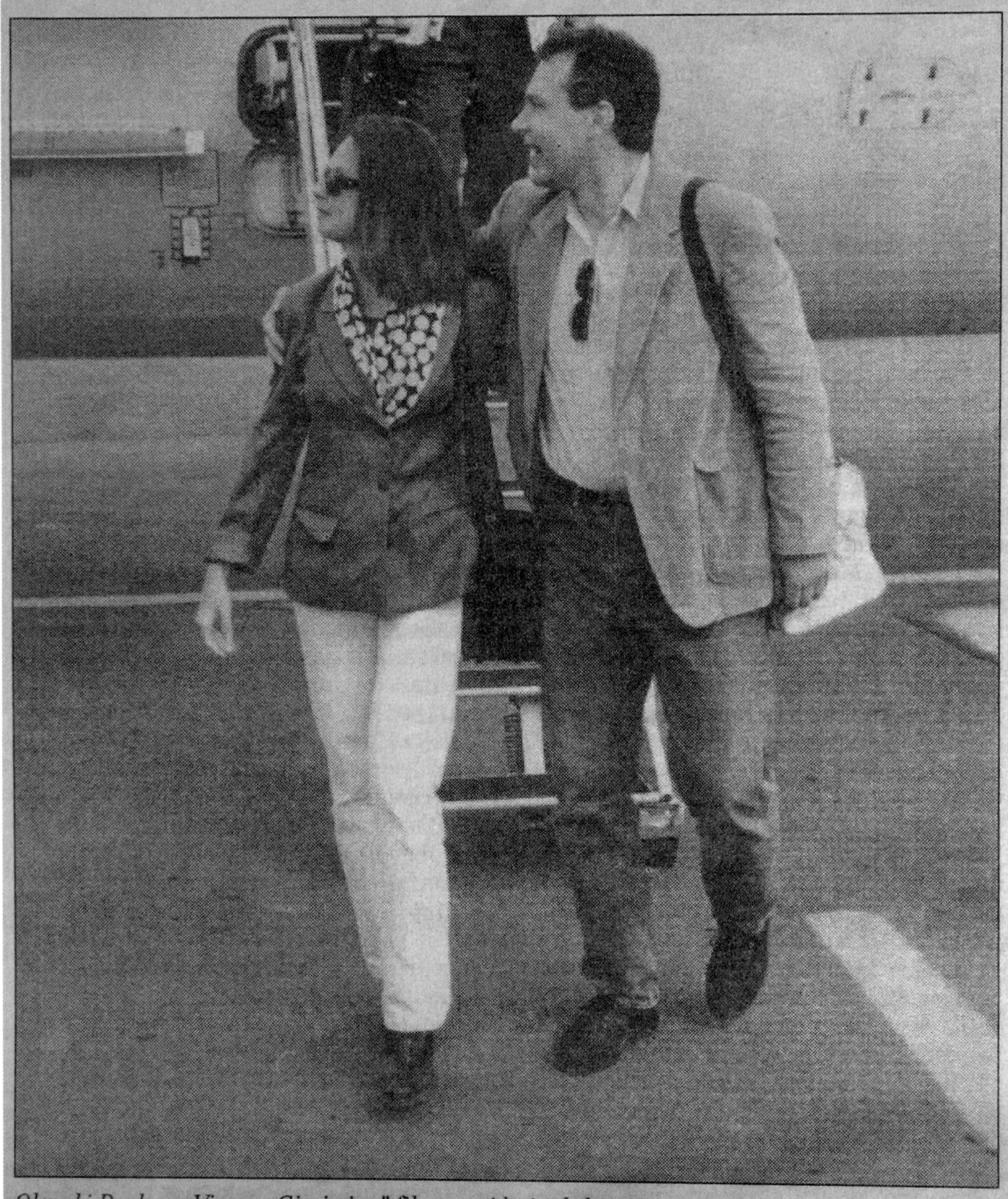

Olandė Barbara Visser „Giminėse" filmavosi kaip daktaro Gastnerio (akt. R.Bagdzevičius) žmona.

M.Vidzbelio nuotr.

Gimines
1995
newspaper clipping

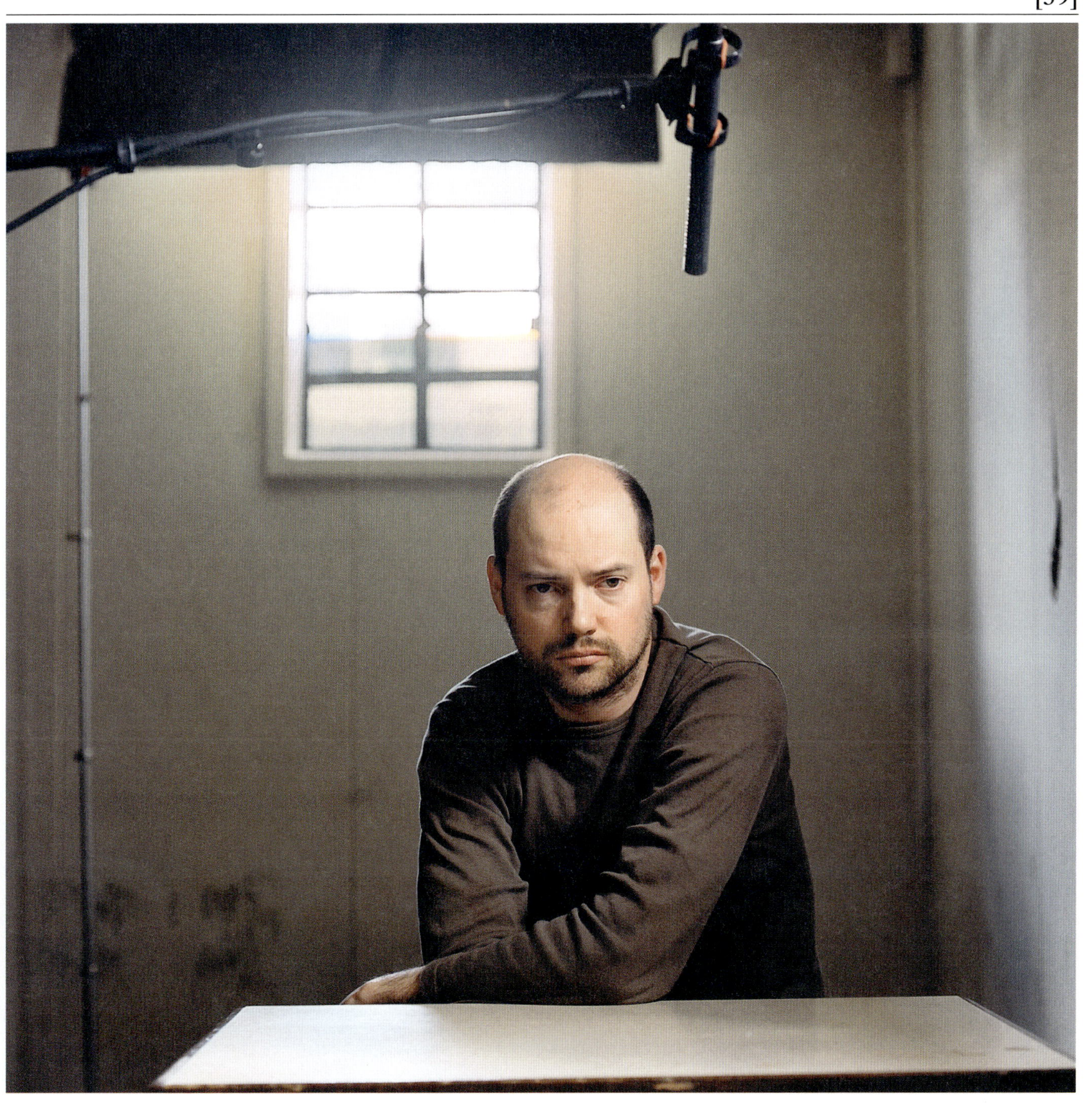

Actor and Liar (Liar)
2003
back-to-back video-projection

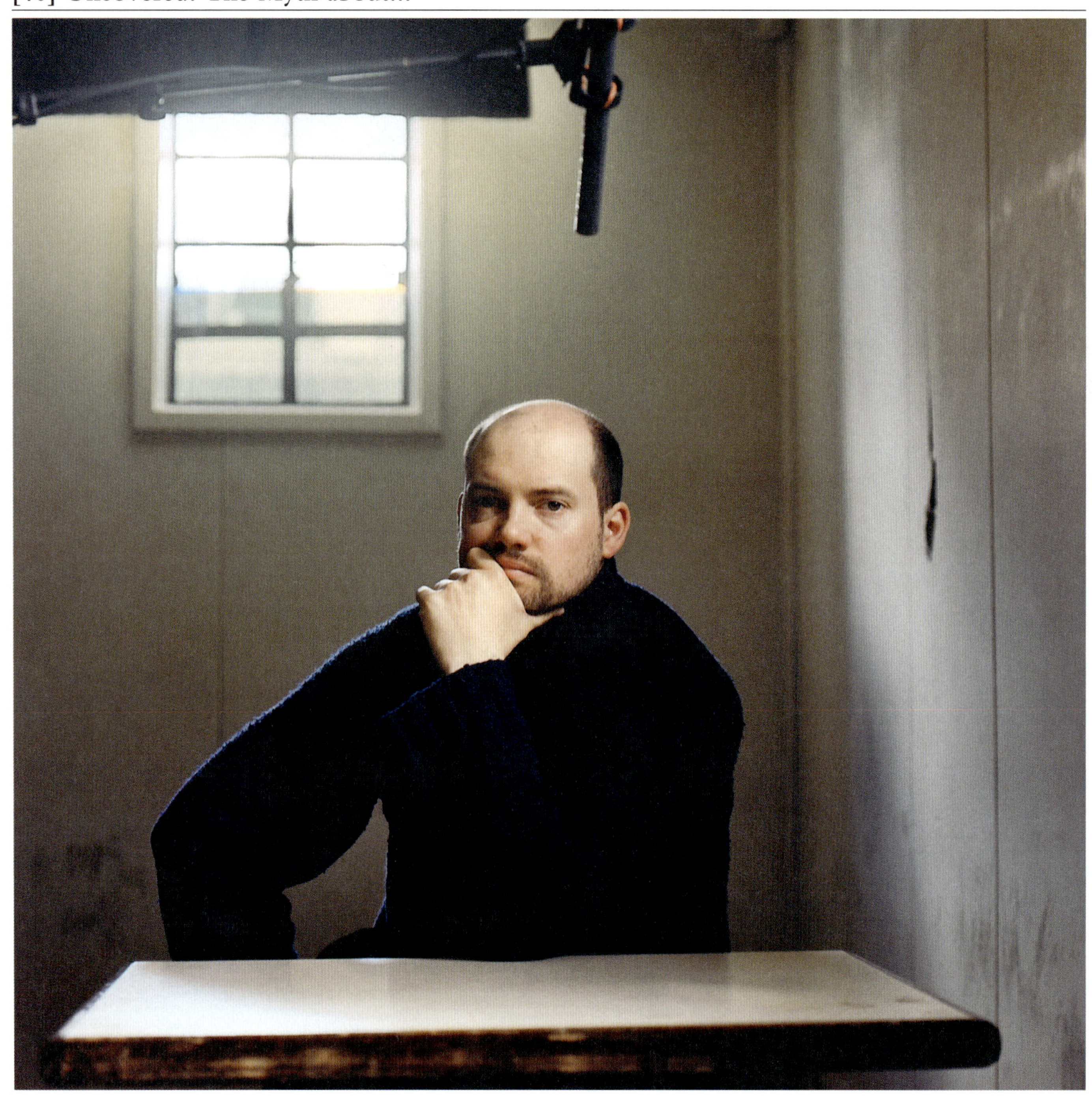

Actor and Liar (Actor)
2003
back-to-back video-projection

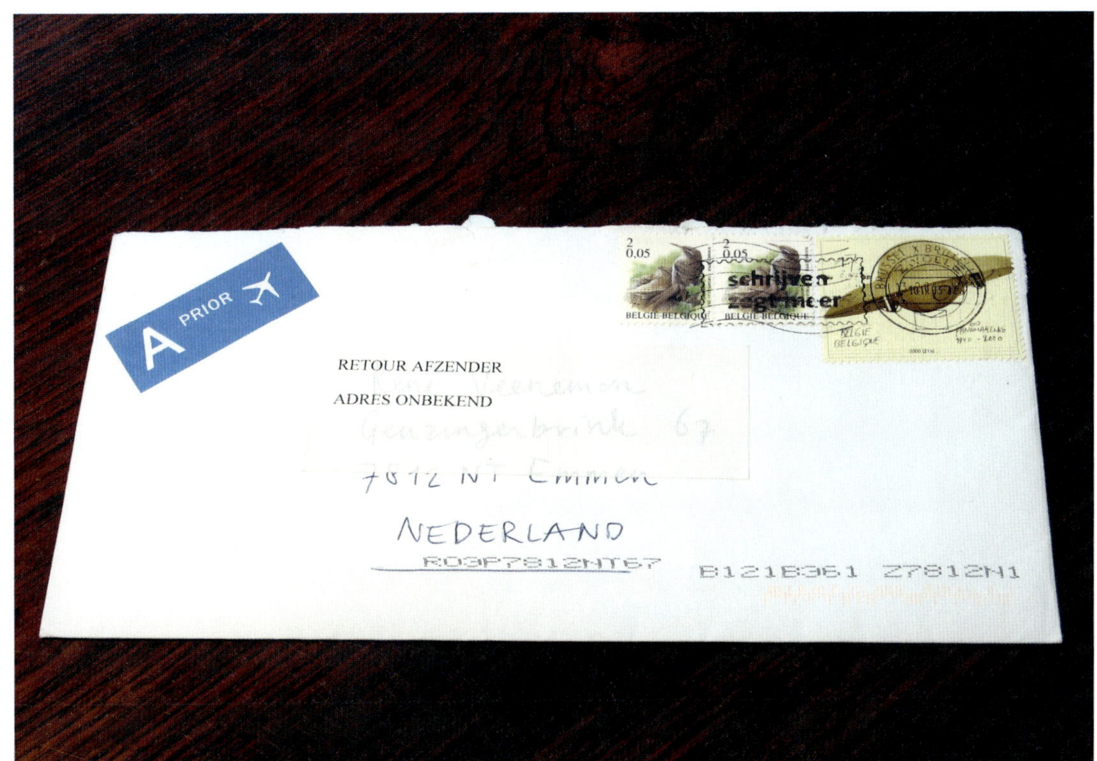

Actor and Liar
2003
document

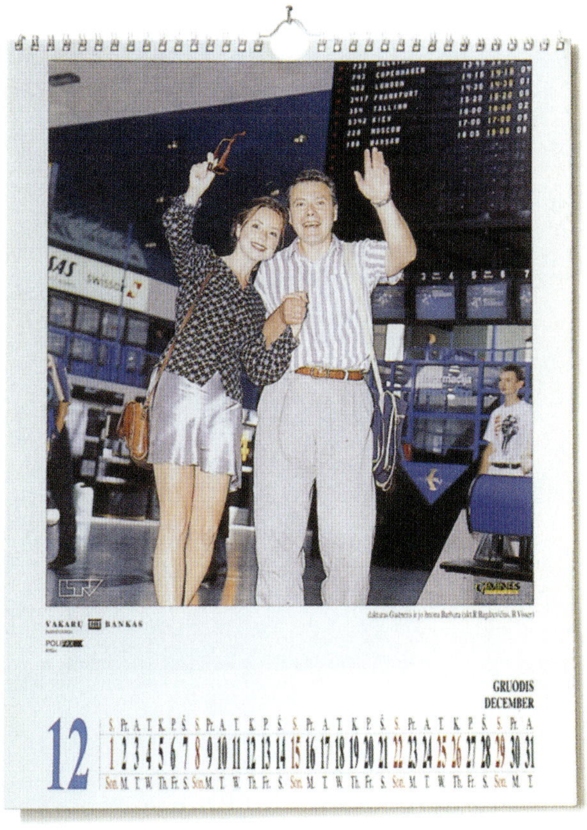

Gimines
1995
calendar of 1996

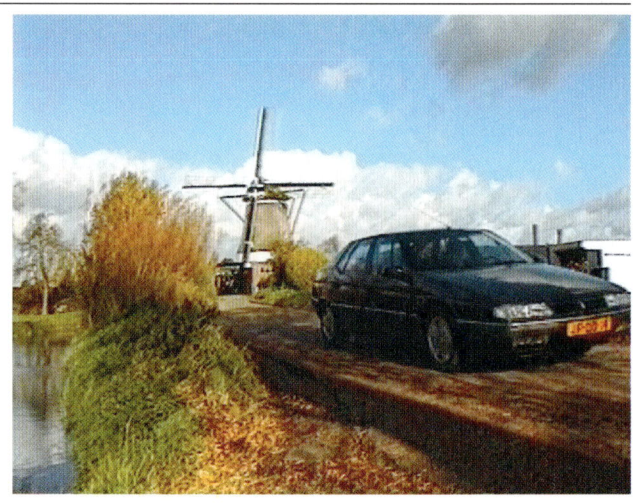

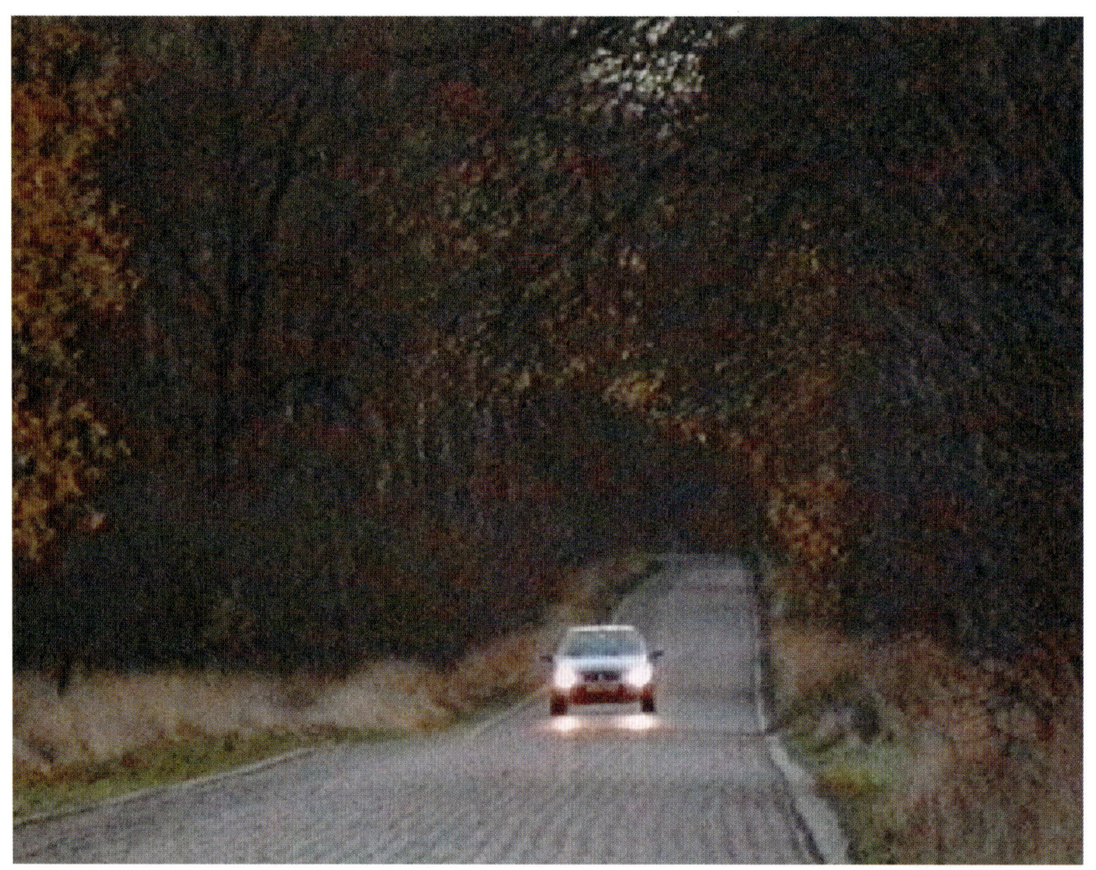

XM
1994
video, still

XM
1994
video, still

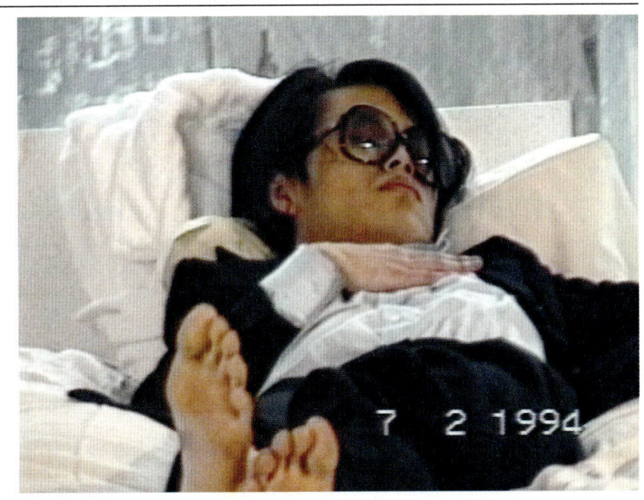

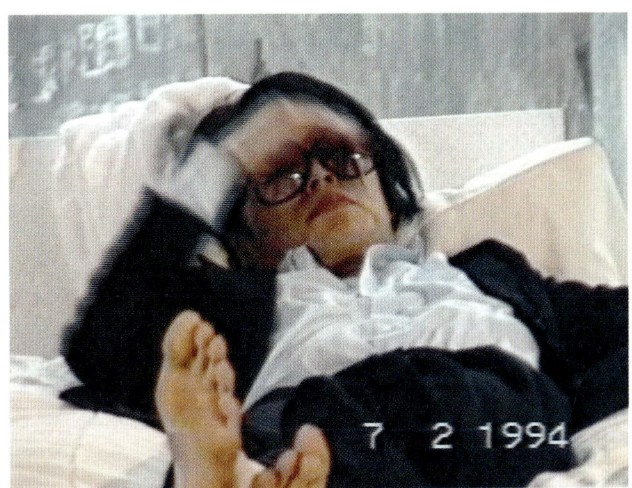

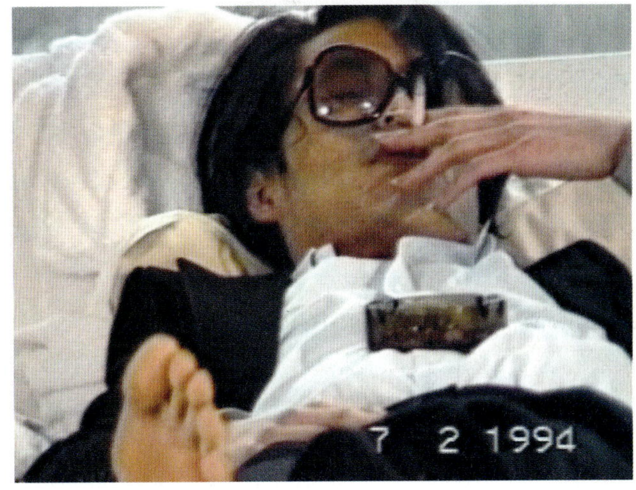

Hilton Piece
1994
video stills

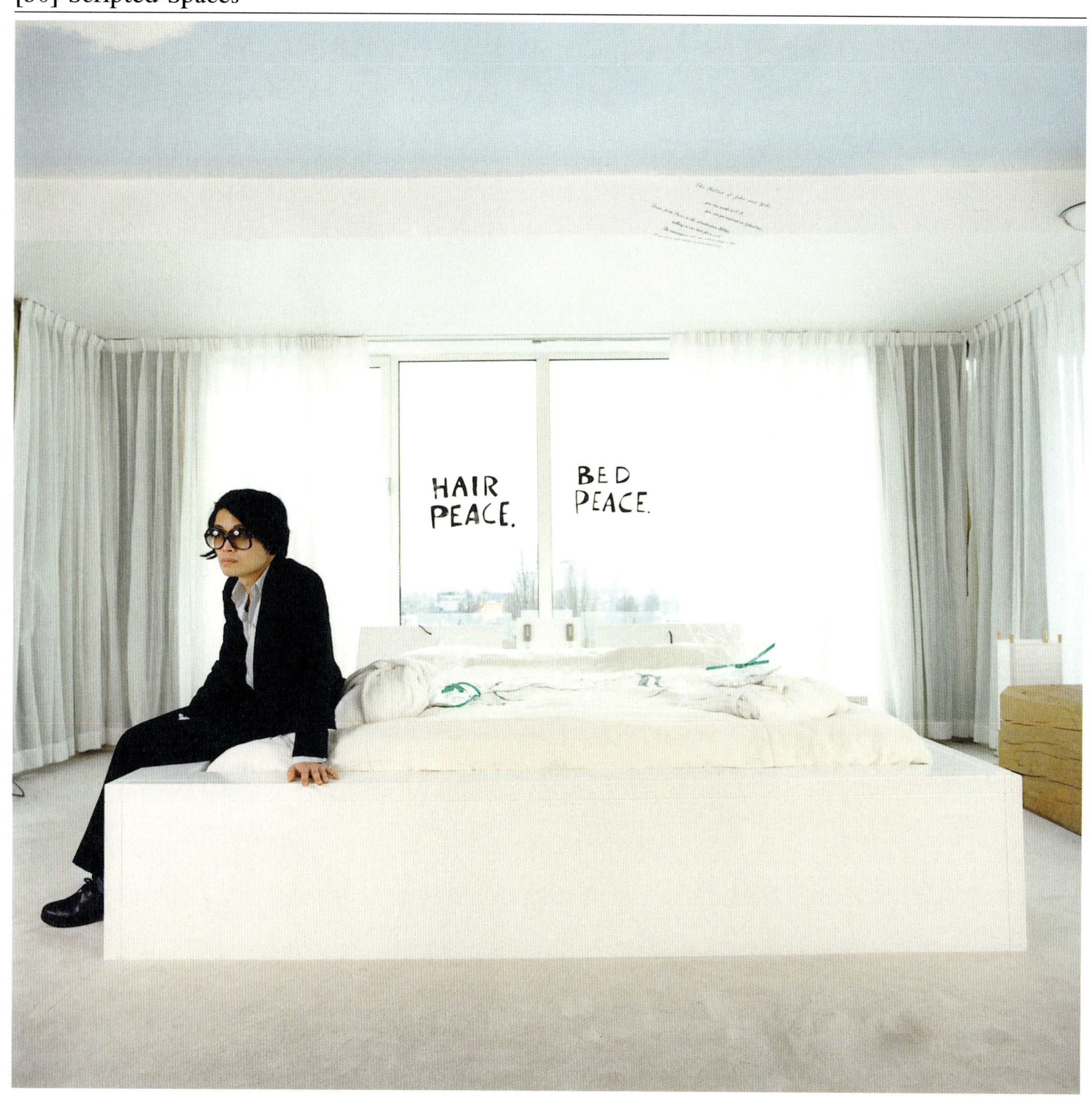

Hilton Piece (Bed II)
1994
three colour photographs

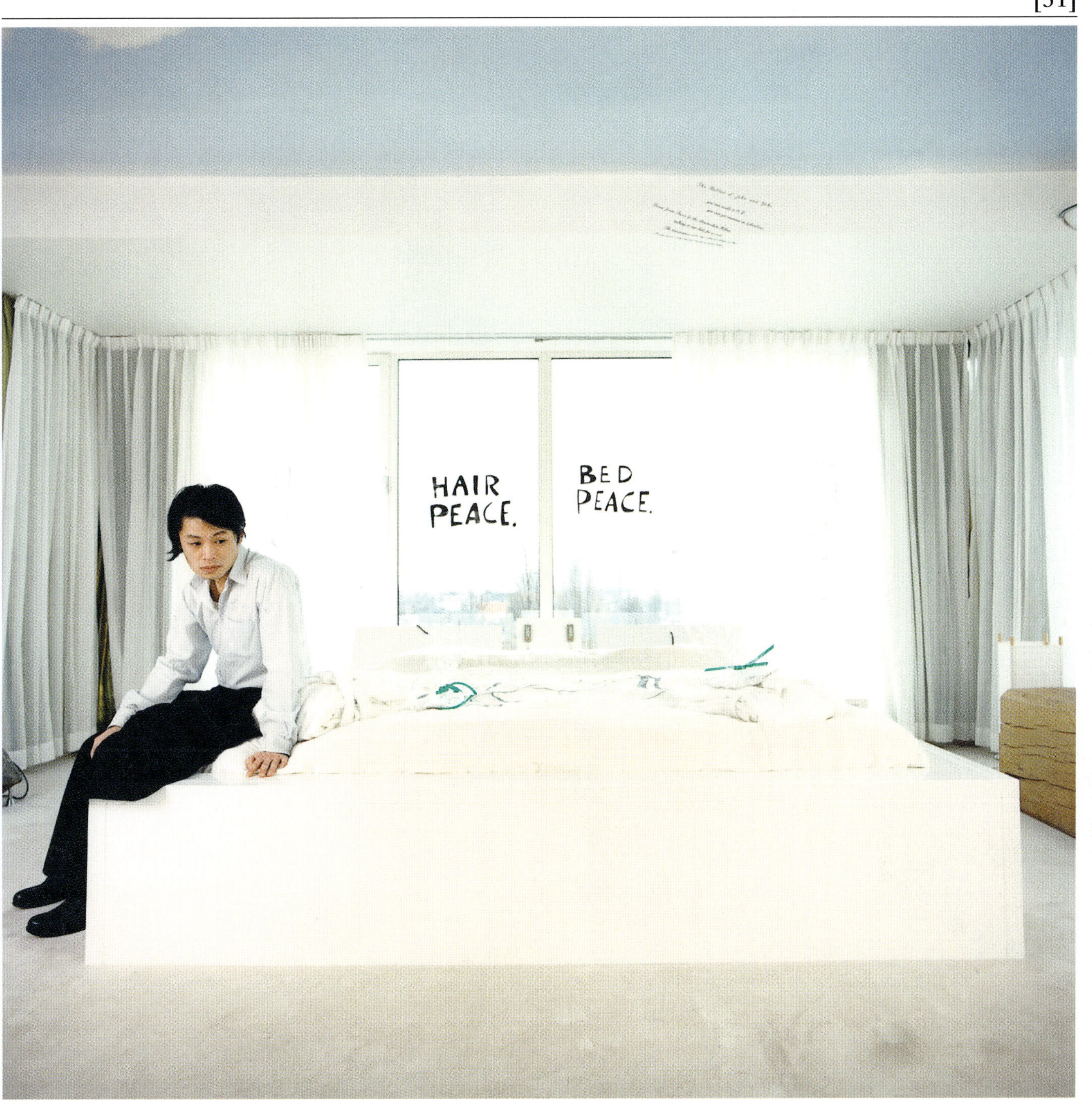

Hilton Piece (Bed II)
1994
three colour photographs

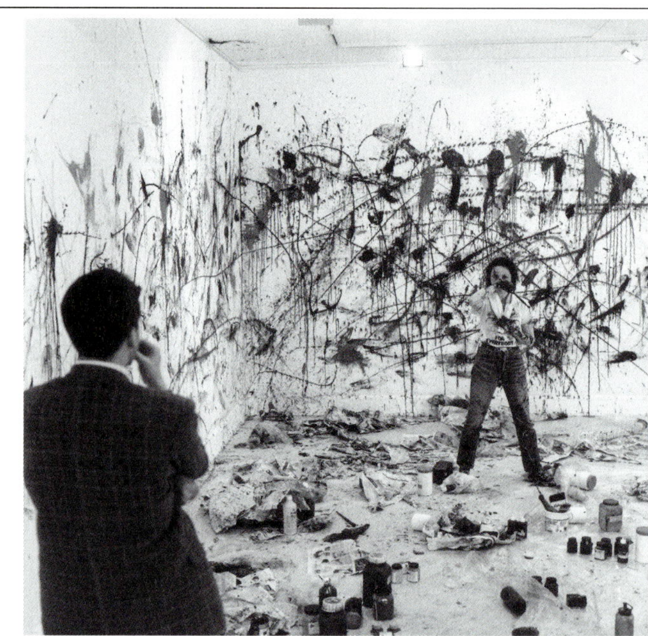

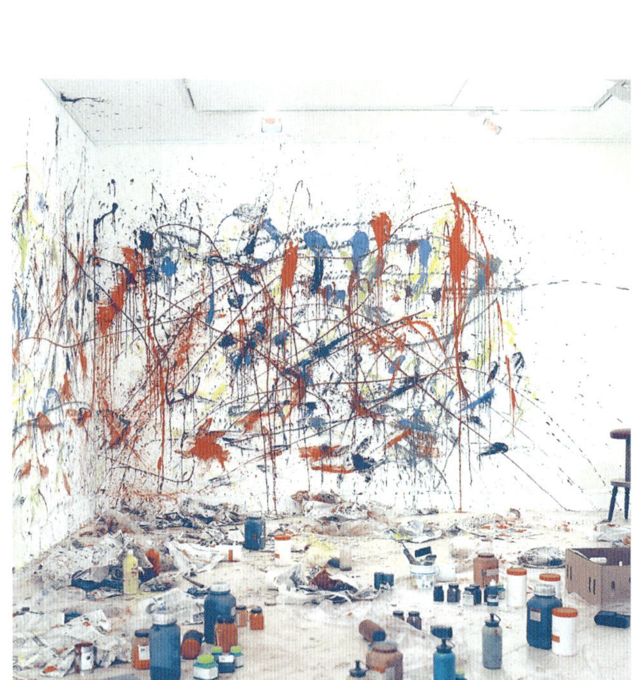

Ars Futura
1994
colour photograph

Ars Futura
1994
set photograph

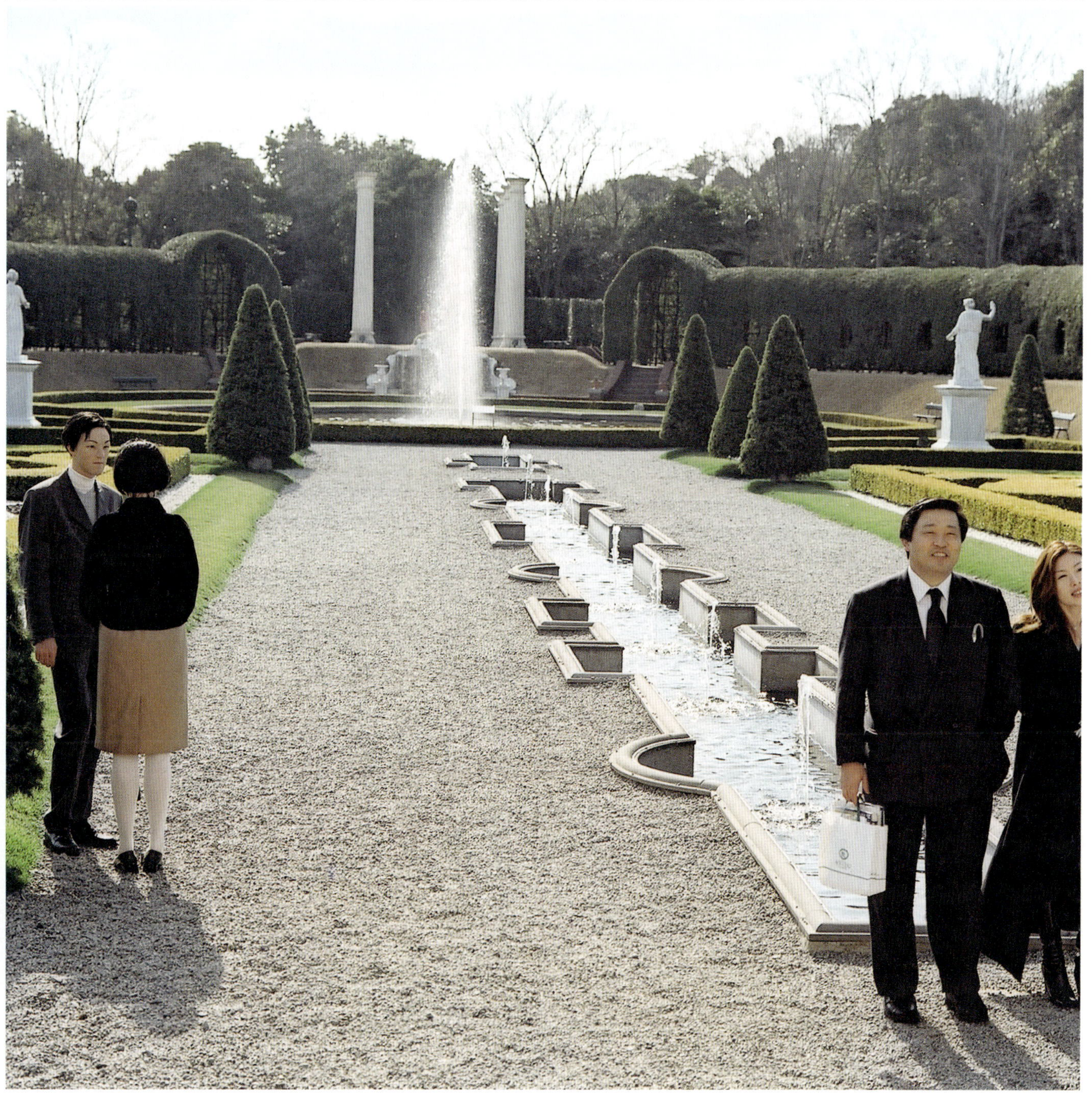

A Day in Holland/Holland in a Day
2001
series of colour photographs

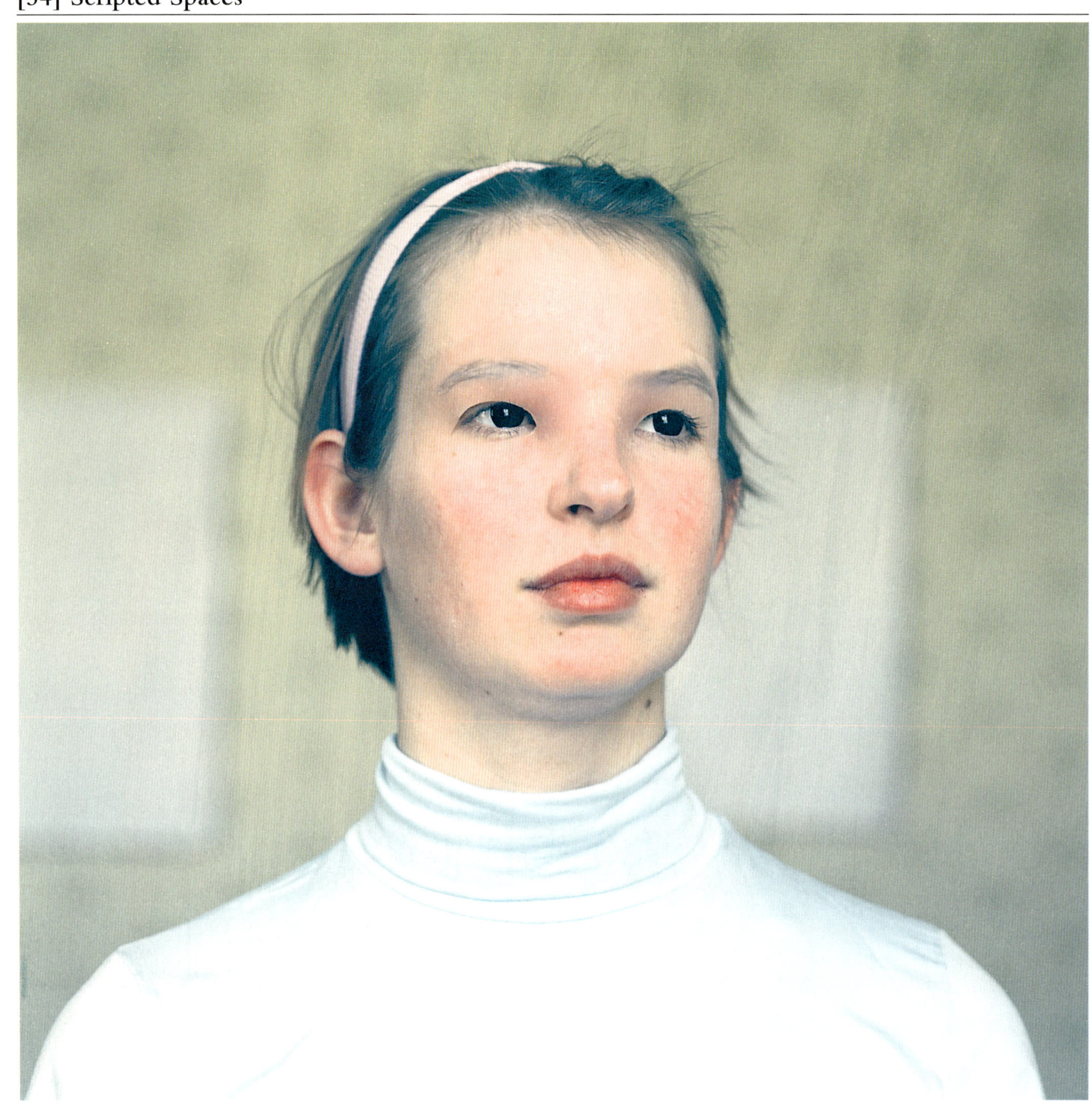

A Day in Holland/Holland in a Day
(Charlotte II)
2001
series of colour photographs

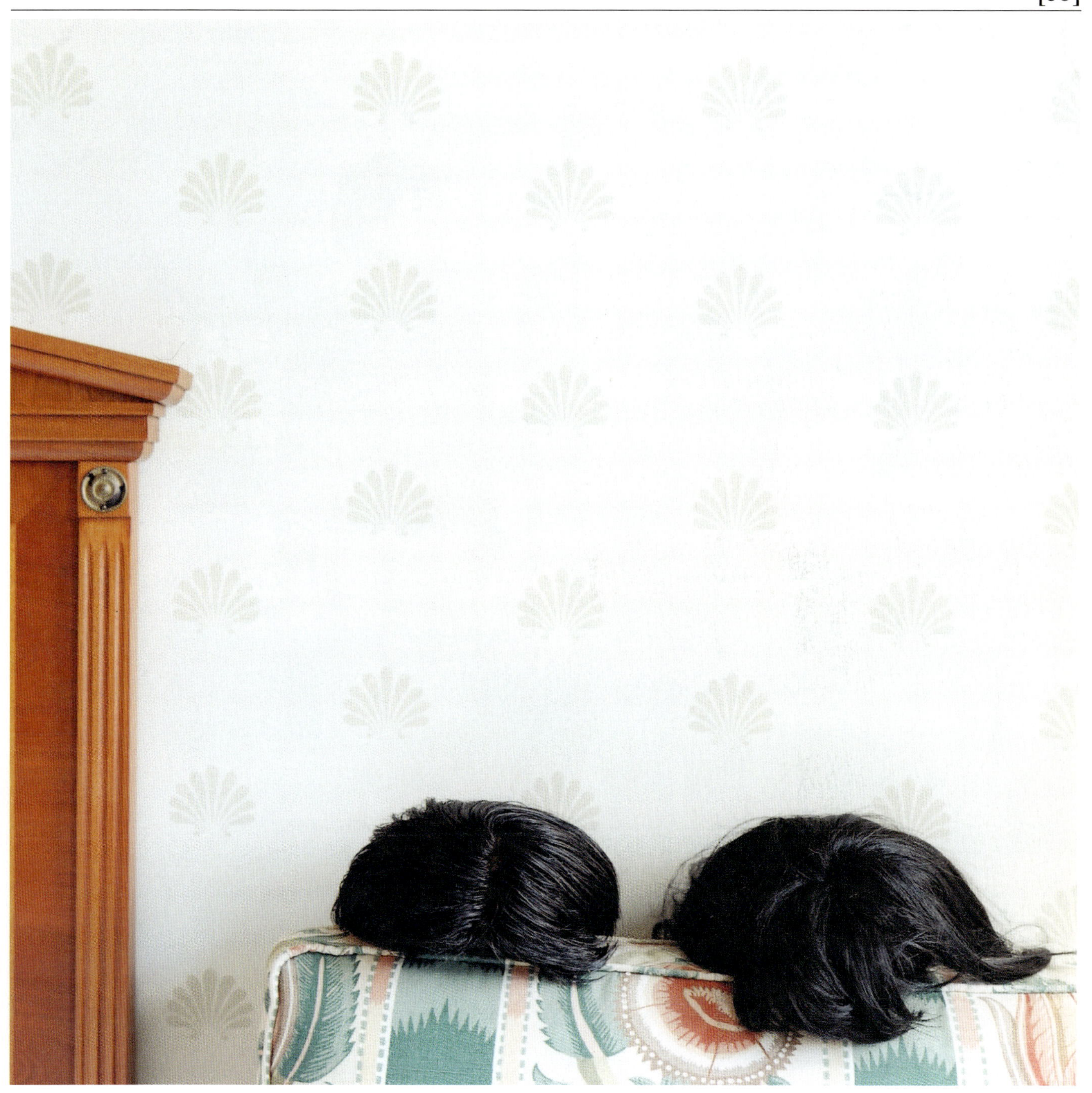

A Day in Holland/Holland in a Day
2001
series of colour photographs

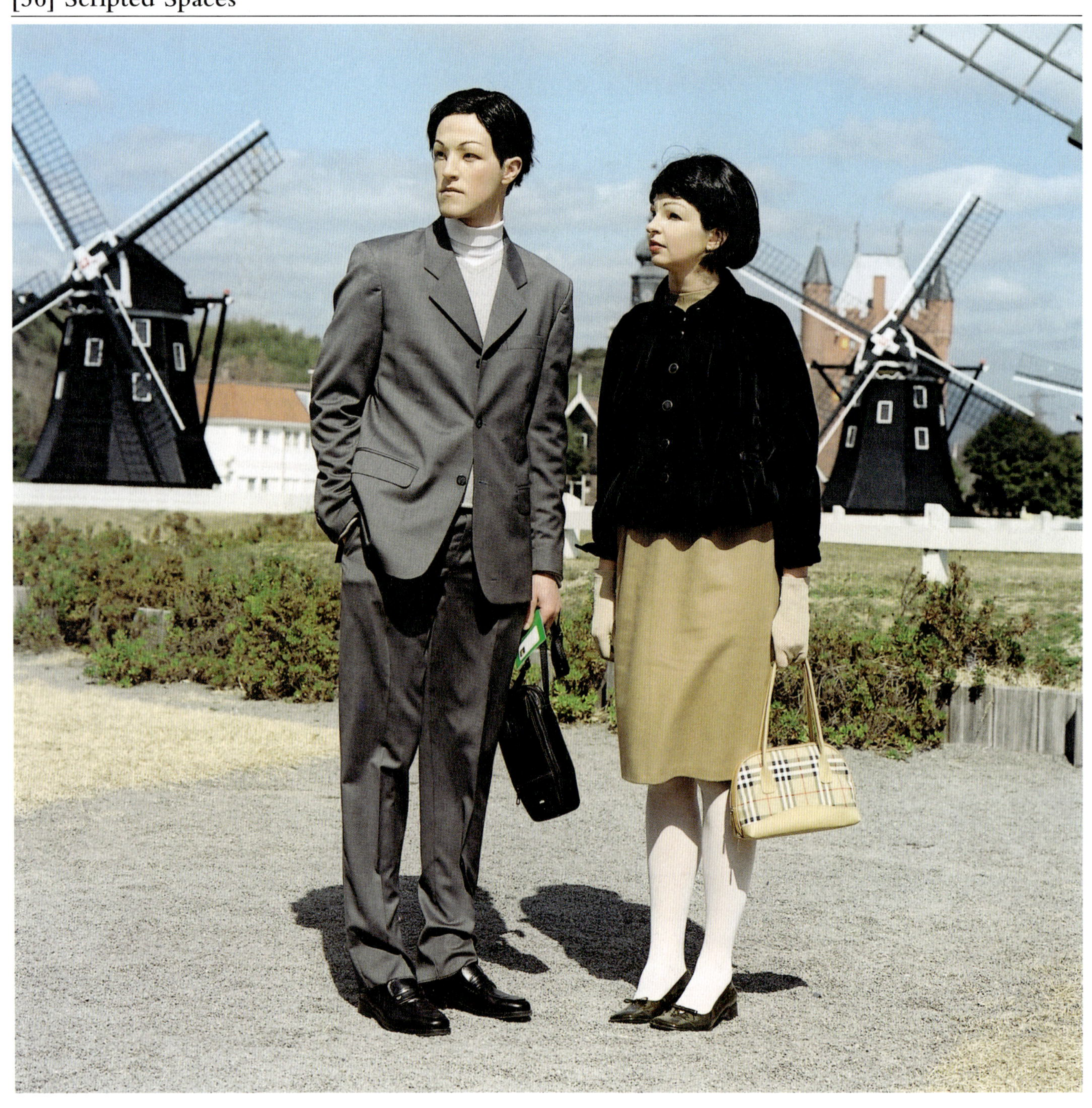

A Day in Holland/Holland in a Day
2001
series of colour photographs

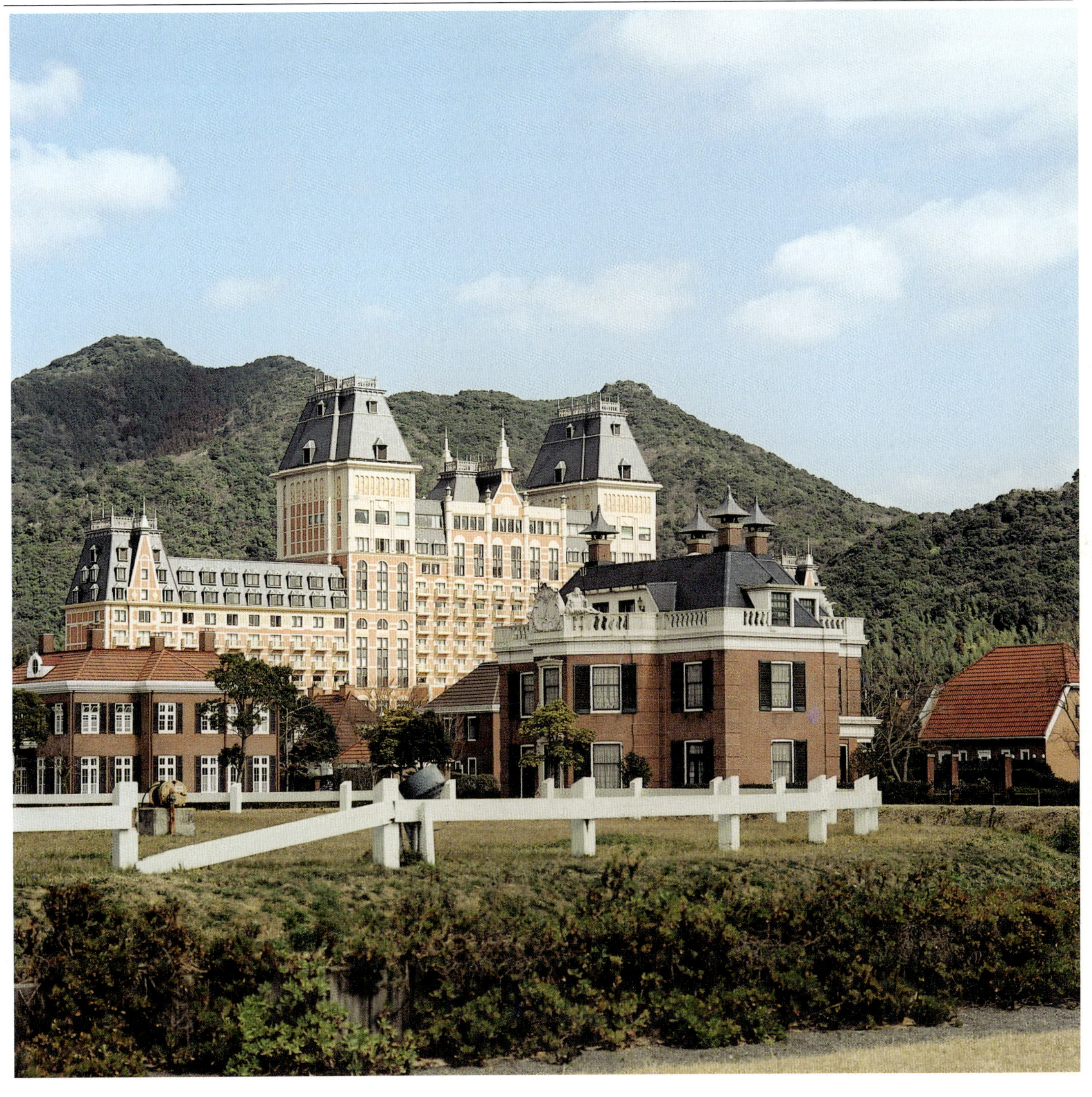

A Day in Holland/Holland in a Day
2001
series of colour photographs

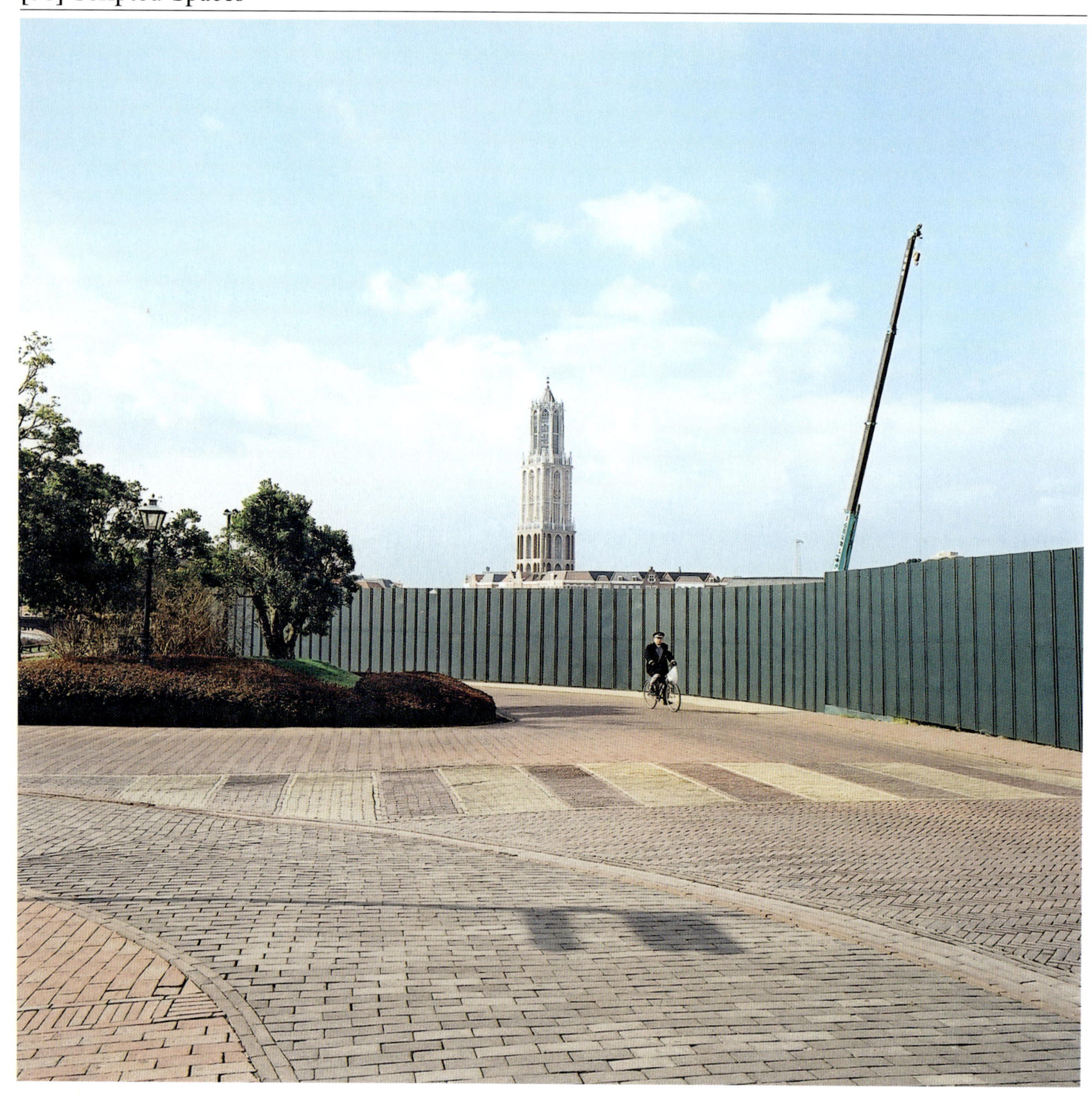

A Day in Holland/Holland in a Day
2001
series of colour photographs

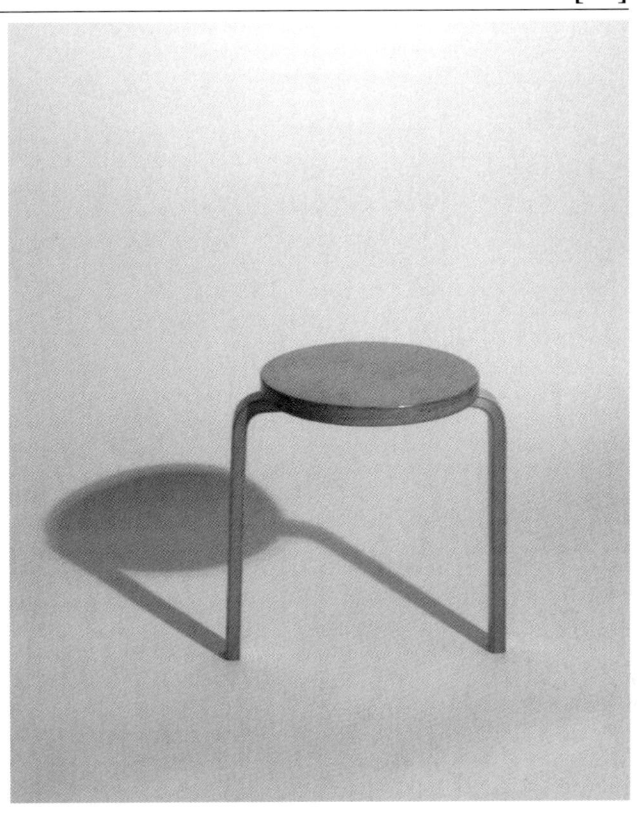

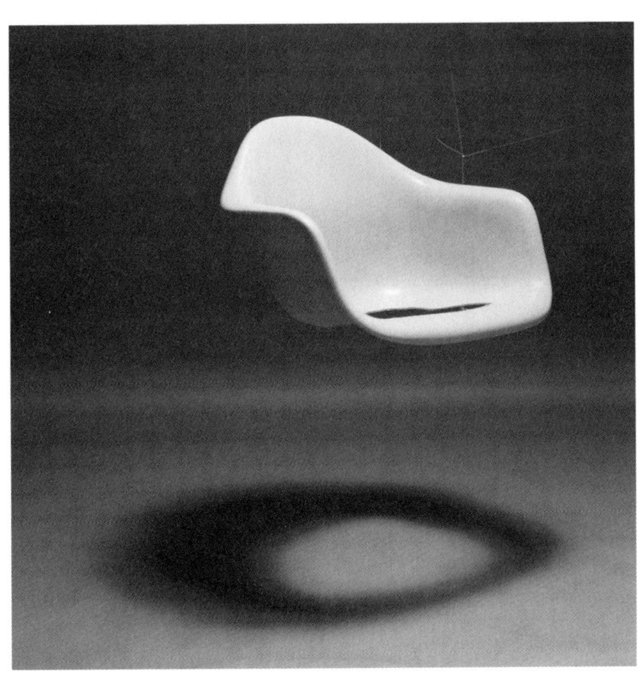

Detitled/EAARS20001205/FT/S/bw
2000
series of photographs

Detitled/AAS19992010/FT/S/bw
2000
series of photographs

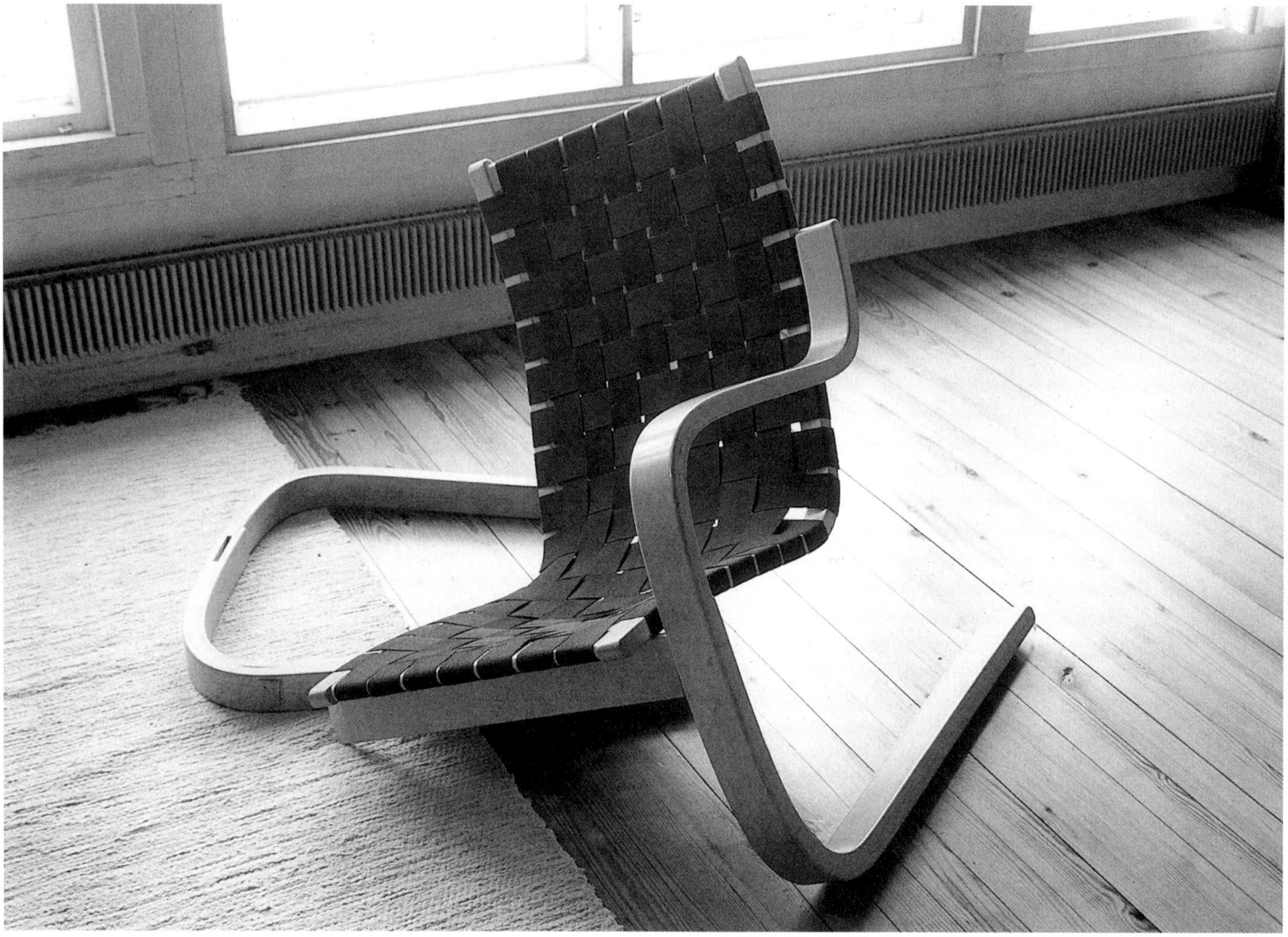

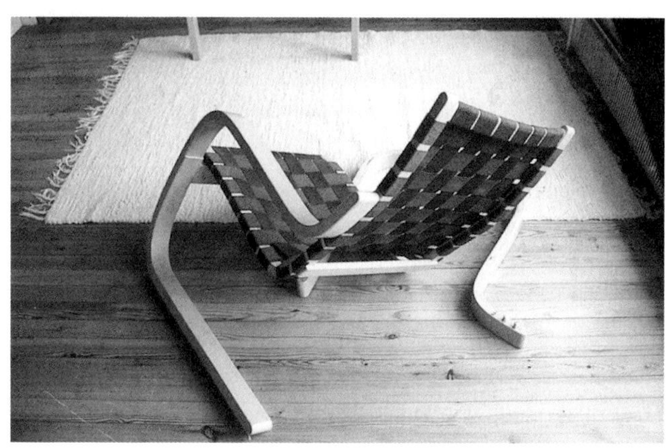

Detitled/AAC19990303/FW/L/bw
2000
series of photographs

Detitled/AAC19990303/RW/L/bw
2000
series of photographs

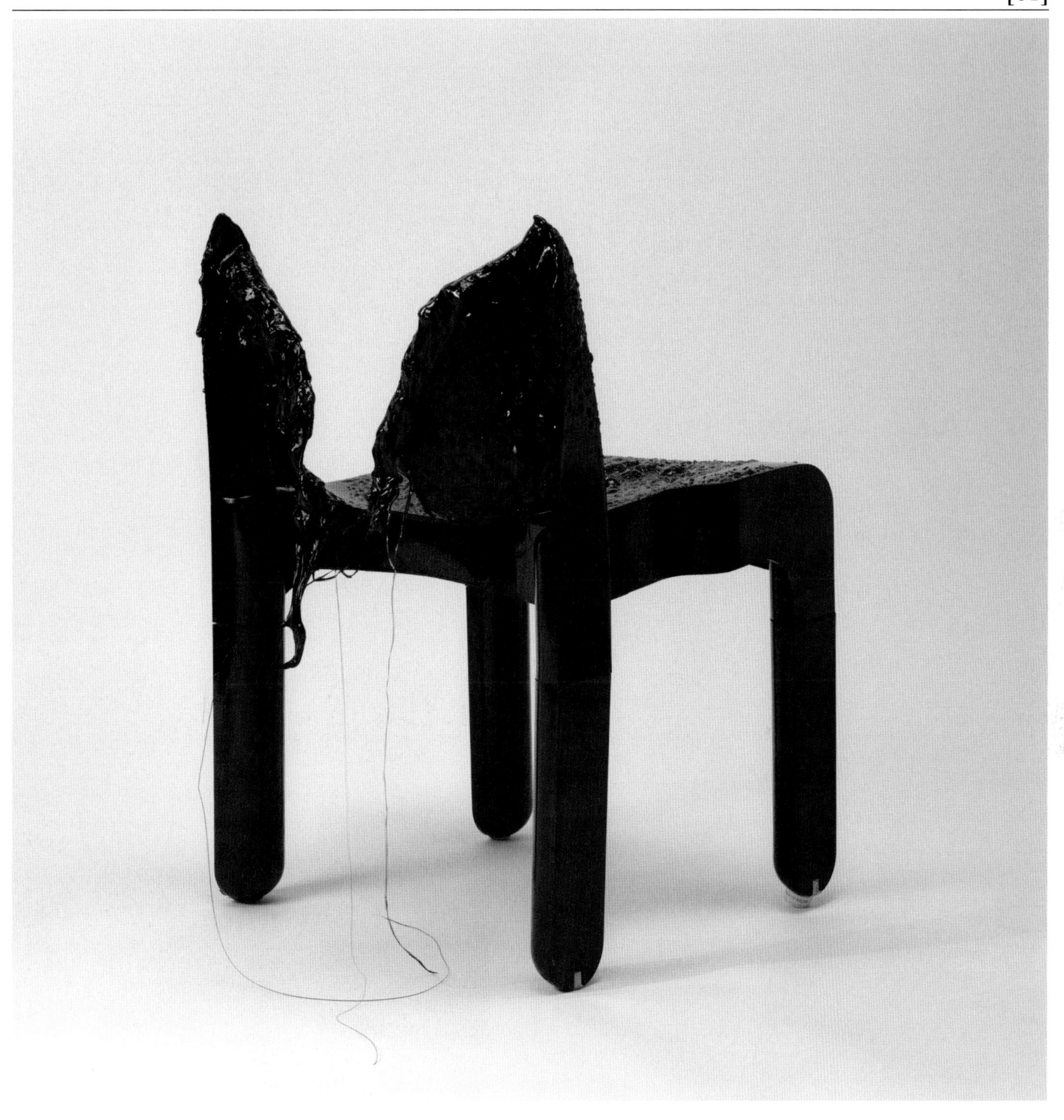

Detitled/JC19991211/RT/S/bw
2000
series of photographs

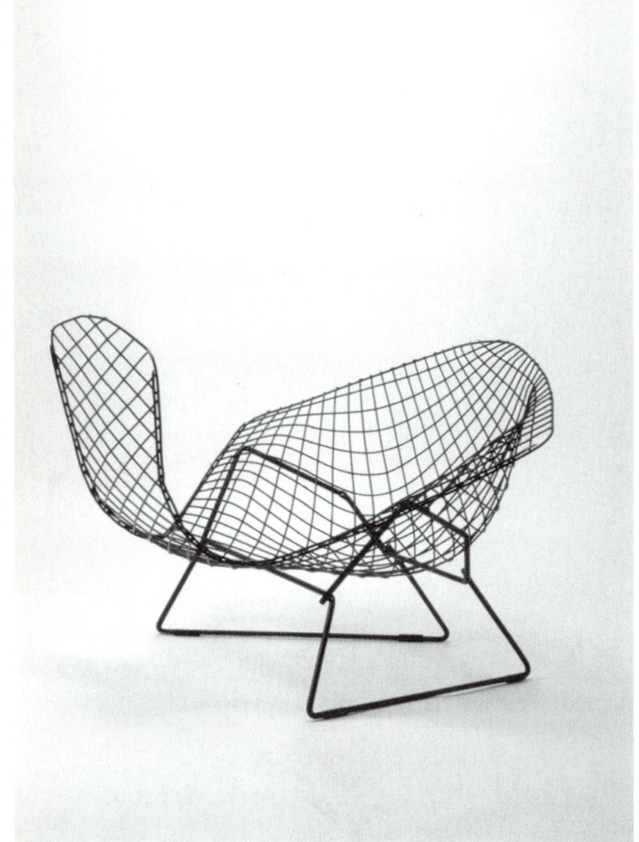

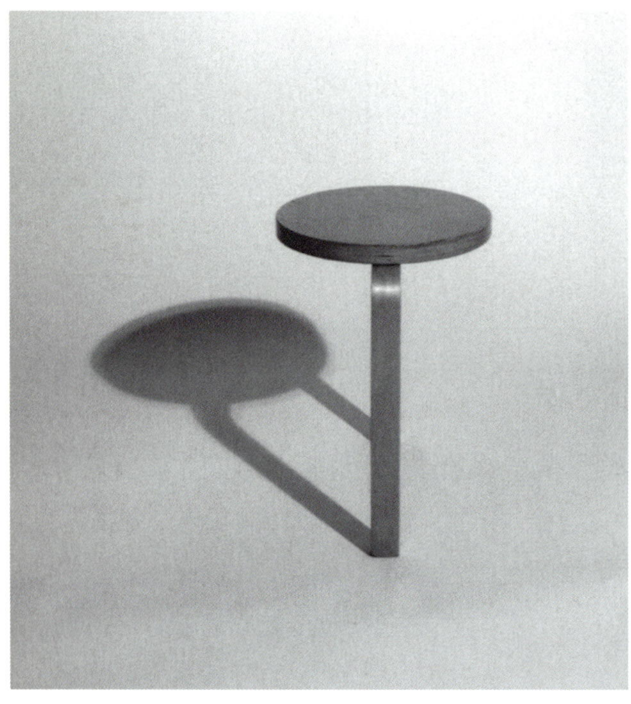

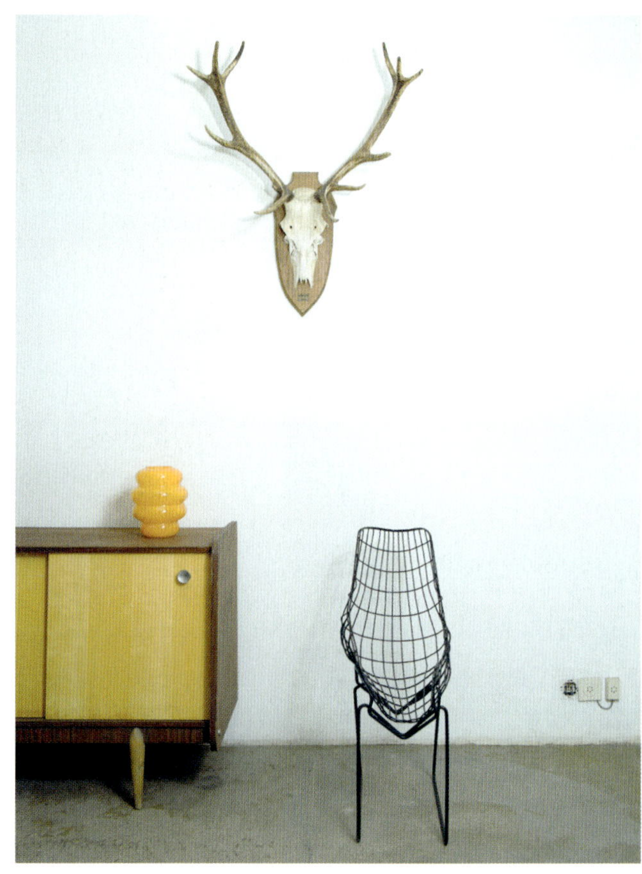

Detitled/BABC19990910/TQT/S/c
Detitled/AAS19992010/ST/S/bw
2000
series of photographs

Detitled/PT-C19992510/FT/L/c
2000
series of photographs

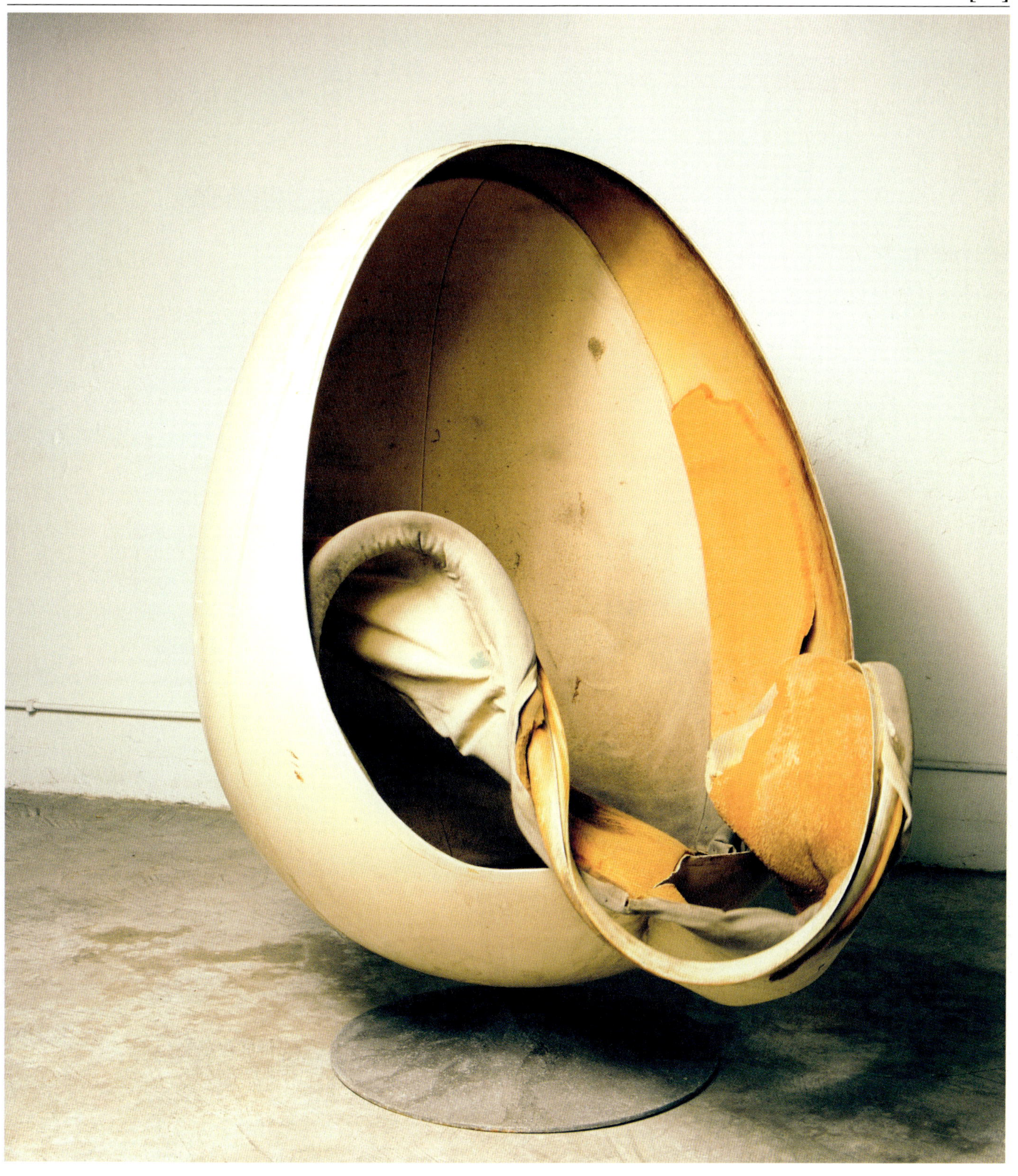

Detitled/EGG19992811/FT/L/c
2000
series of photographs

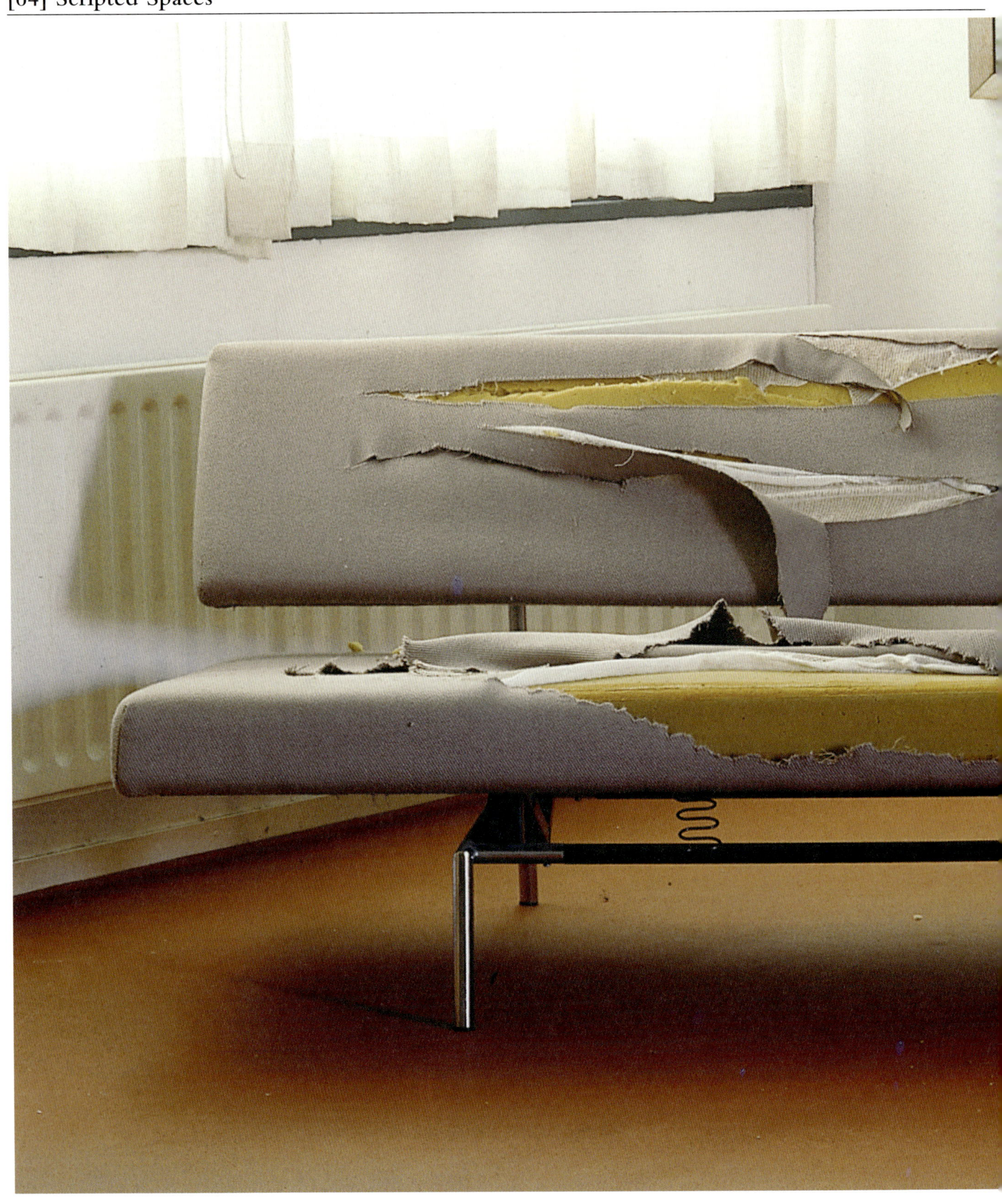

Detitled/MVB20001505/FT/S/c
2000
series of photographs

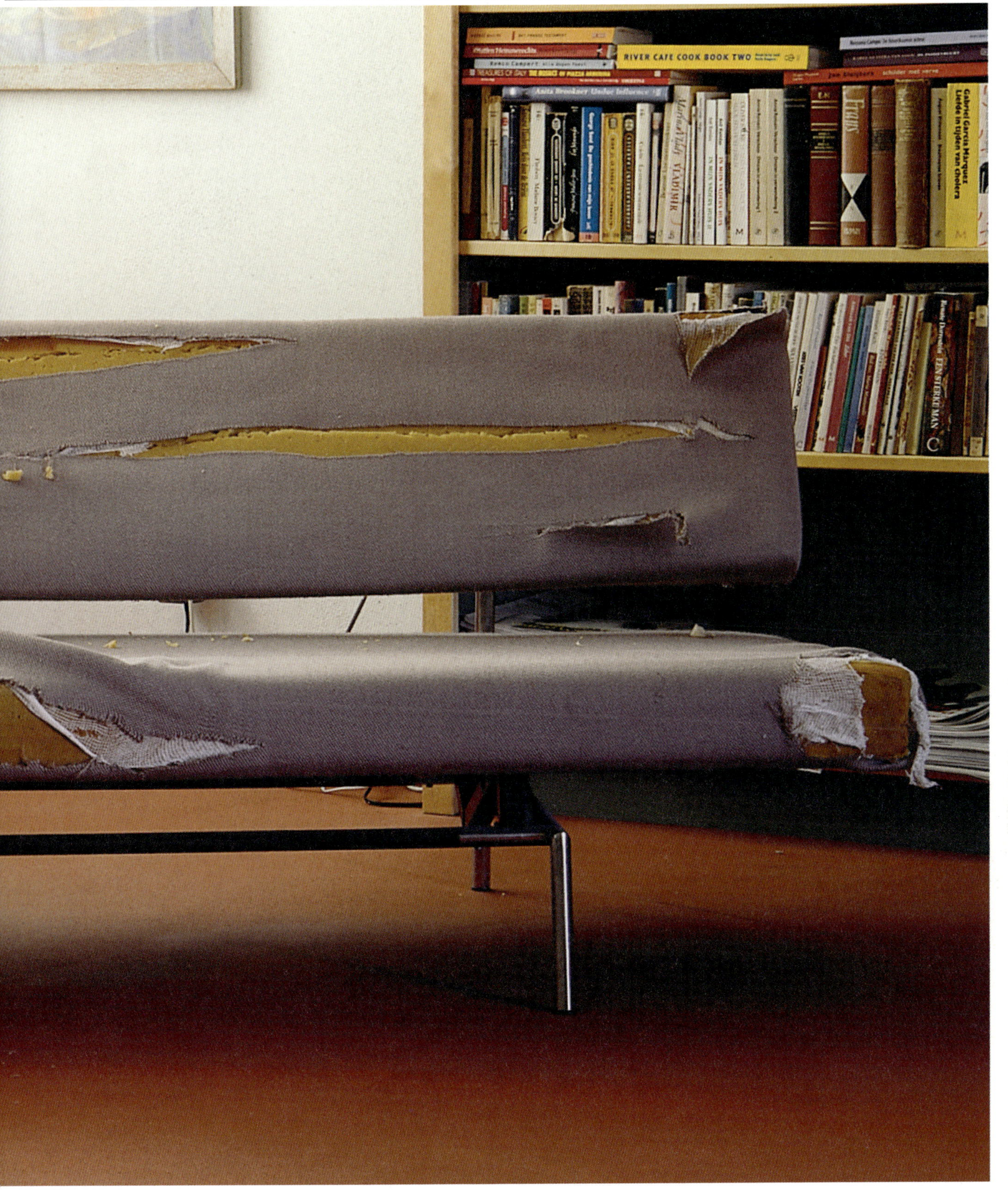

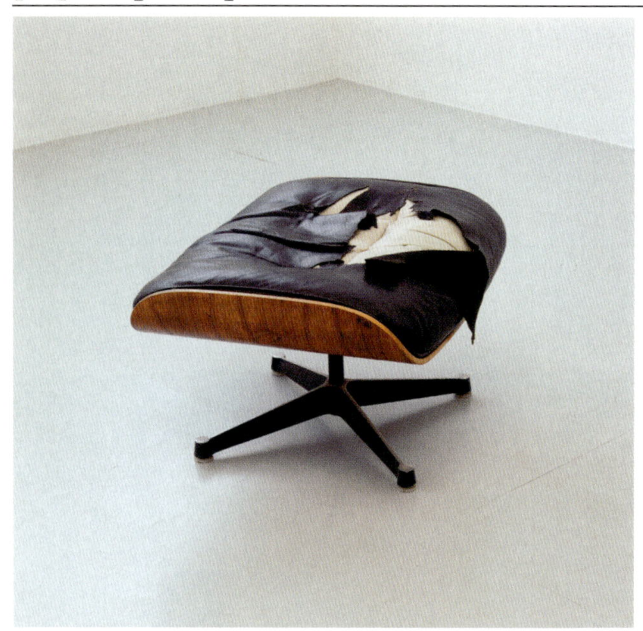

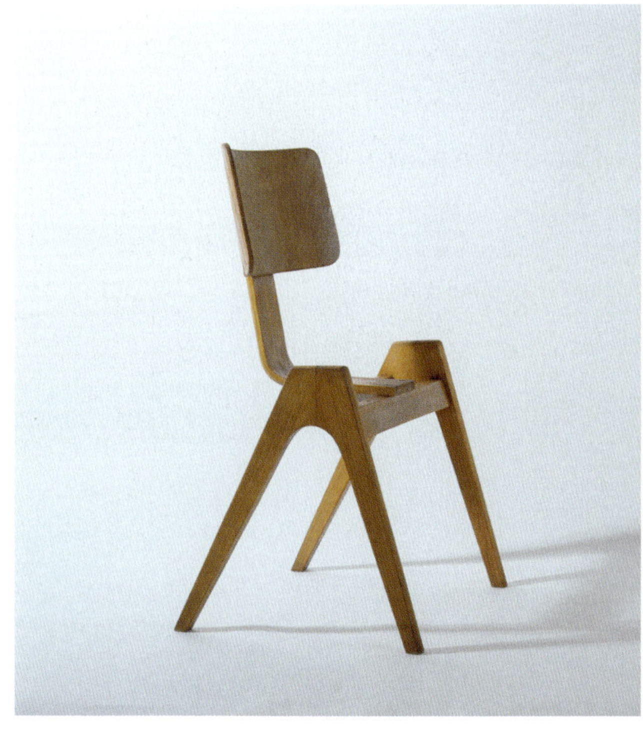

Detitled/EAFS19991012/ST/L/c
2000
series of photographs

Detitled/RDH19990410/ST/S/c
2000
series of photographs

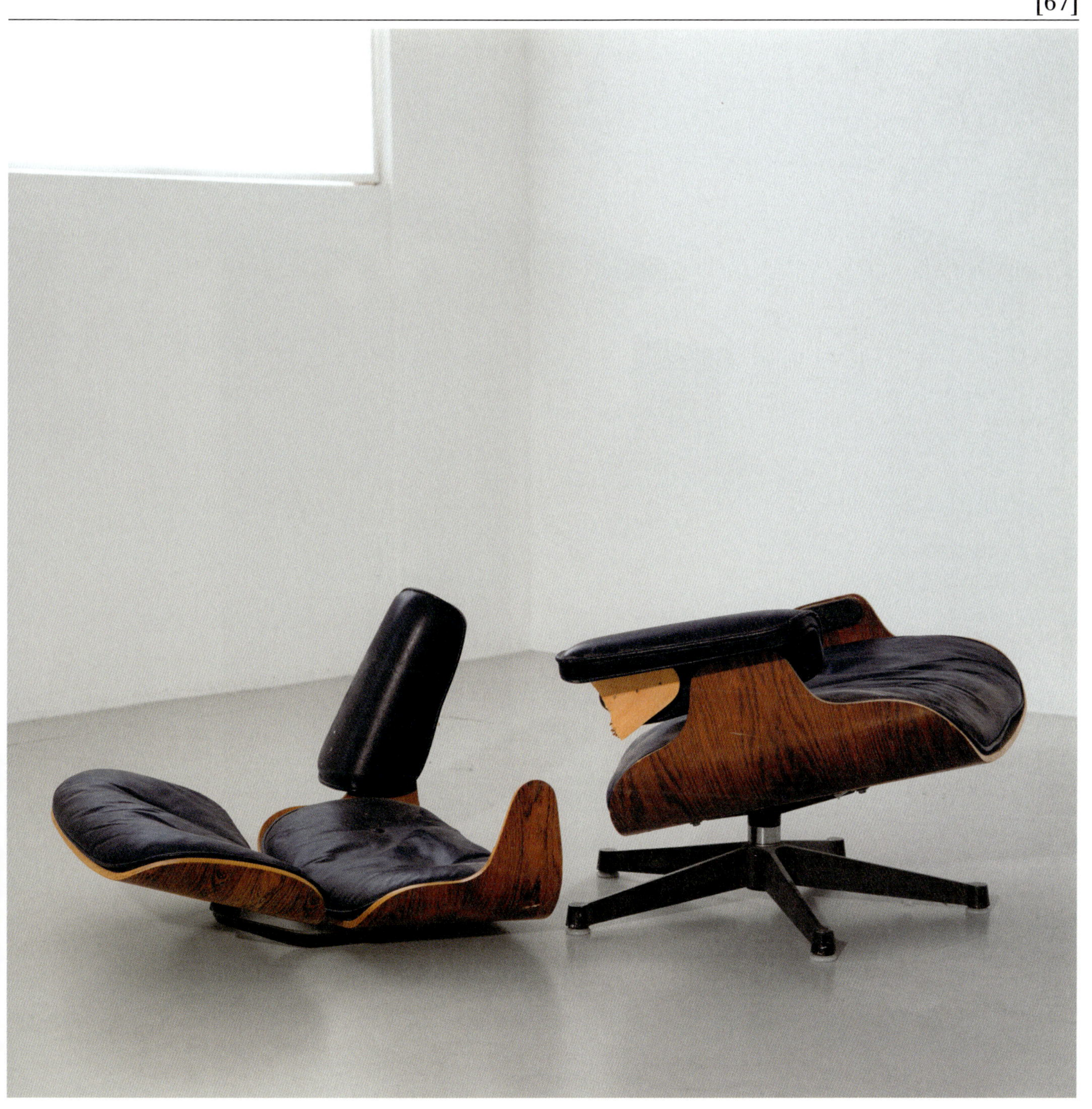

Detitled/EACH19991012/ST/L/c
2000
series of photographs

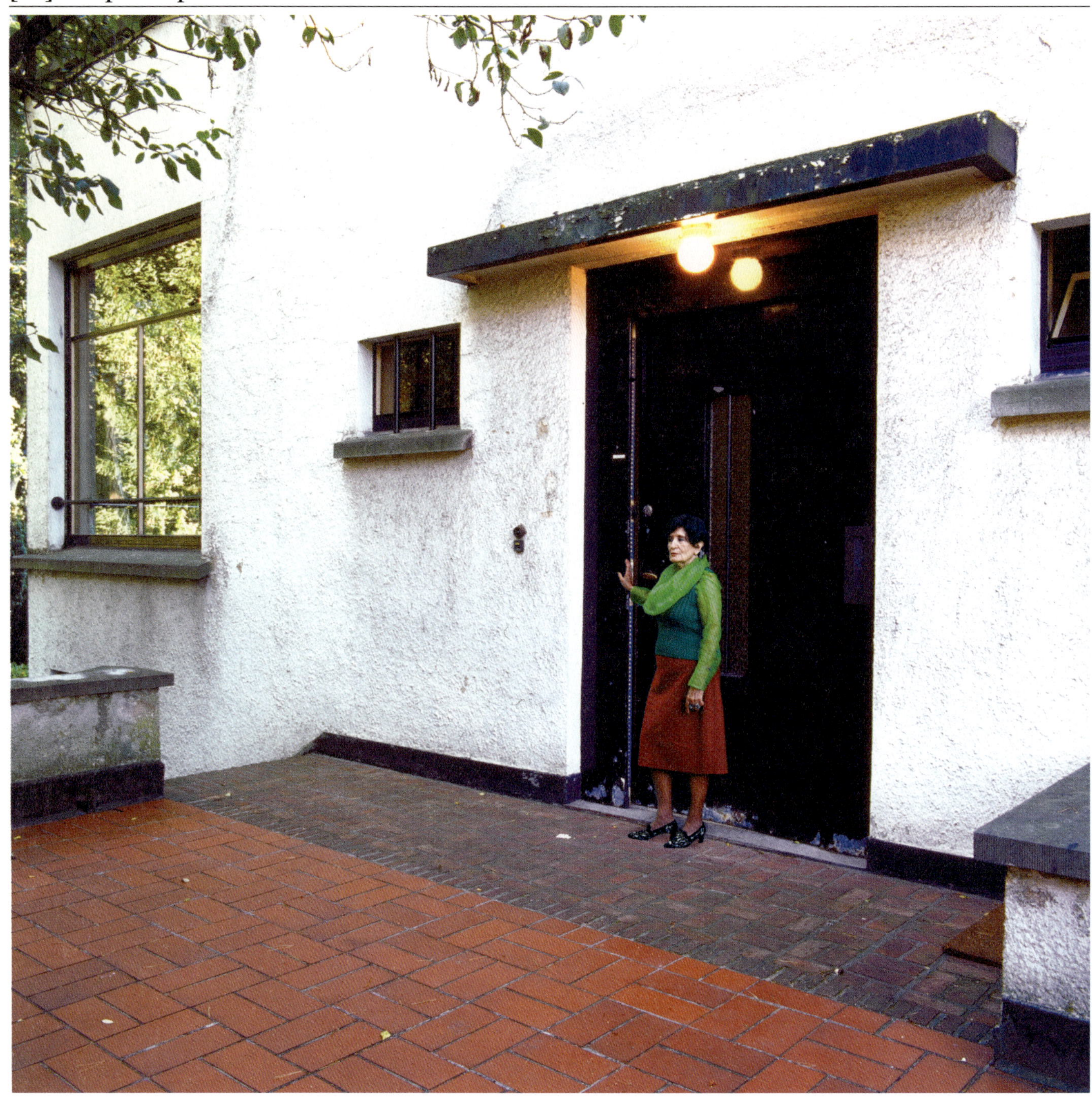

Maison Grégoire 118%
2000
colour photograph

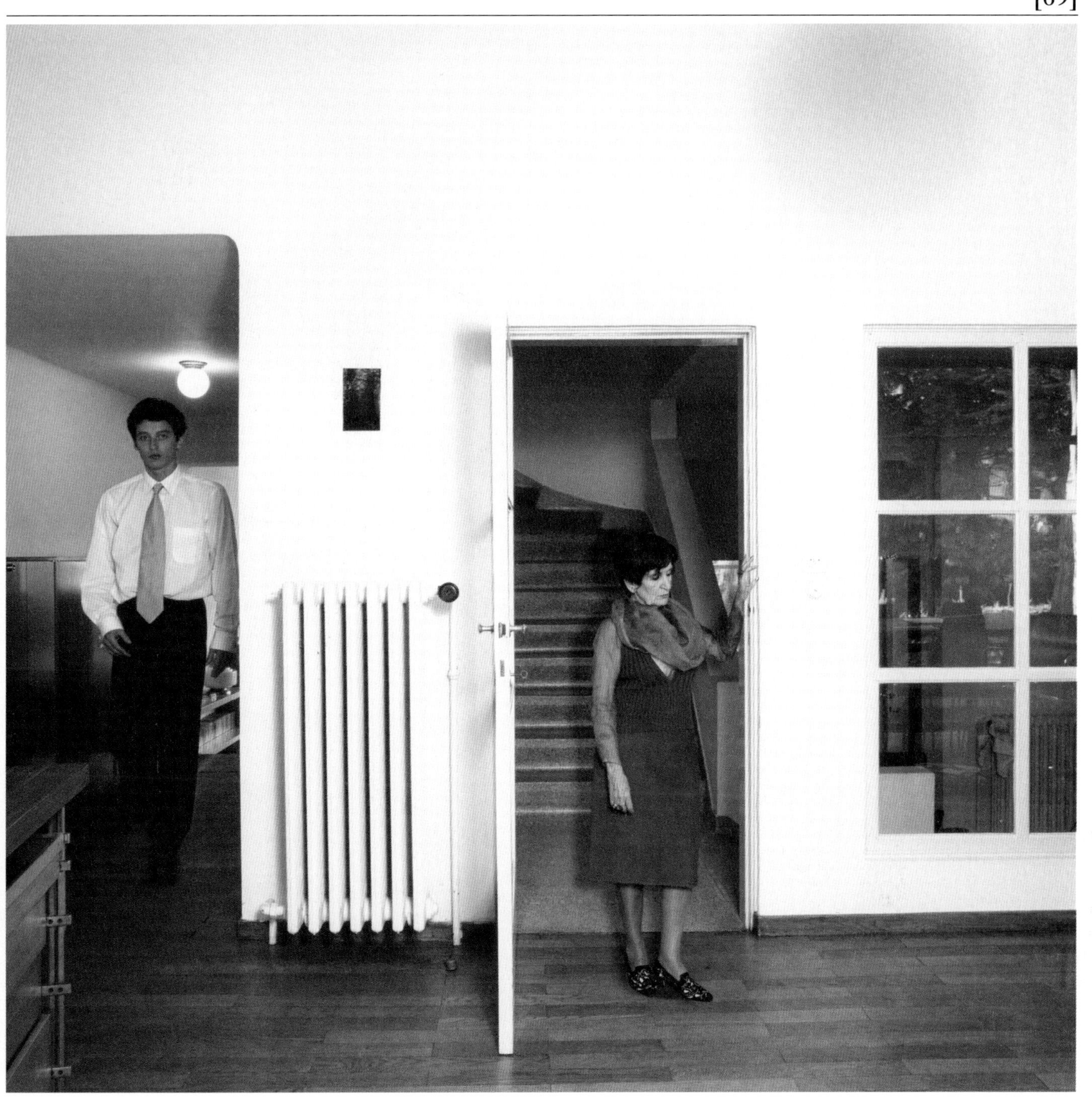

Maison Grégoire 118%
2000
b/w photograph

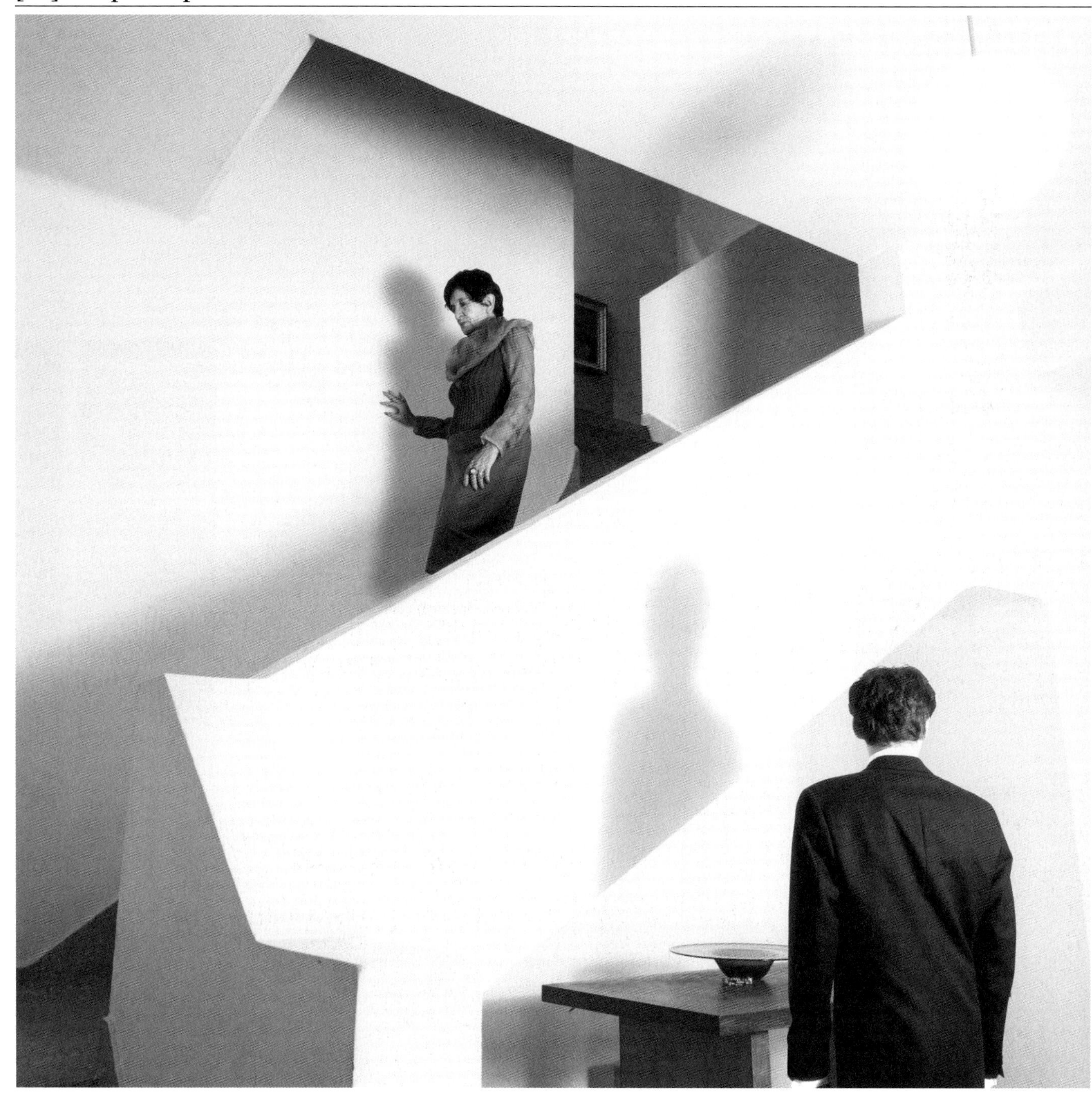

Maison Grégoire 118%
2000
b/w photograph

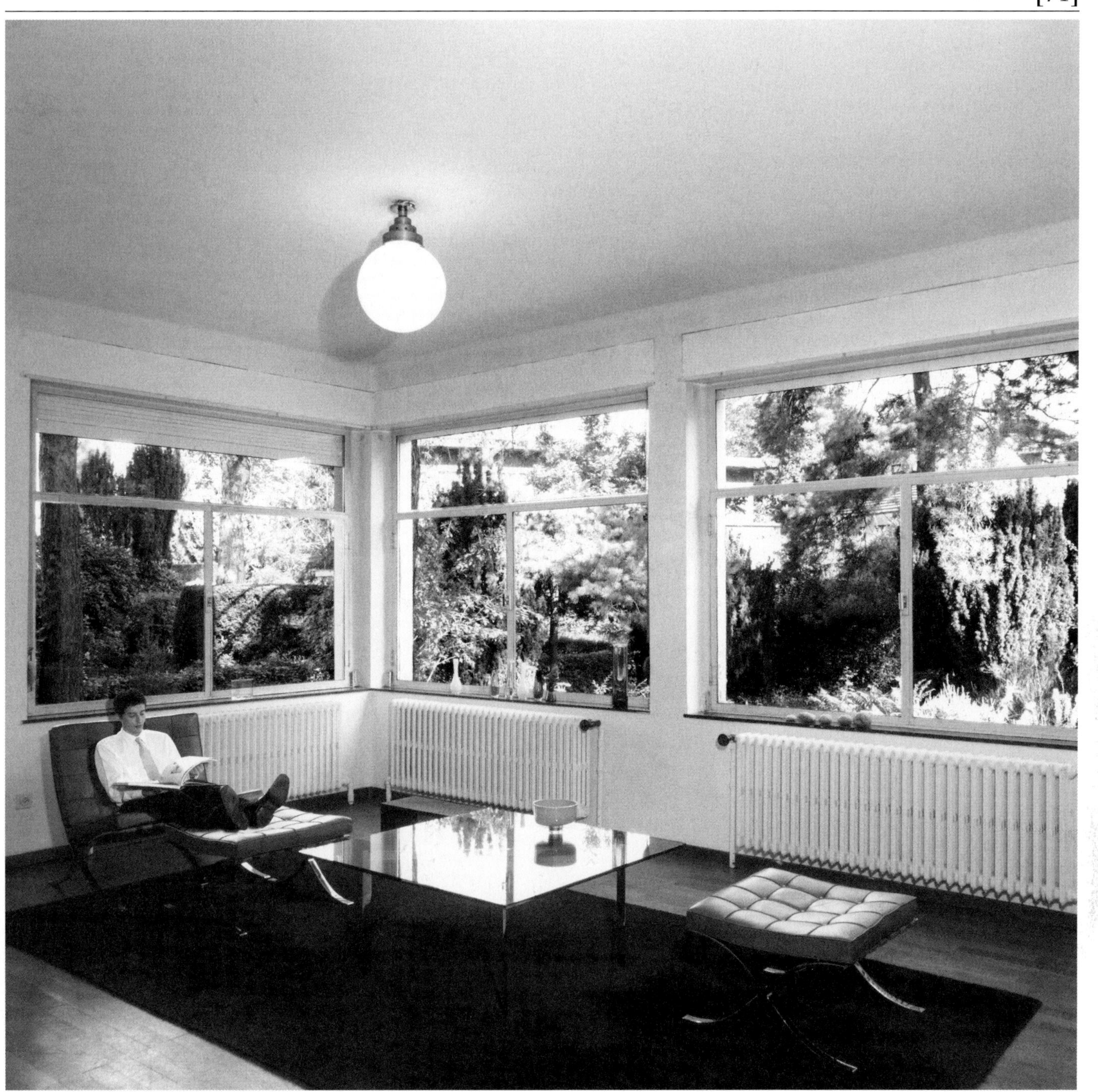

Maison Grégoire 118%
2000
b/w photograph

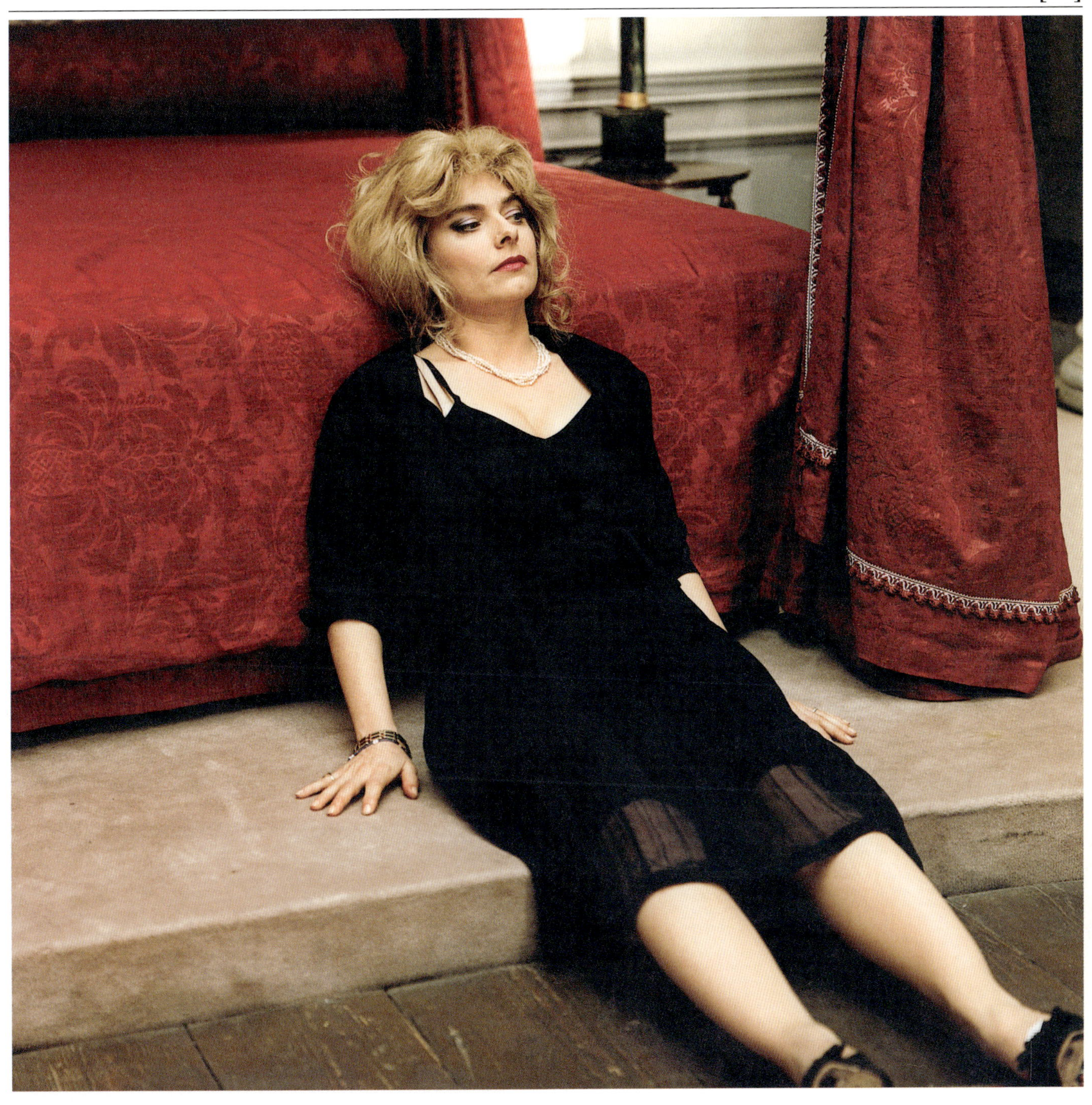

Philippa
1998
video, set photograph

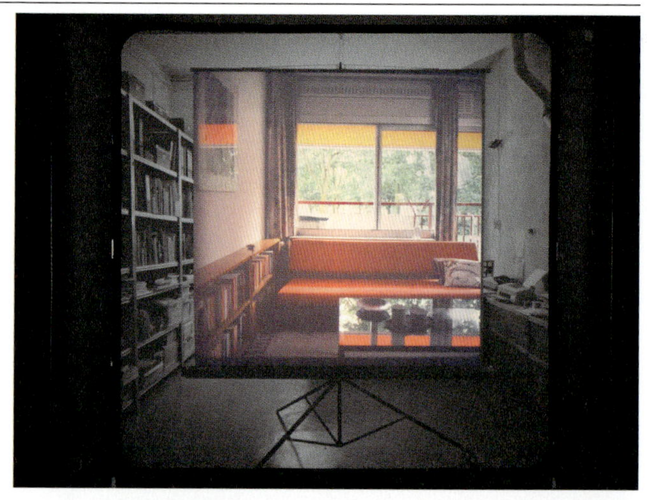

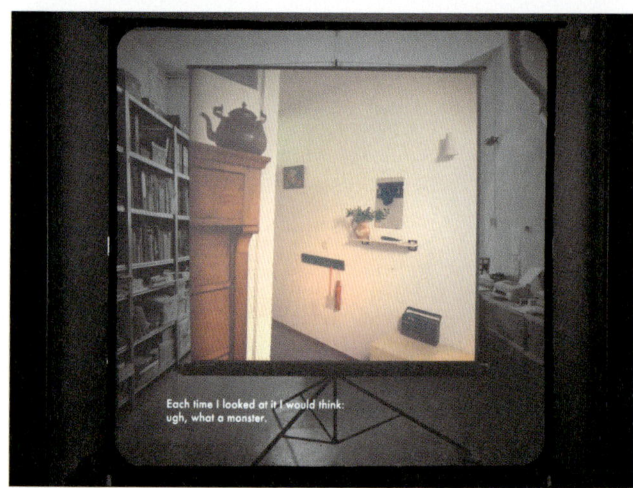

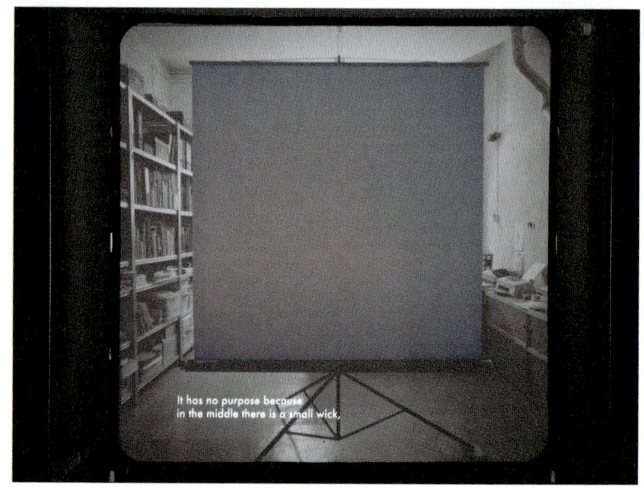

Twee Projecties / Two Projections
2005
video and slide projection with sound

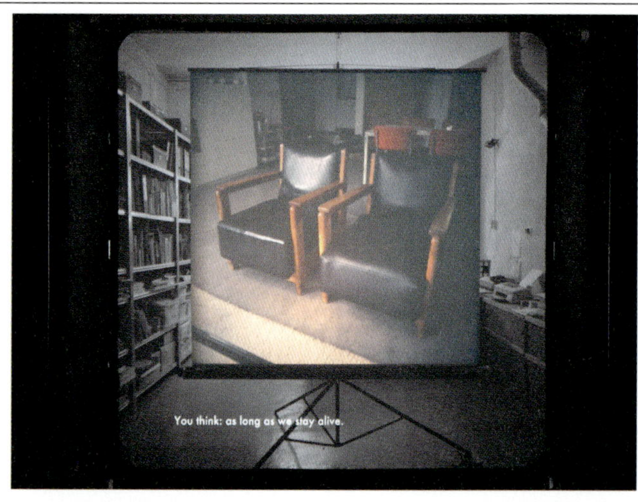

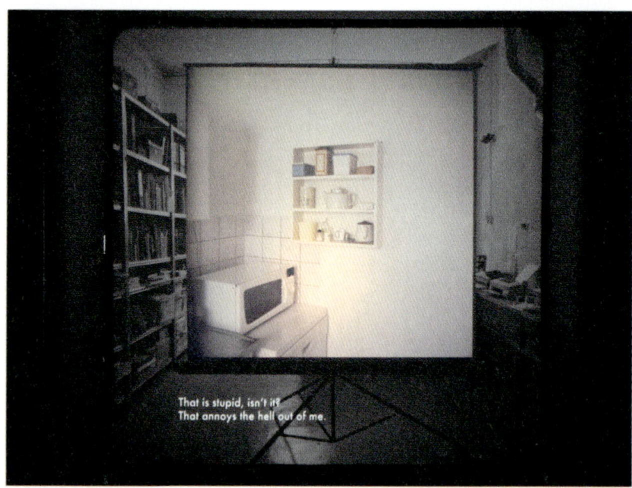

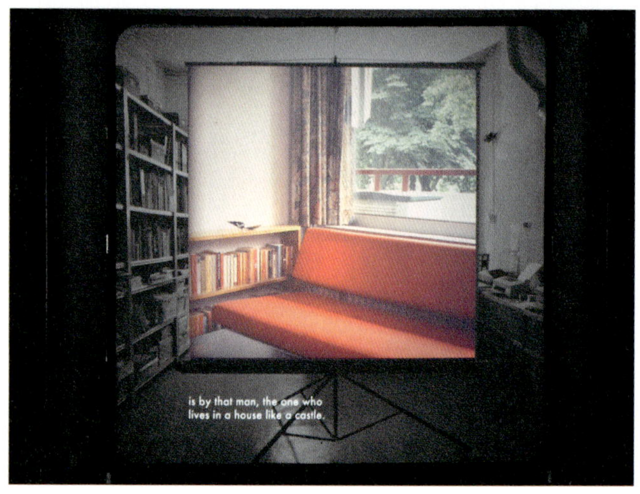

Twee Projecties / Two Projections
2005
video and slide projection with sound

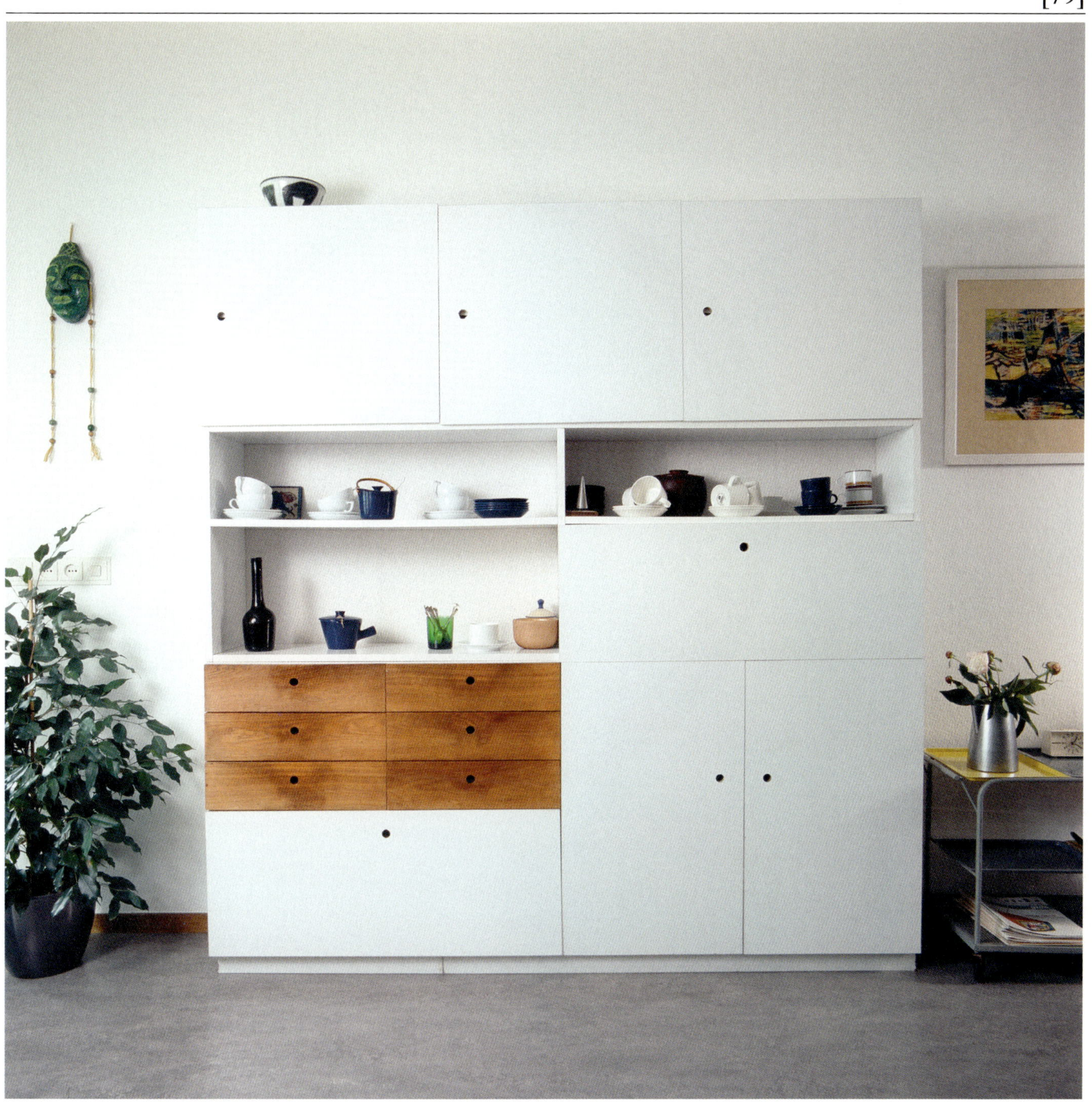

Twee Projecties / Two Projections
2005
single slide

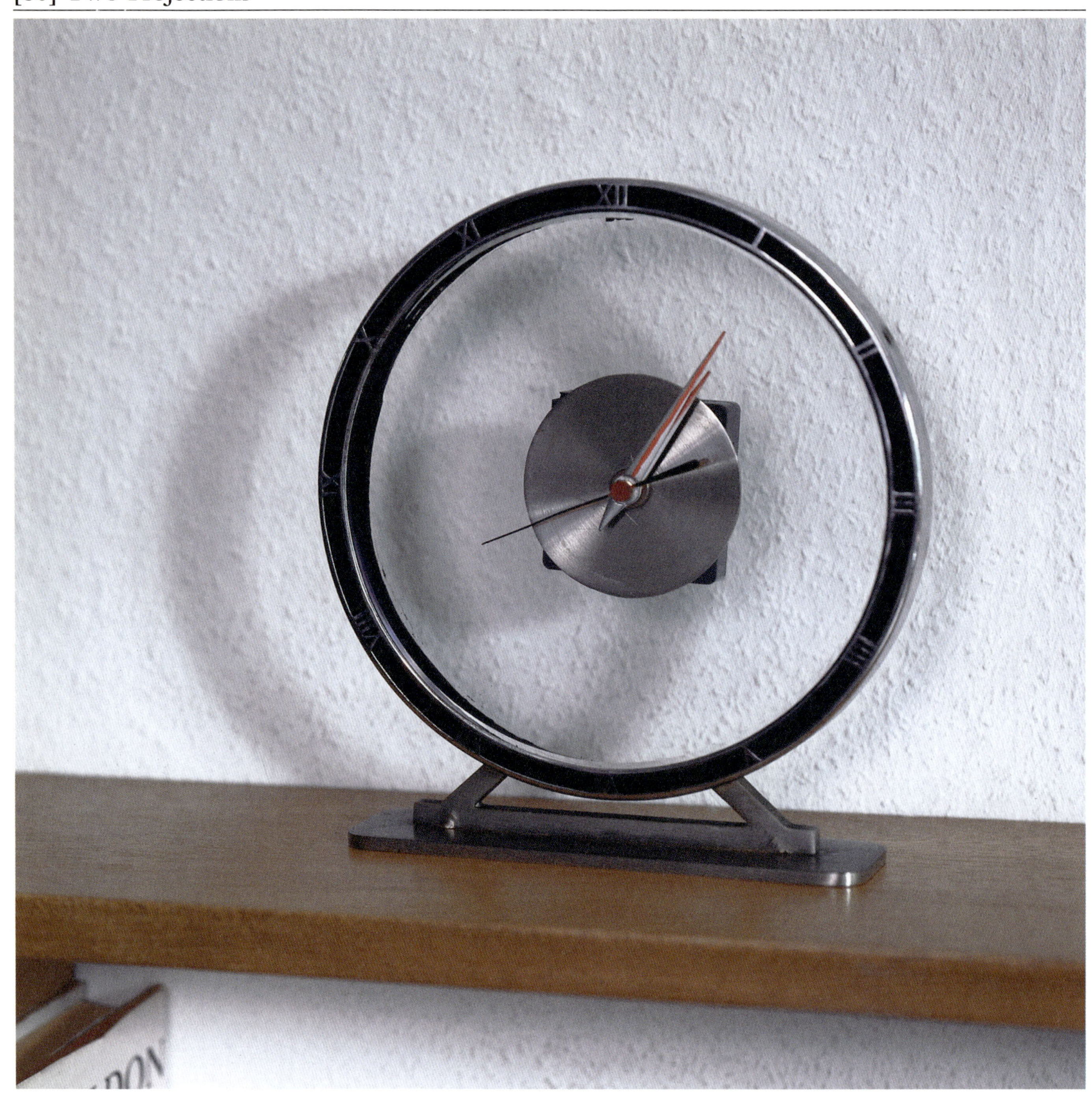

Twee Projecties / Two Projections
2005
single slide

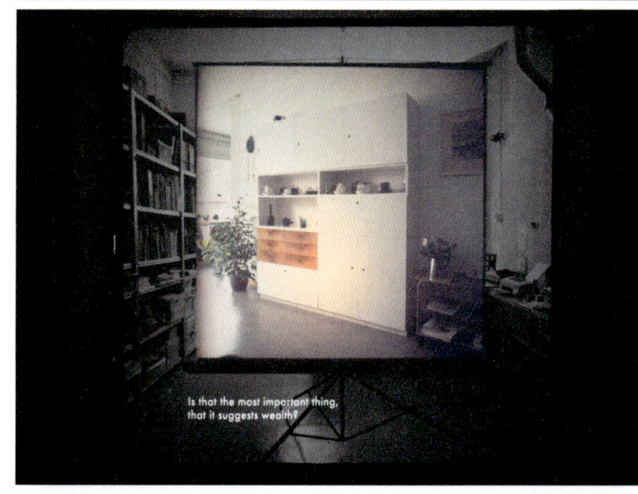

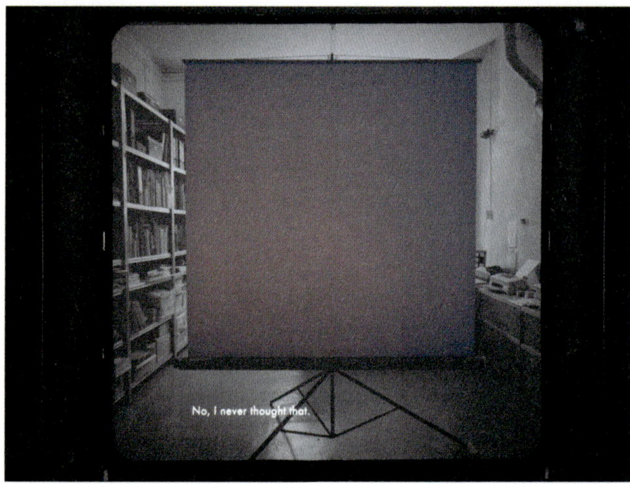

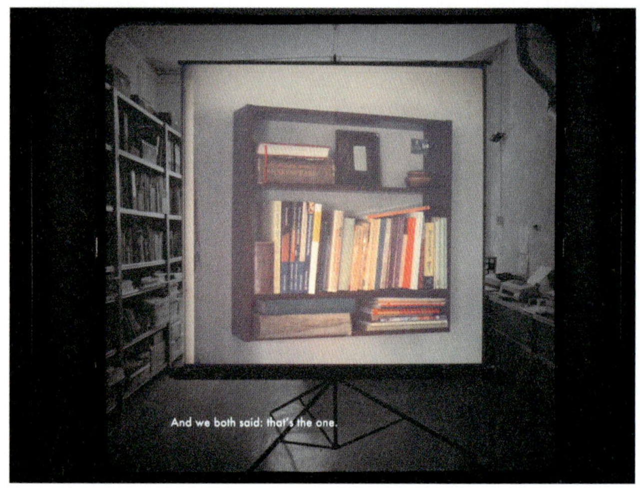

Twee Projecties / Two Projections
2005
video and slide projection with sound

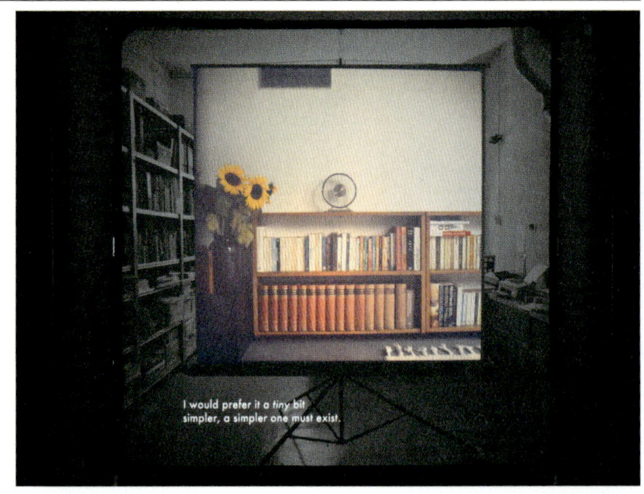

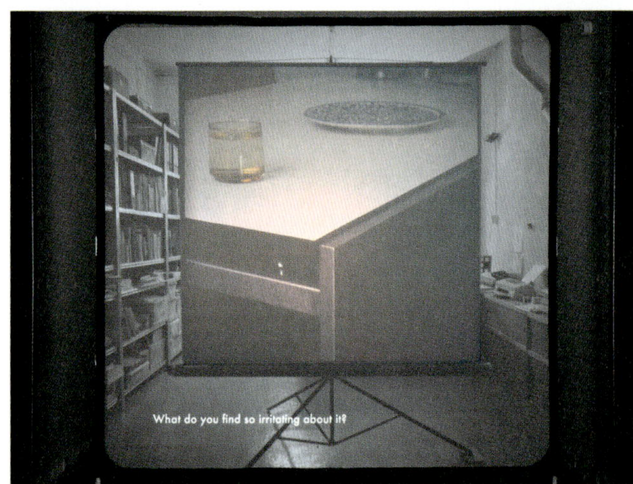

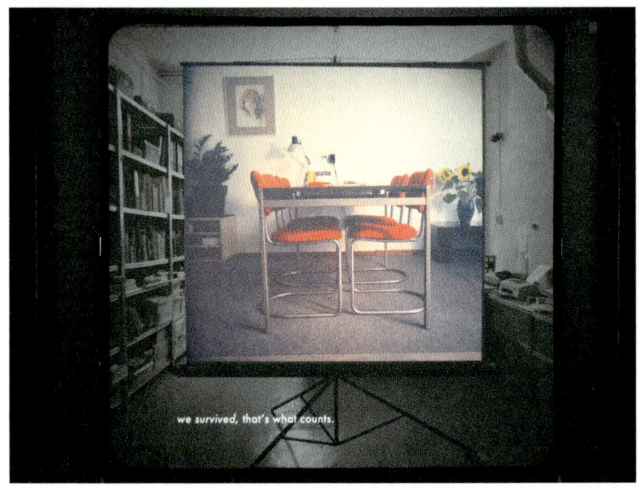

Twee Projecties / Two Projections
2005
video and slide projection with sound

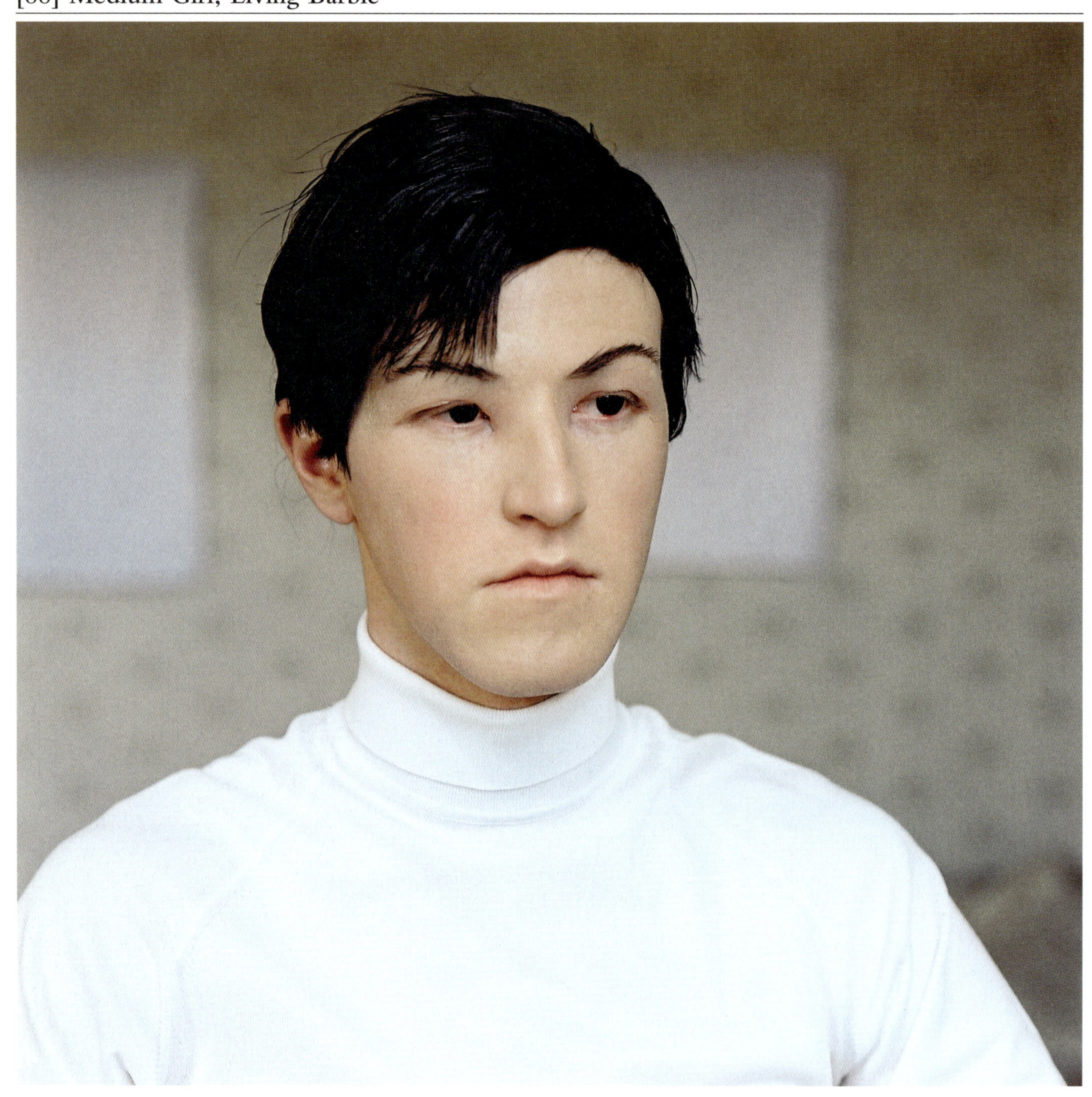

A Day in Holland/Holland in a Day
(Jan IV)
2001
series of colour photographs

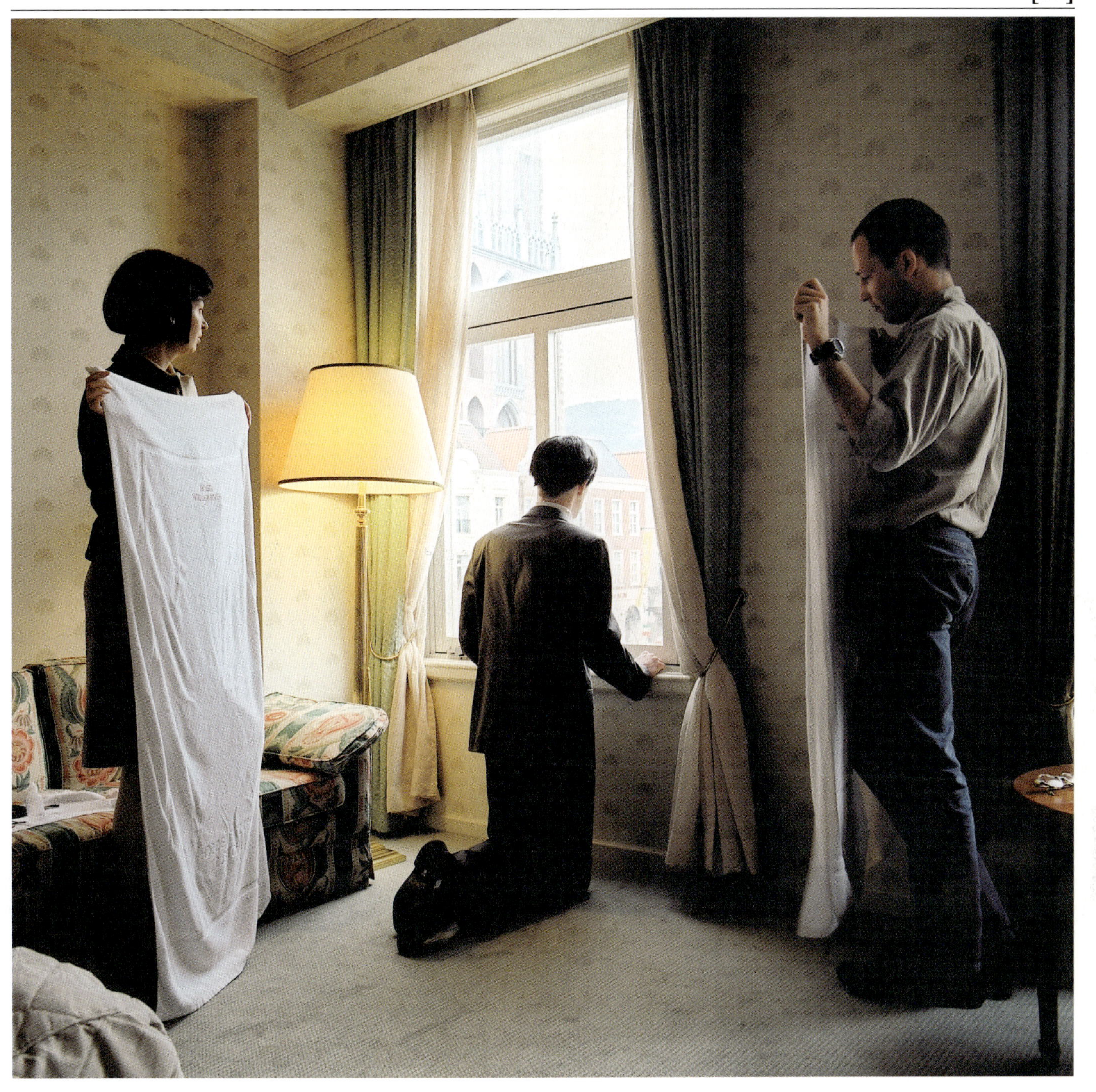

A Day in Holland/Holland in a Day
2001
series of colour photographs

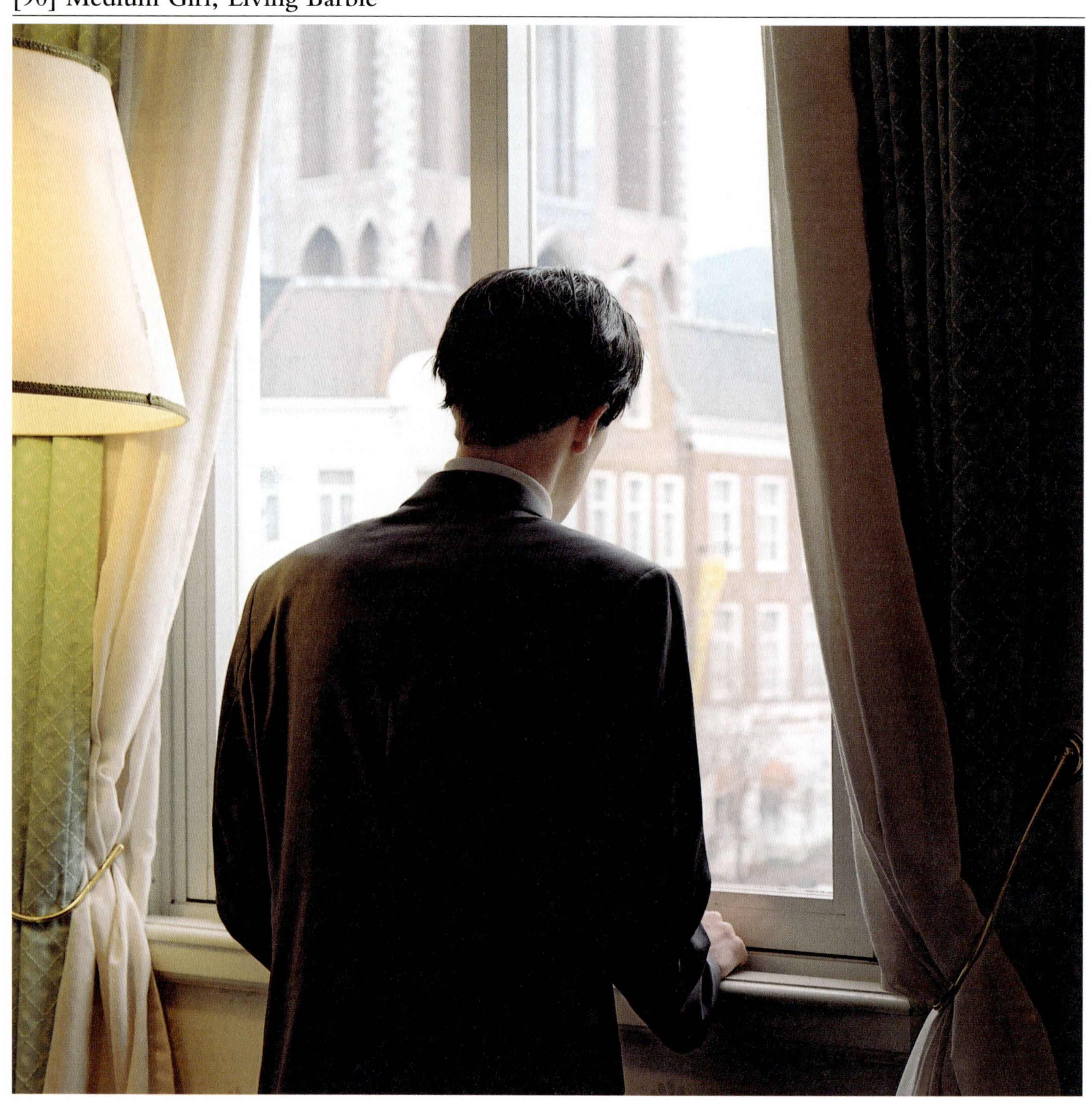

A Day in Holland/Holland in a Day
2001
series of colour photographs

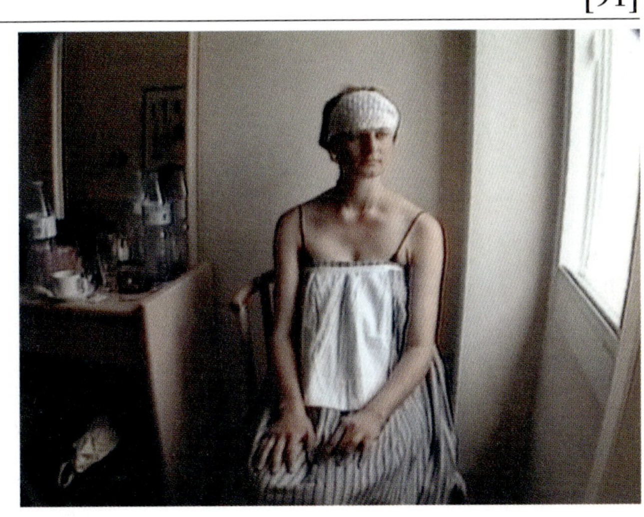

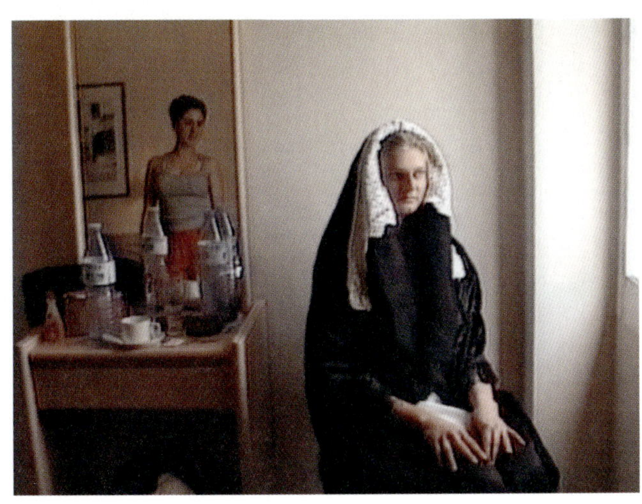

Medium Girl
1996
video, still

Medium Girl
1996
video, still

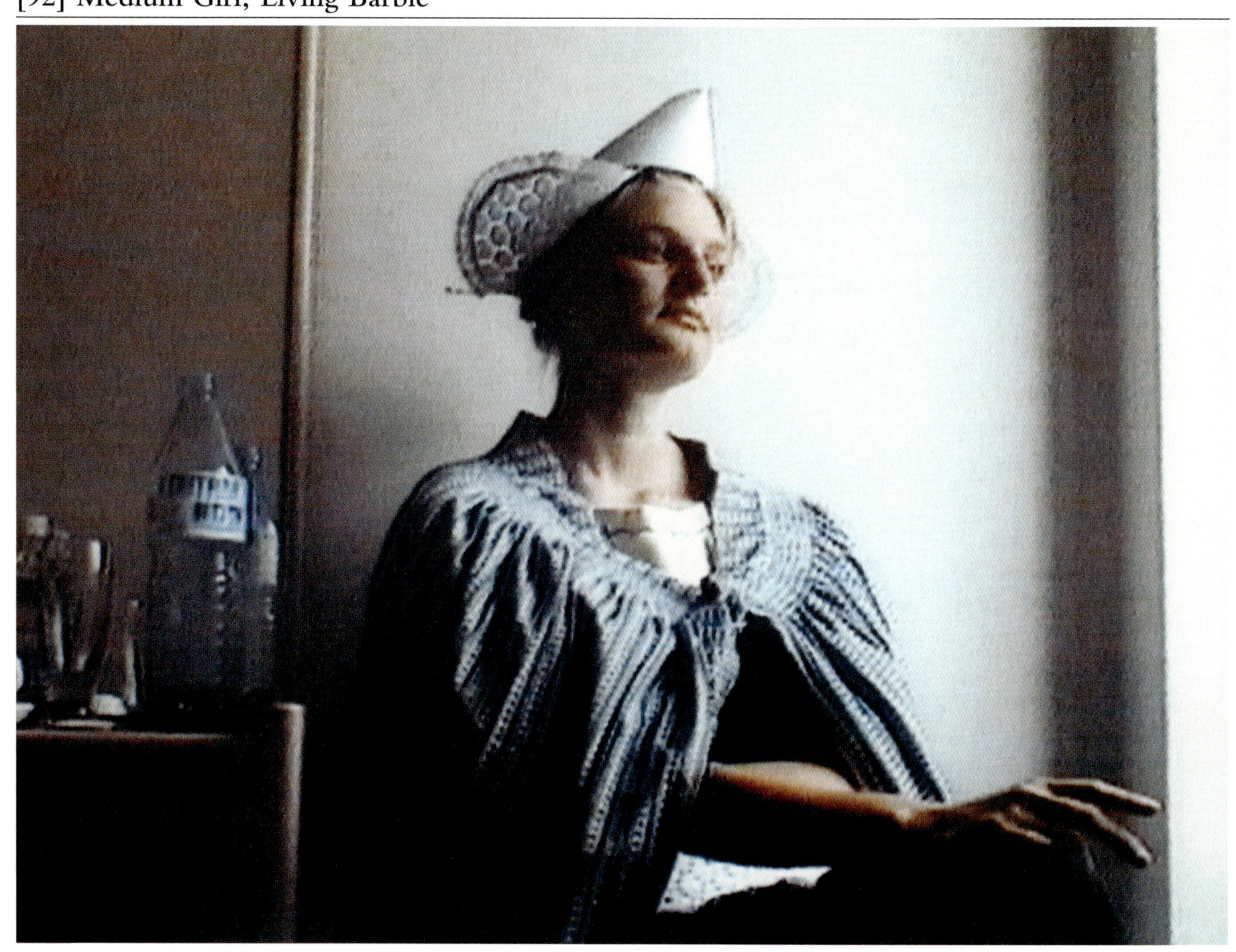

Medium Girl
1996
video, still

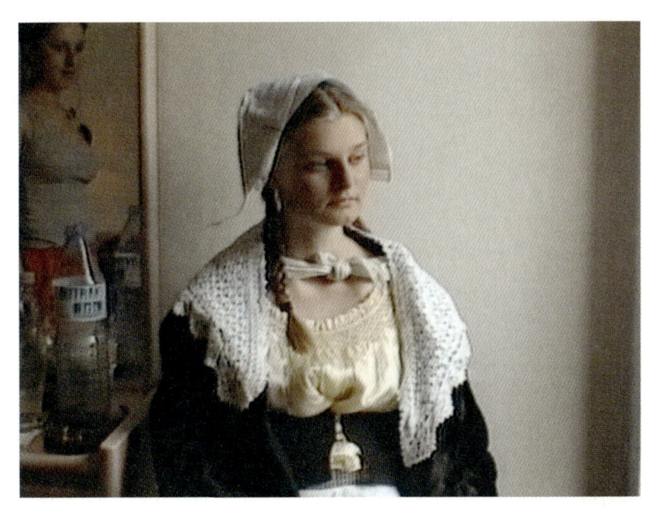

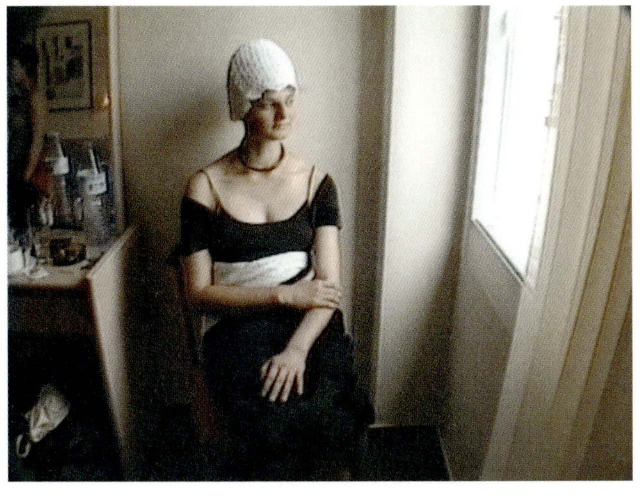

Medium Girl
1996
video, still

Medium Girl
1996
video, still

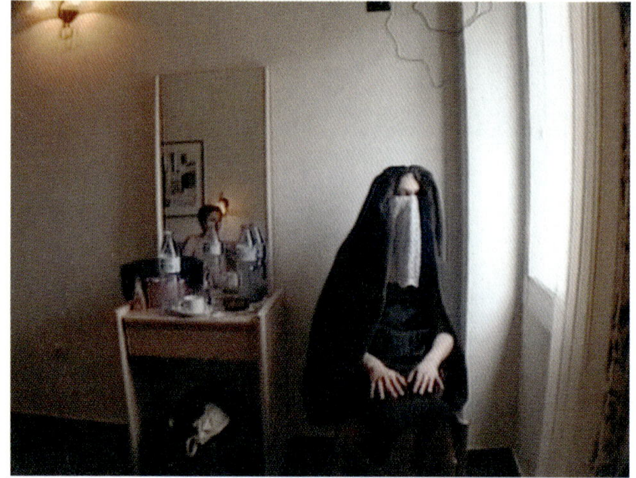

Medium Girl
1996
video, still

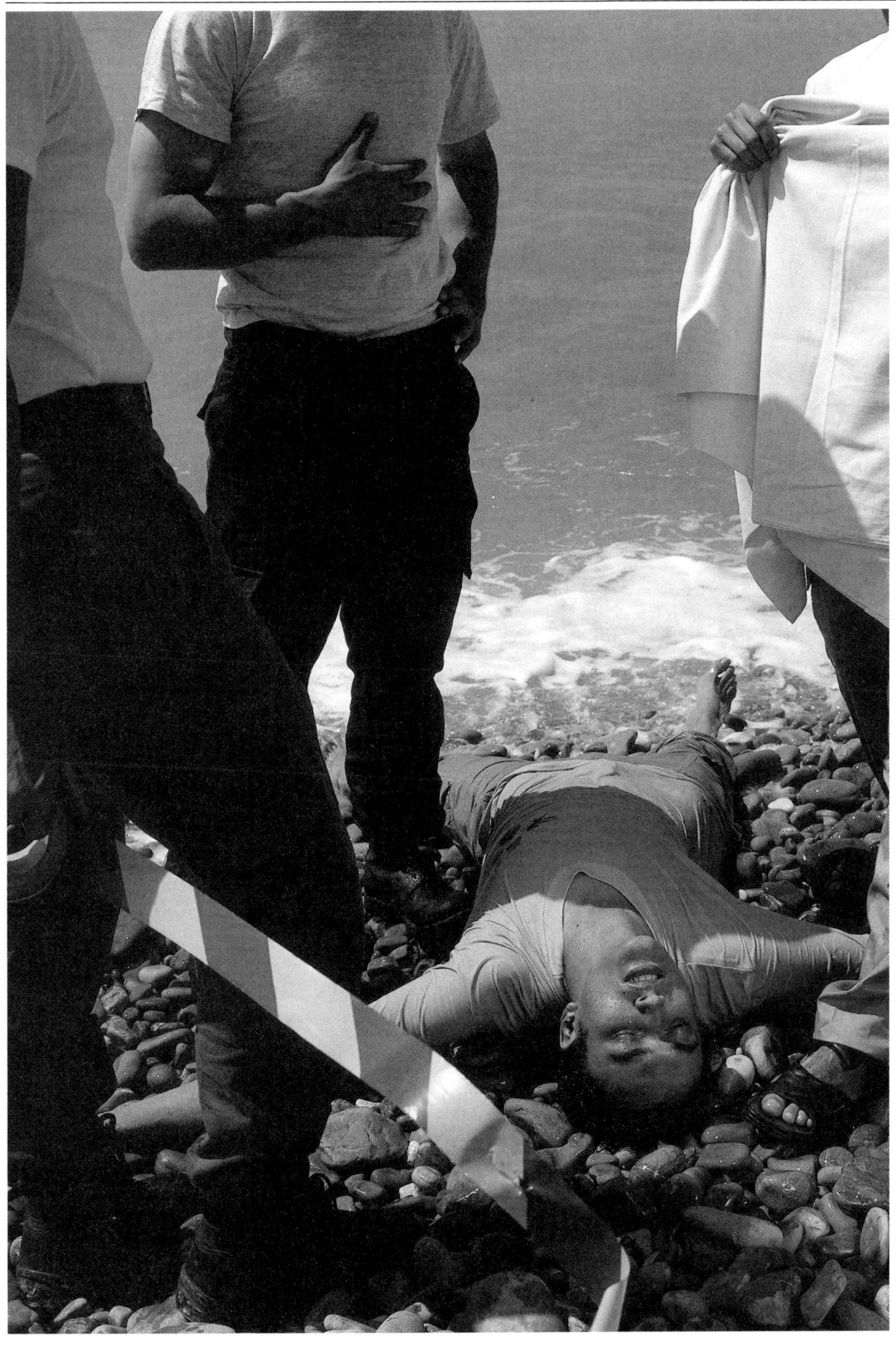

Le monde appartient à ceux qui se lèvent tôt/
The world belongs to early risers
2002
5 full colour offset posters

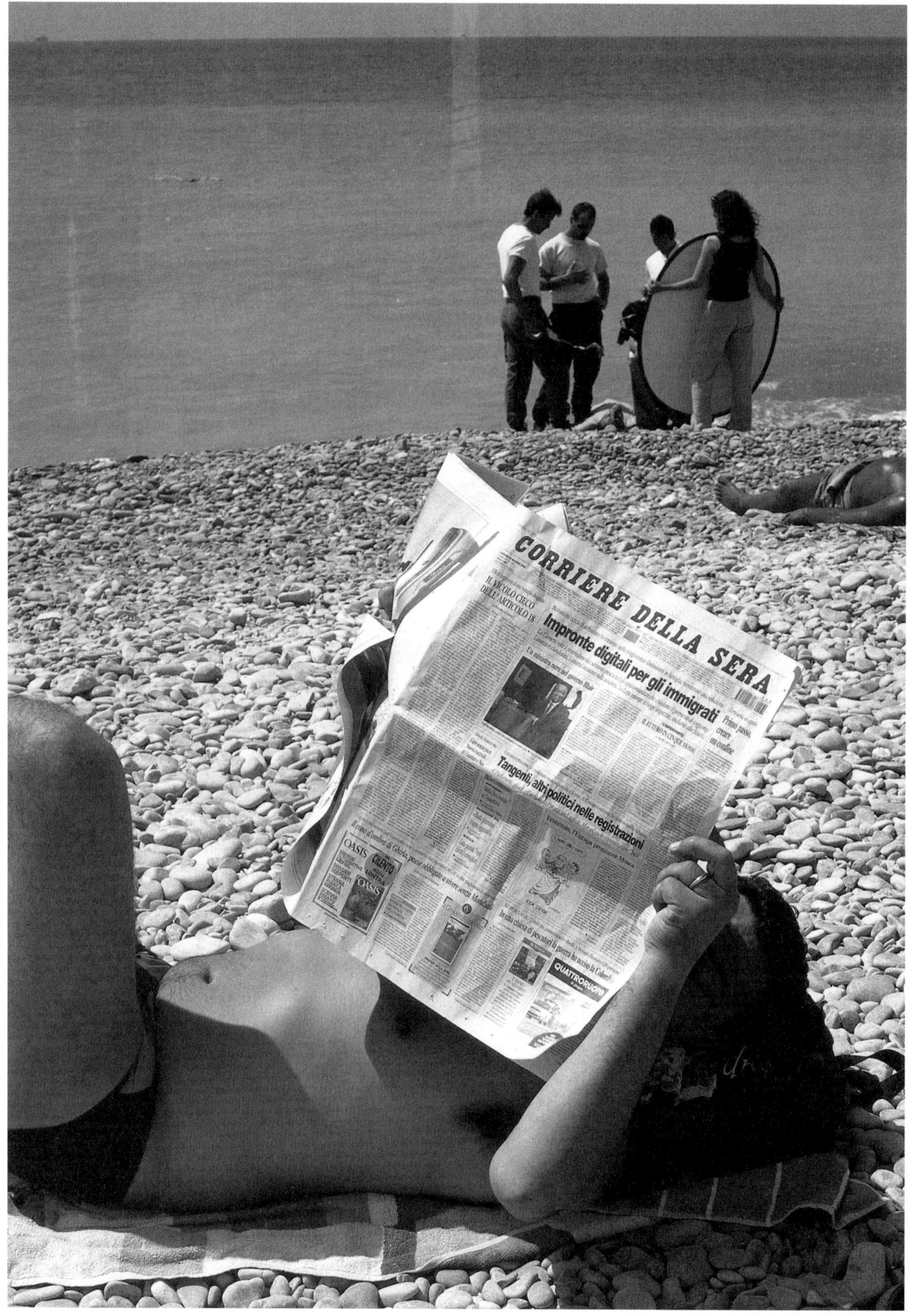

Le monde appartient à ceux qui se lèvent tôt/
The world belongs to early risers
2002
5 full colour offset posters

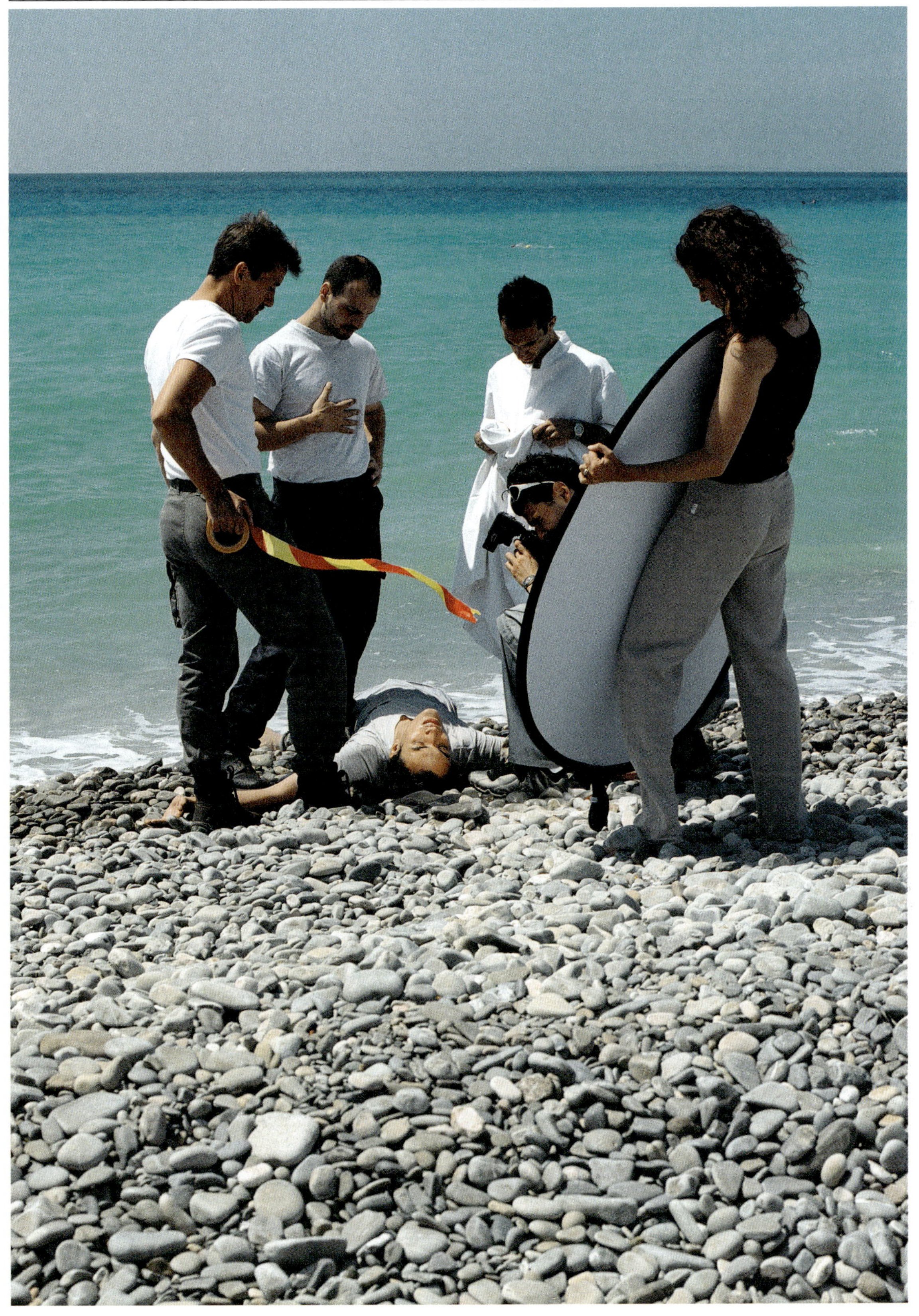

Le monde appartient à ceux qui se lèvent tôt/
The world belongs to early risers
2002
5 full colour offset posters

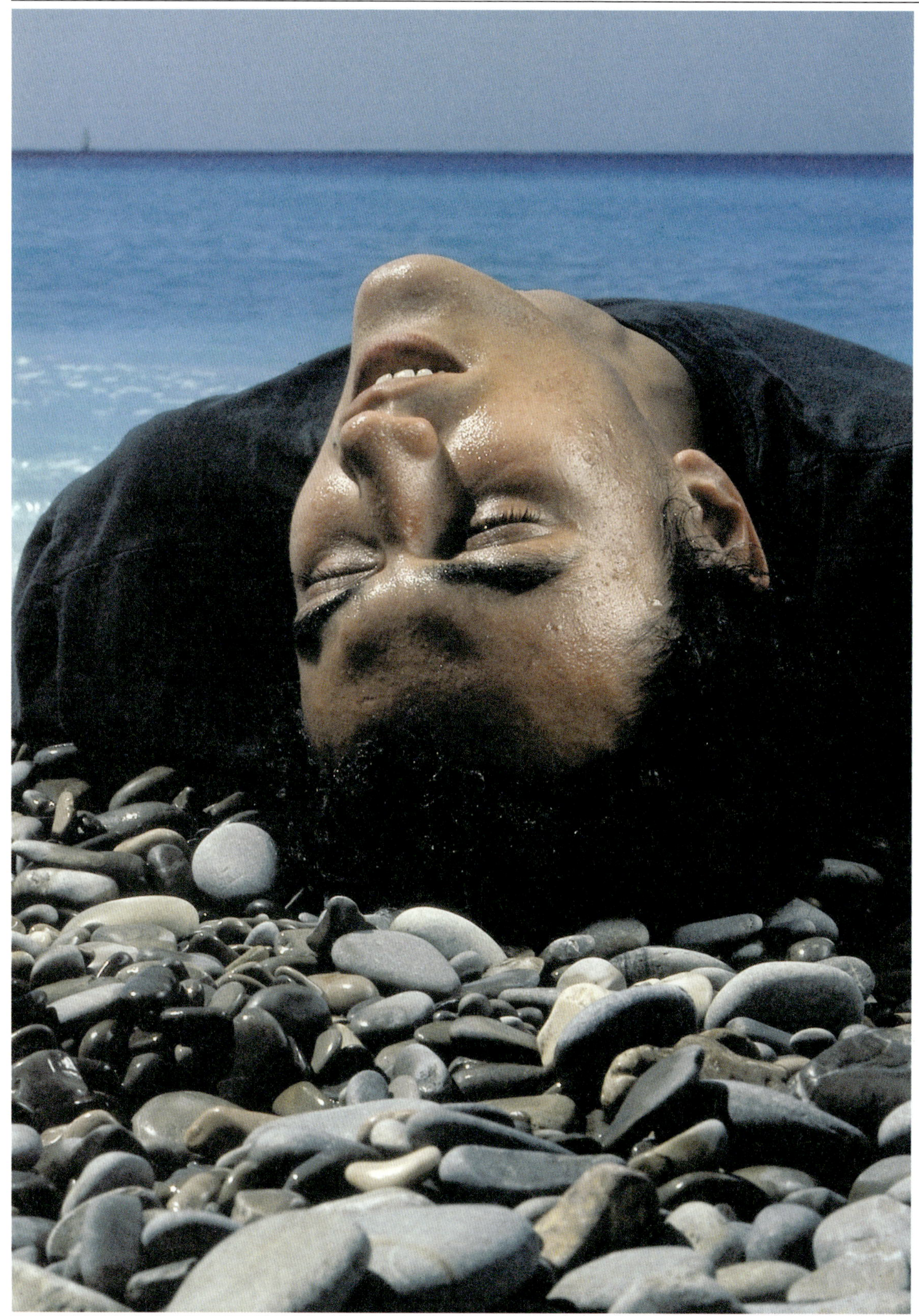

Le monde appartient à ceux qui se lèvent tôt/
The world belongs to early risers
2002
5 full colour offset posters

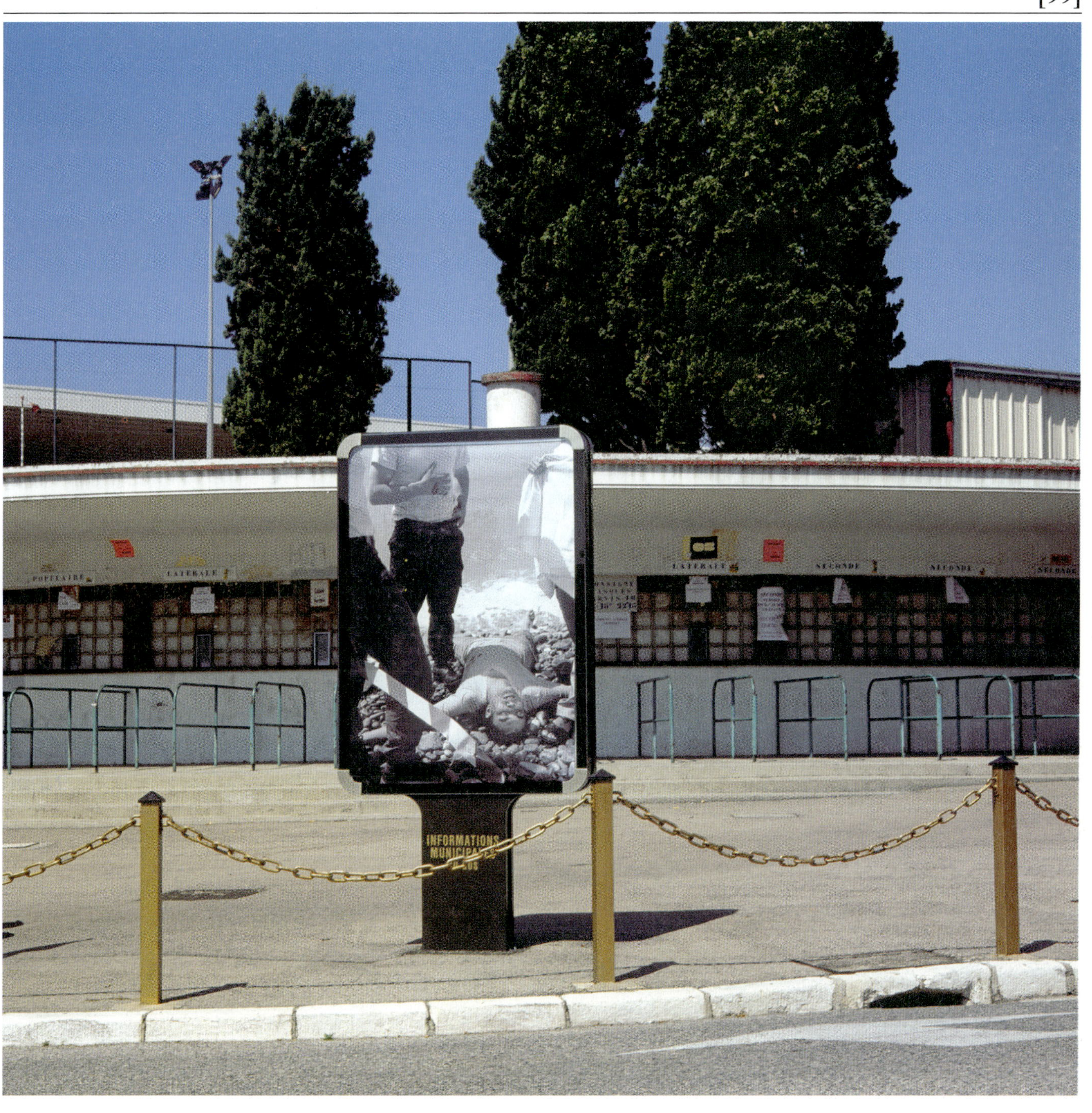

Le monde appartient à ceux qui se lèvent tôt/
The world belongs to early risers
2002
colour photograph

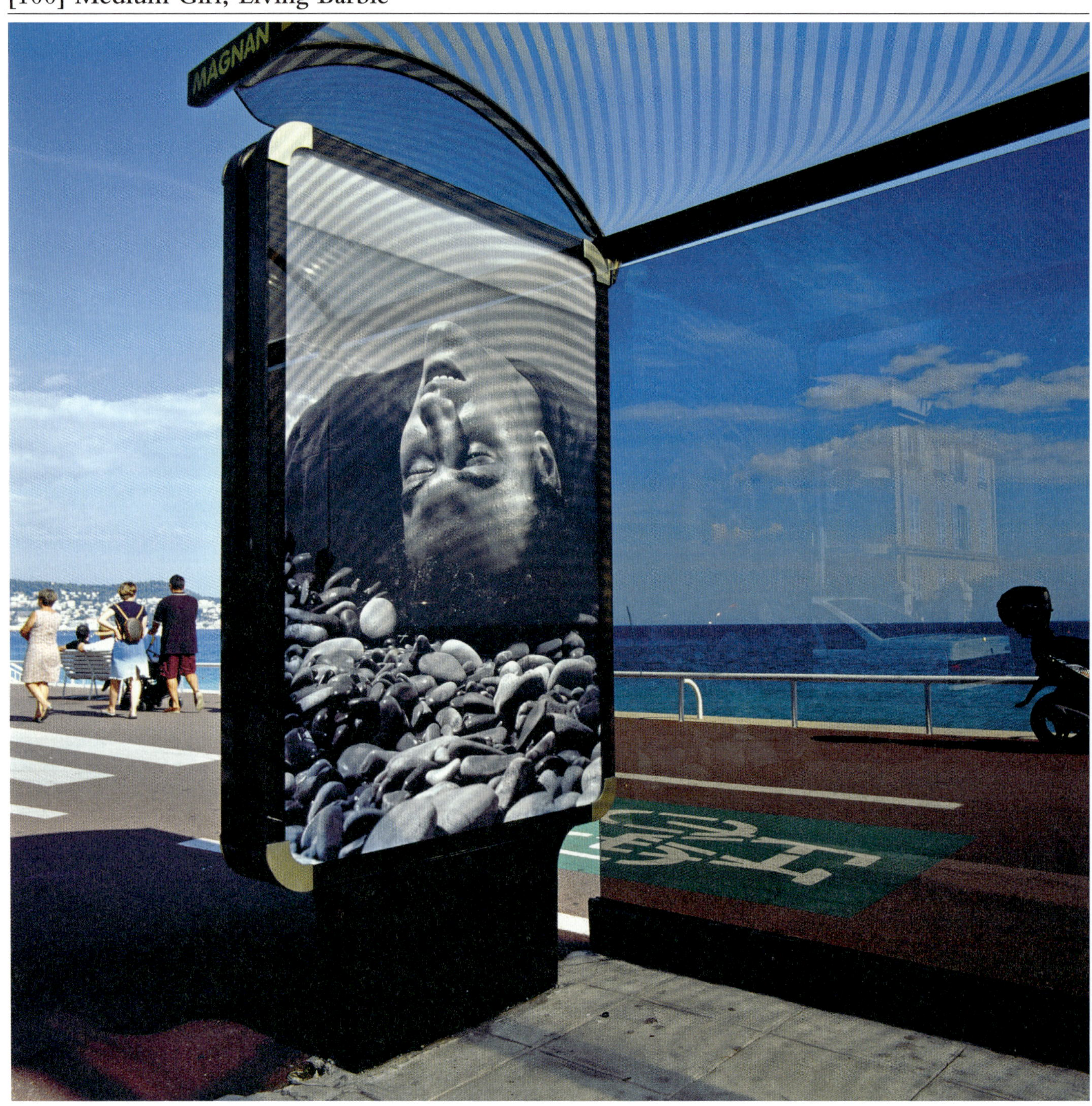

Le monde appartient à ceux qui se lèvent tôt/
The world belongs to early risers
2002
colour photograph

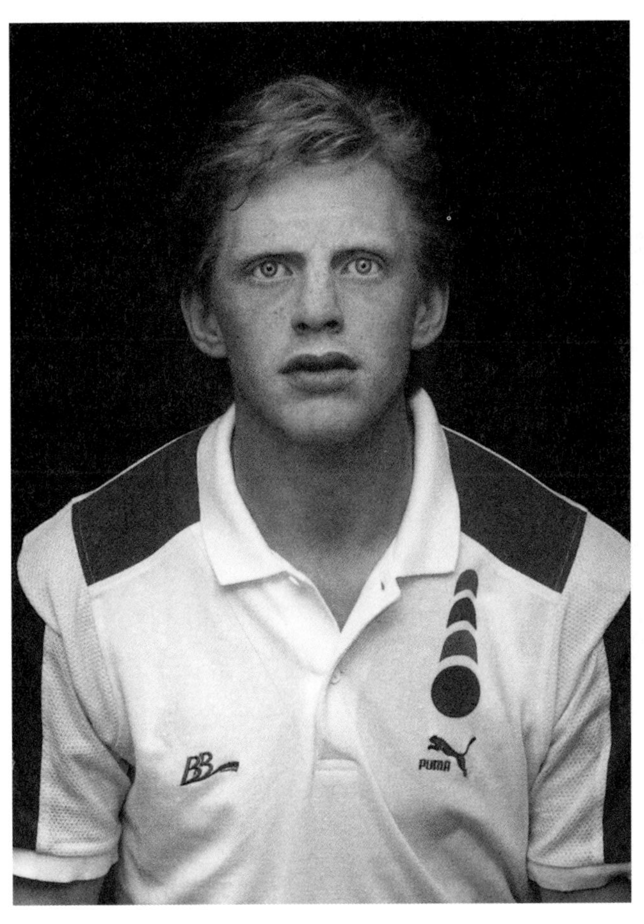

Boris
1991
b/w photograph, postcard

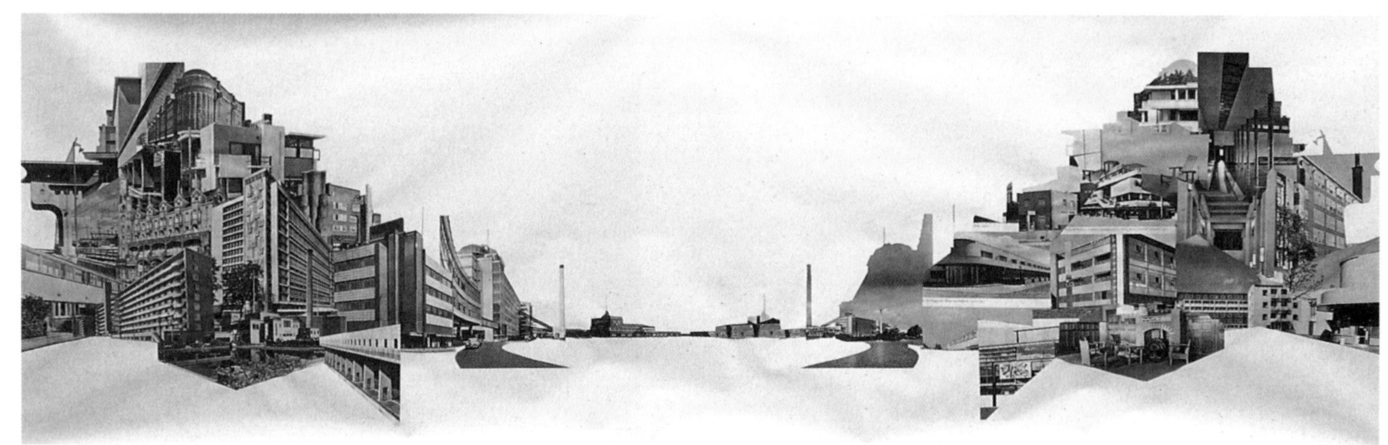

Collage 1
2001
panorama

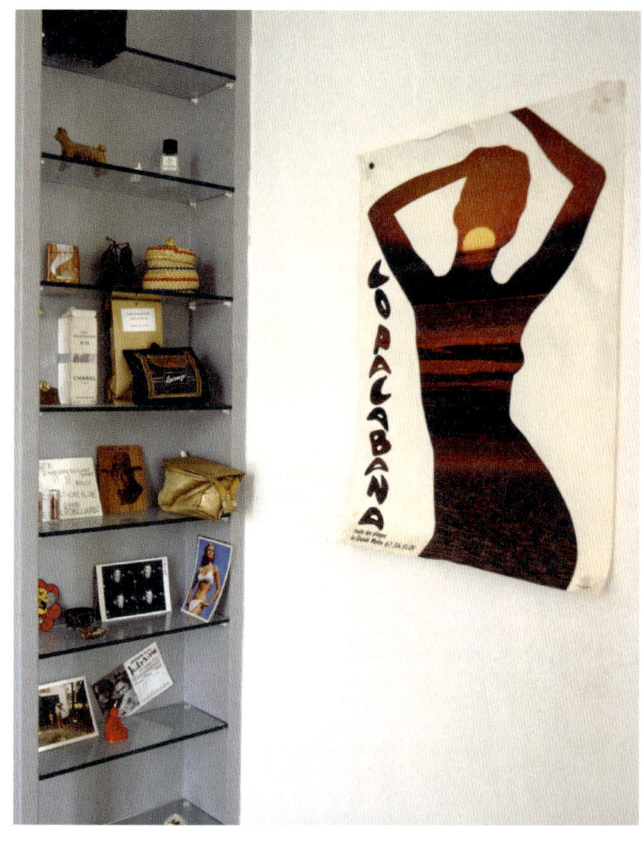

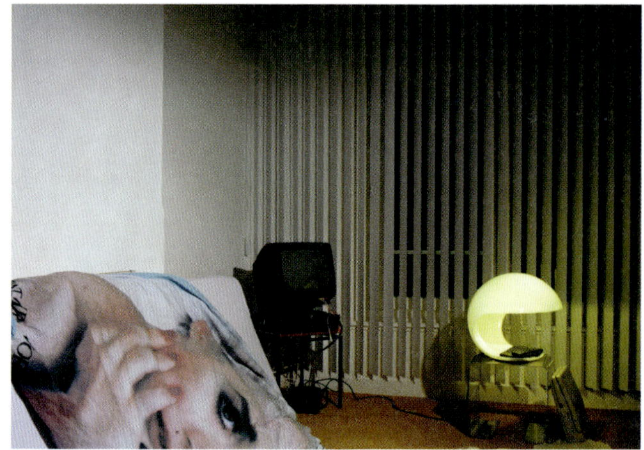

Interieurs/Interiors
1995
colour photographs

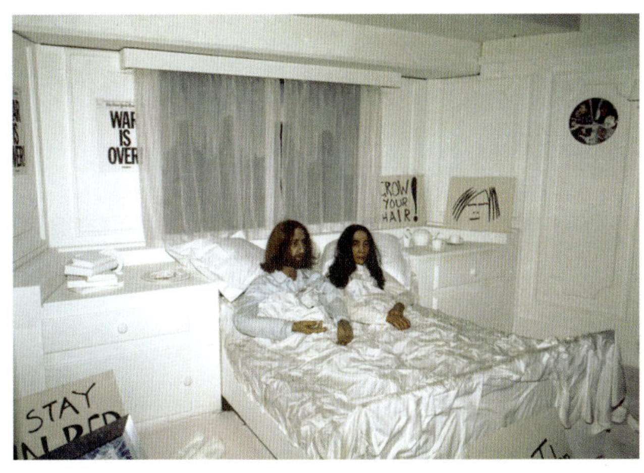

John & Yoko, Paris 1993
1993
colour photograph

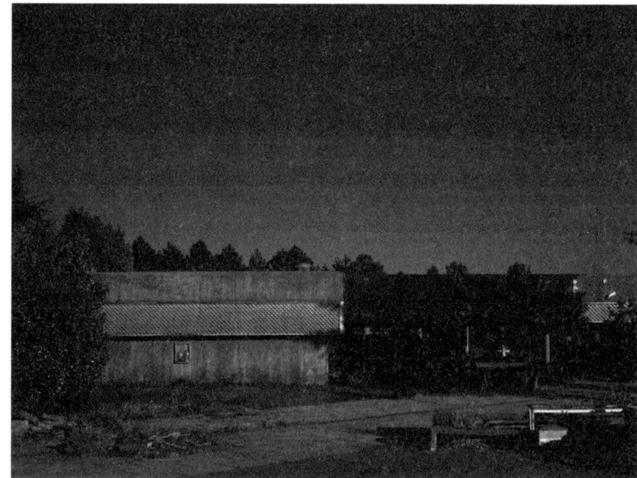

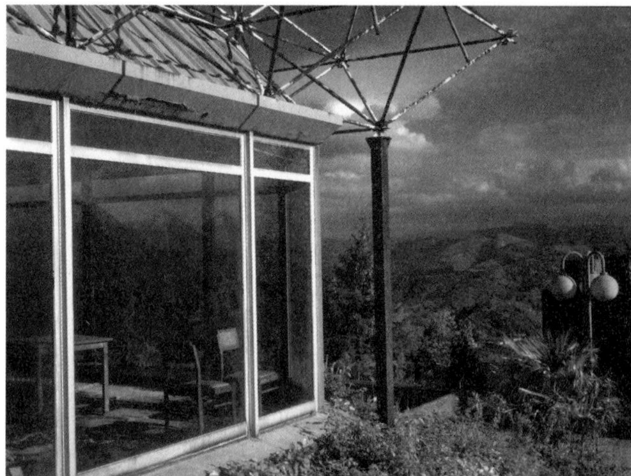

Lot, Frankrijk/Lot, France
1994
series of b/w photographs

Luna Park
2006
series of colour and b/w photographs

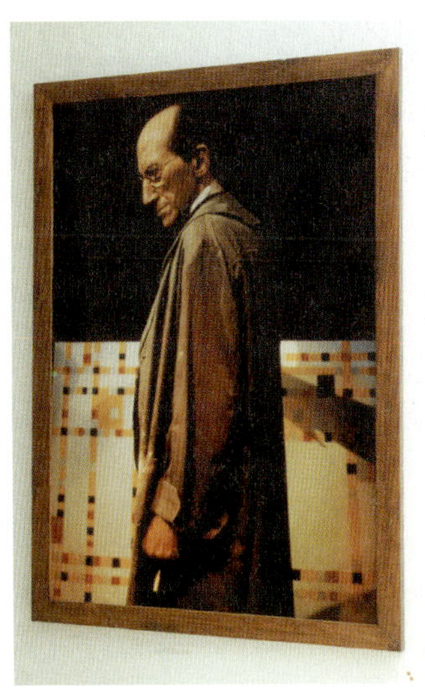

Mondriaan
1991
colour photograph

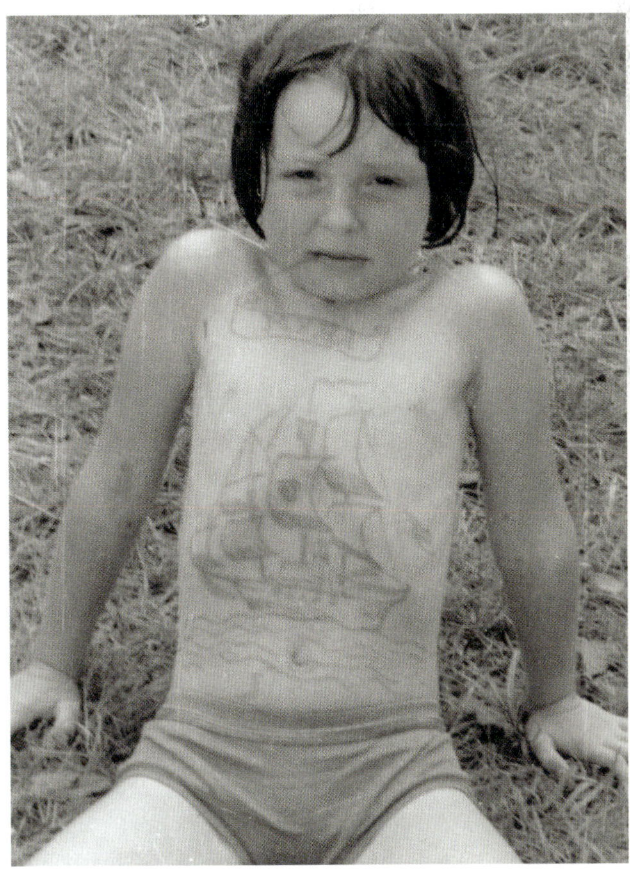

Myra
1991
b/w photograph

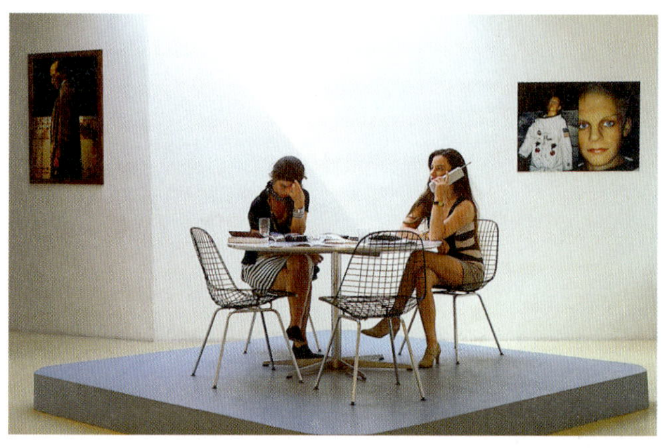

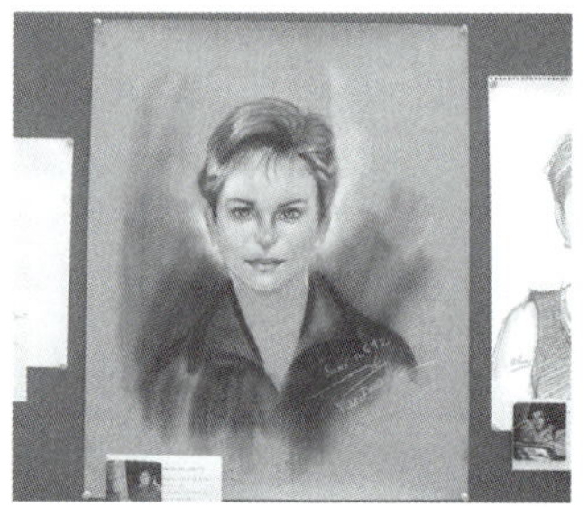

Podium
1993
installation at Bloom Gallery, photograph

Portret van de Kunstenaar/
Portrait of the Artist
1992
18 drawings, photographs, text

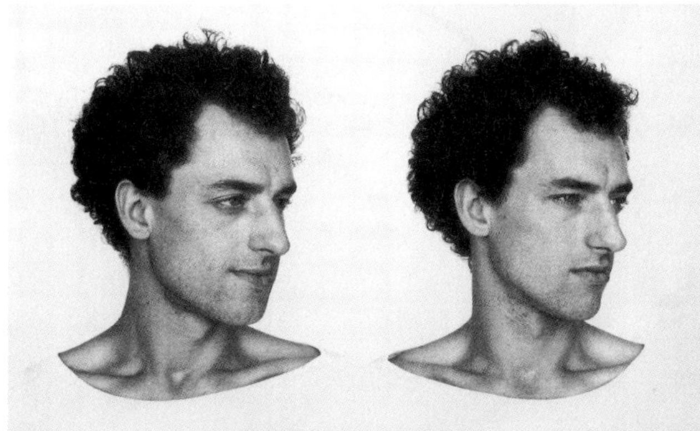

Rutger
1989
two b/w photographs

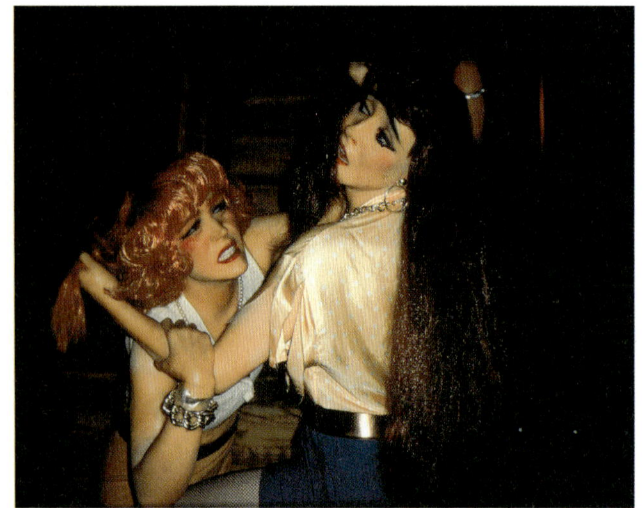

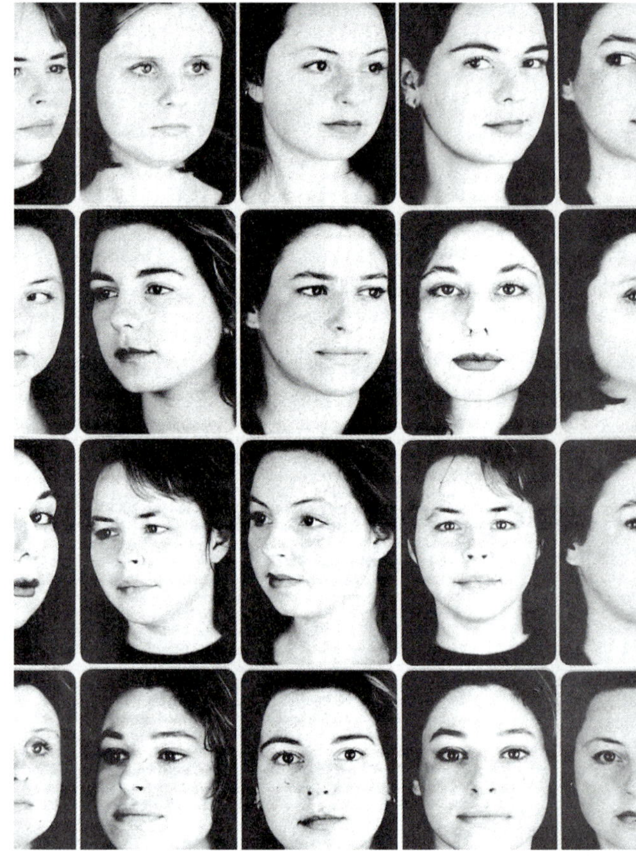

Two Fighting Prostitutes
1991
colour photograph

Z.T. (Zusjes)/ N.T. (Sisters)
1990–91
87 b/w photographs